CONCEPTUAL PHYSICS

Laboratory Manual

Paul Robinson
San Mateo High School
San Mateo, California

Cover Photograph: roller coaster, Jeremy Sutton-Hibbert/Alamy; background, Shutterstock.

Many of the designations used by manufacturers and sellers to distinguish their products are claimed as trademarks. Where such a designation appears in this book and the publisher was aware of a trademark claim, the designation has been printed in initial capital letters (e.g., Macintosh).

Pearson® is a trademark, in the U.S. and/or in other countries, of Pearson plc or its affiliates.

Prentice Hall® is a trademark, in the U.S. and/or in other countries, of Pearson Education, Inc., or its affiliates.

Boston, Massachusetts
Chandler, Arizona
Glenview, Illinois
Upper Saddle River, New Jersey

Contributors

Clarence Bakken (retired)
Gunn High School
Palo Alto, California

Tim Cooney
Price Laboratory School
Cedar Falls, Iowa

Roy Unruh (retired)
University of Northern Iowa
Cedar Falls, Iowa

Consultants

Dan Burns
Los Gatos, High School
Los Gatos, California

Paul Doherty
Exploratorium
San Francisco, California

Stephanie Finander
Woodside High School
Woodside, California

Kenneth Ford (retired)
Germantown Academy
Fort Washington, Pennsylvania

David Kagan
California State University, Chico
Chico, California

Jay Obernolte
FarSight Studies
Big Bear Lake, California

Cover Photograph: **roller coaster**, Jeremy Sutton-Hibbert/Alamy; **background**, Shutterstock.

13-digit ISBN 978-0-13-364752-5
10-digit ISBN 0-13-364752-8
10 V056 15

Acknowledgments

Most of the ideas in this manual come from teachers who share their ideas at American Association of Physics Teachers (AAPT) meetings that I have attended since my first year of teaching. This sharing of ideas and cooperative spirit is a hallmark of our profession.

Many more individuals have contributed their ideas and insights freely and openly than I can mention here. The greatest contributors are Roy Unruh and Tim Cooney, principal authors of the PRISMS (Physics Resources and Instructional Strategies for Motivating Students) Guide. I am especially thankful to them and others on the PRISMS team: Dan McGrail, Ken Shafer, Bob Wilson, Peggy Steffen, and Rollie Freel. For contributions and feedback to the first edition, I am grateful to Brad Huff, Bill von Felten, Manuel Da Costa, and Clarence Bakken, as well as the students of Edison Computech High School who provided valuable feedback. I am especially indebted to my talented former student Jay Obernolte (founder of FarSight Studios), who developed computer software that originally accompanied this manual.

For helpful lab ideas I thank Dean Baird, Rio Americano High School; Evan Jones, Sierra College; Dave Wall, City College of San Francisco; David Ewing, Southwestern Georgia University; and Sheila Cronin, Avon High School, CT, for her adaptations of CASTLE curriculum. Thanks go to Paul Tipler; Verne Rockcastle, Cornell University; the late Lester Hirsch; and to the late Frank Crawford, University of California, Berkeley for their inspiration. I am especially grateful to Ken Ford, who critiqued the third edition.

For suggestions on integrating the computer in the physics laboratory, I am grateful to my AAPT colleagues Dewey Dykstra, Robert H. Good, Charles Hunt, and Dave and Christine Vernier. Thanks also to Dave Griffith, Kevin Mather, and Paul Stokstad of PASCO Scientific for their professional assistance. For production assistance I thank Lisa Poole and Helen Yan.

I am grateful to my computer wizard and long time friend Skip Wagner for his creative expertise on the computer.

For the fourth edition, I am grateful to David Kagan, California State University, Chico, for his thorough reading and critiquing of all the labs new to this edition; and also to Lonnie Grimes of Oakmont High School for his careful review and feedback. Special thanks go to Paul Doherty, Director of the Teacher Institute at the Exploratorium in San Francisco and to my PTSOS colleague Stephanie Finander of Woodside High School and Dan Burns, Los Gatos High School, for lending their advice. I'd also like to tip my hat to my students at San Mateo High School for making teaching such a pleasurable experience and who constantly challenge and inspire me.

Love and thanks to my parents for their encouragement and support, to my children—David, Kristen, and Brian—and my dear wife Ellyn Daugherty—for her tireless energy and encouragement.

Paul Robinson

Contents

To the Student

You need to know the rules of a game before you can fully enjoy it. Likewise with the physical world—to fully appreciate nature you need to know its rules—what physics is about. Read your textbook and enjoy!

Also like a game, to fully understand physics, you need to know how to keep score. This involves observing, measuring, and expressing your findings in numbers. That's what this lab manual is about. *Do* physics and understand!

Visit the author's web site at laserpablo.com

Goals

The laboratory part of the *Conceptual Physics* program should

1) Provide you with hands-on experience that relates to physics concepts.

2) Provide training in making measurements, recording, organizing, and analyzing data.

3) Provide you with the experiences in elementary problem solving.

4) Show you that all this can be interesting and worthwhile—*doing* physics can be quite enjoyable!

This lab manual contains 62 *activities* and 43 *experiments*. Most *activities* are designed to provide you with hands-on experience that relates to a specific concept. *Experiments* are usually designed to give you practice using a particular piece of apparatus. The goals for activities and experiments, while similar, are in some ways different.

The chief goal of activities is to acquaint you with a particular physical phenomenon which you may or may not already know something about. The emphasis during an activity is for you to observe relationships, identify variables, and develop tentative explanations of phenomena in a qualitative fashion. In some cases, you will be asked to design experiments or formulate models that lead to a deeper understanding.

Experiments are more quantitative in nature and generally involve acquiring data in a prescribed manner. Here, a greater emphasis is placed on learning how to use a particular piece of equipment, making measurements, identifying and estimating errors, organizing your data, and interpreting your data.

Graphing

When you look at two columns of numbers that are related some way, they probably have little meaning to you. A *graph* is a visual way to see how two quantities are related. You can tell at an instant what the stock market has been doing by glancing at a plot of the Dow Jones Industrial Average plotted as a function of time.

Often you will take data by changing one quantity, called the *independent variable*, in order to see how another quantity, called the *dependent variable*, changes. A graph is made by plotting the values of the independent variable on the *horizontal axis*, or *x-axis* with values of the dependent variable on the *vertical axis*, or *y-axis*. When you make a graph, it is always important to label each of the axes with the quantity and units used to express it. The graph is completed by sketching the best smooth curve or straight line that fits all the points.

To eliminate confusion and increase learning efficiency, your teacher will guide you before each experiment as to how to label the axes and choose a convenient scale. Often you will work in groups and graph your data *as you perform the experiment*. This has the chief advantage of providing immediate feedback if an erroneous data point is made. This gives you time to adjust the apparatus and make the necessary adjustments so that your data are more meaningful. Provided everyone uses the same scale for each axes, the results of the entire class can be compared by simply overlapping the graphs on an overhead projector. This method also has the added benefit of eliminating graphing as a homework assignment!

Use of the Computer

The computer provides a powerful tool in collecting and analyzing your data and displaying it graphically. Data plotting software or spreadsheets enable you to input data easily and to plot the corresponding graph in minutes. The computational power of the computer can make revealing the relationships between variables much easier and efficient than doing so by hand.

In this course you will be encouraged to use the computer as a laboratory instrument. A variety of sensors enable the computer to accurately measure time, force, magnetic fields, and temperature—just to name a few quantities. Though not required for any of the labs, the use of probeware greatly facilitates data collection and processing.

Lab Reports

Your teacher may ask that you write up a lab report. Be sure to follow your teacher's specific instructions on how to write a lab report. The general guideline for writing a lab report is: Could another student taking physics at some other school read your report and understand what you did well enough to replicate your work? Other guidelines include:

Lab number and title   Write your name, date, and period in the upper right-hand corner of your report. Include the names of your lab partners underneath.

Purpose   Write a brief statement of what you were exploring, verifying, measuring, investigating, etc.

Method   Make a rough sketch of the apparatus you used and a brief description of how you planned to accomplish your lab.

Data   Show a record of your observations and measurements, including all data tables.

Analysis   Show calculations performed, any required graphs, and answers to questions. Summarize what you accomplished in the lab.

Safety in the Physics Laboratory

By following certain common sense in the physics lab, you can make the lab safe not only for yourself but for all those around you.

1. Never work in the lab unless a teacher is present and aware of what you are doing.

2. Prepare for the lab activity or experiment by reading it over first. Ask questions about anything that is unclear to you. Note any cautions that are stated.

3. Dress appropriately for a laboratory. Avoid wearing bulky or loose-fitting clothes or dangling jewelry. Pin or tie back long hair, and roll up loose sleeves.

4. Keep the work area free of any books and materials not needed for what you are working on.

5. Wear safety goggles when working with flames, heated liquids, or glassware.

6. Never throw anything in the laboratory.

7. Use the apparatus only as instructed in the manual or by your teacher. If you wish to try an alternate procedure, obtain your teacher's approval first.

8. If a thermometer breaks, inform your teacher immediately. Do not touch either the mercury or the glass with your bare skin.

9. Do not force glass tubing or thermometer into dry rubber stopper. The hole and the glass should both be lubricated with glycerin (glycerol) or soapy water, and the glass should be gripped through a paper towel to protect the hands.

10. Do not touch anything that may be hot, including burners, hot plates, rings, beakers, electric immersion heaters, and electric bulbs. If you must pick up something that is hot, use a damp paper towel, a pot holder, or some other appropriate holder.

11. When working with electric circuits, be sure that the current is turned off before making adjustments in the circuit.

12. If you are connecting a voltmeter or ammeter to a circuit, have your teacher approve the connections before you turn the current on.

13. Do not connect the terminals of a dry cell or battery to each other with a wire. Such a wire can become dangerously hot.

14. Report any injuries, accidents, or breakages to your teacher immediately. Also report anything that you suspect may be malfunctioning.

15. Work quietly so that you can hear any announcements concerning cautions and safety.

16. Know the locations of fire extinguishers, fire blankets, and the nearest exit.

17. When you have finished your work, check that the water and gas are turned off and that electric circuits are disconnected. Return all materials and apparatus to the places designated by your teacher. Follow your teacher's directions for disposal of any waste materials. Clean the work area.

See the following page for descriptions of the safety symbols you will see throughout this laboratory manual.

Safety Symbols

These symbols alert you to possible dangers in the laboratory and remind you to work carefully.

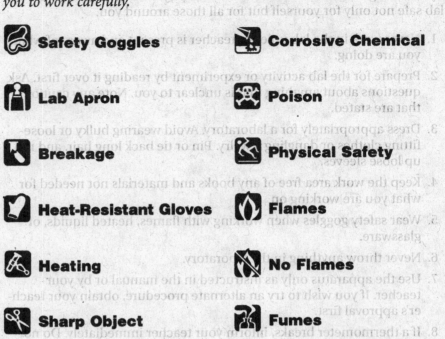

Safety Goggles	Corrosive Chemical
Lab Apron	Poison
Breakage	Physical Safety
Heat-Resistant Gloves	Flames
Heating	No Flames
Sharp Object	Fumes
Electric Shock	General Safety Awareness

Emergency Procedures

Report all injuries and accidents to your teacher immediately. Know the locations of fire blankets, fire extinguishers, the nearest exit, first aid equipment, and the school's office nurse.

Situation	Safe Response
Burns	Flush with cold water until the burning sensation subsides.
Cuts	If bleeding is severe, apply pressure or a compress directly to the cut and get medical attention. If cut is minor, allow to bleed briefly and wash with soap and water.
Electric Shock	Provide fresh air. Adjust the person's position so that the head is lower than the rest of the body. If breathing stops, use artificial resuscitation.
Eye Injury	Flush eye immediately with running water. Remove contact lenses. Do not allow the eye to be rubbed.
Fainting	See Electric Shock.
Fire	Turn off all gas outlets and disconnect all electric circuits. Use a fire blanket or fire extinguisher to smother the fire. Caution: Do not cut off a person's air supply. Never aim fire extinguisher at a person's face.

1 Amassing a Penny's Worth

Purpose

To formulate a hypothesis, accumulate data, and then develop a conclusion

Required Equipment/Supplies

balance (capable of measuring to the nearest hundredth of a gram)
20 pennies: 10 dated before 1982; 10 dated after 1982
graph paper

Discussion

Making measurements sometimes leads to important discoveries that might otherwise go unnoticed. In this activity you will measure the mass of some pennies and plot a histogram of your results. The results may be surprising.

The *mass* of an object refers to the amount of matter it possesses. The *weight* of an object, on the other hand, refers to the force of gravity on the object. Even though the mass of something remains constant, its weight can vary, since the gravitational force on an object depends on its location on Earth. We weigh a little bit less at the top of a mountain because we're farther from the center of Earth. So weight depends on location, whereas mass doesn't.

It is customary to measure the weight of things by how much they stretch a spring. S*pring scales* measure the weight (although they are typically calibrated in mass units such as grams). It is customary to measure the mass of an object by comparing it to a *standard mass*. Masses may be compared using a *beam balance.* Whereas a spring scale will give different readings in regions of different gravitation, a beam balance will accurately compare masses anywhere. A kilogram will balance a kilogram just as accurately at the top of a mountain as it will at sea level.

Procedure

Step 1: Adjust your beam balance so that it balances with no load. This is *zeroing* the balance. After zeroing the balance, find the mass of a penny to the nearest hundredth of a gram and write down your measurement for each penny and the penny's date of issue. Repeat for all of the pennies.

Step 2: Note that the pennies do not have identical masses. To see if there is any pattern to the data, make a *histogram*. A histogram is a plot of the frequency of each measurement in a series of measurements. Label the horizontal axis as the mass and the vertical axis as the number

Penny	Mass (g)	Date
1		
2		
3		
4		
5		
6		
7		
8		
9		
10		
11		
12		
13		
14		
15		
16		
17		
18		
19		
20		

of times that measurement occurred (sometimes called the "frequency" axis). The horizontal axis should range from the smallest to the largest mass in tenths of a gram. Number the vertical axis from 0 to 10. Place a dot above the value on the horizontal axis for the number of times each mass measurement occurs.

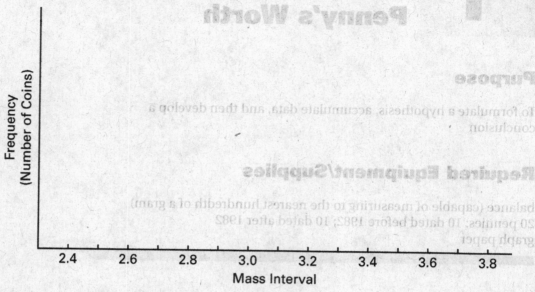

Analysis

1. Does your histogram reveal any information about the pennies that was not apparent by just looking at them? Do the coins *look* the same? Do they *feel* as though they have the same mass?

   _____

   _____

   _____

2. How do you account for the measured differences of the masses of the coins? What impact may the date of issue have on the mass of the pennies?

   _____

   _____

3. What other manufactured items besides pennies might exhibit variations in mass?

   _____

Penny	Mass (g)	Date
1		
2		
3		
4		
5		
6		
7		
8		
9		
10		
11		
12		
13		
14		
15		
16		
17		
18		
19		
20		

Chapter 2: Mechanical Equilibrium

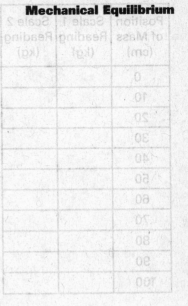

Position of Mass (cm)	Scale 1 Reading (kg)	Scale 2 Reading (kg)
0		
10		
20		
30		
40		
50		
60		
70		
80		
90		
100		

2 Smart Ropes

Purpose

To explore mechanical equilibrium

Required Equipment/Supplies

2 digital balances, preferably with a minimum of 1-kg capacity
meterstick
1-kg mass

Discussion

As a former boxer, uranium prospector, and cartoonist, the author of your textbook Paul Hewitt certainly had an unusual route into physics. He was inspired to learn about the subject by a fellow sign painter, Burl Grey, who was a science buff. Hewitt would engage in lively discussions about fascinating topics in science. It was these discussions in part that inspired Paul Hewitt to attend the Lowell Technological Institute in Massachusetts, where he began his physics career at the age of 26 with no scientific knowledge whatsoever.

During one of his discussions with Burl, Hewitt thought about what would happen to the tension in a rope suspended on either end of a wooden plank, like the kind used to suspend sign painters. It seemed reasonable enough that if you stood in the center, the tension of each rope would be the same. But what would the tension in each rope be if the painter walked closer to one rope or the other? Would the tension in the rope near to the painter be greater and the tension in the other, more distant rope, less? If so, how much greater? And how much less would the tension be in the other rope? More importantly, was the amount the tension *increases* in one rope the same as the amount the tension *decreases* in the other? How did each rope "know" how much to change? If so, what makes the ropes so *smart*?

Procedure

Step 1: Place the balances so that they are about 1 meter apart. Turn on the balances and make sure that they read "zero." Carefully position the meterstick so that each end is in the middle of the balance pan.

Step 2: Look at the mass reported on each balance. They should read about the same. Press the tare button. This resets the balance to zero. Doing this enables you to take readings that don't include the mass of the stick.

Position of Mass (cm)	Scale 1 Reading (kg)	Scale 2 Reading (kg)
0		
10		
20		
30		
40		
50		
60		
70		
80		
90		
100		

Step 3: Place a 1-kg mass on the 50-cm mark of the meterstick. Record the mass data reported on each scale in the data table.

Step 4: Move the 1-kg mass to the 40-cm mark. What mass is reported on each balance now? Continue to record mass measurements on each balance as you move the 1-kg mass to the 30-cm mark, the 20-cm mark, the 10-cm mark, and the 0-cm mark.

Step 5: Move the 1-kg mass back to the 50-cm mark. Take mass measurements on each balance as in Step 4, but with the 1-kg mass at the 60-cm mark, the 70-cm mark, the 80-cm mark, the 90-cm mark, and finally the 1-m (or 100-cm) mark.

Analysis

1. Study your data. Do you see a pattern? How does the amount of increase on one scale compare to the decrease on the other? What is the sum of the readings from each scale? Summarize your results below.

   _____

   _____

   _____

2. Make a "dual" plot line graph—that is, plot the readings from the left scale and the right scale versus the positions on the meterstick on the same graph. Make different data point marks on the graph such as squares for the left balance data and circles for the right balance data. Where do the plots intersect?

   _____

   _____

3. Write a generalization that explains why you think this is so.

   _____

   _____

   _____

3 24-Hour Towing Service

Purpose

To find a technique for moving a car when its wheels are locked

Required Equipment/Supplies

7 m to 10 m of chain or strong rope
tree or other strong vertical support
automobile or other large movable mass
1-, 2-, 5-kg masses

Discussion

You can exert a force on a parked automobile if you push or pull on it with your bare hands. You can do the same with a rope, but with more possibilities. Even without using pulleys, you can multiply the forces you exert. In this activity, you will try to show that you can exert a far greater force with brains than with brawn.

Procedure

Step 1: Park a car on a level surface with a tree in front of it, the brakes locked, and the gear selector set on "park" or in first gear.

Step 2: Your goal is to move the car closer to the tree. You will do this by exerting force on a rope, chain, or cable tied to the car's front end. How and where the force is exerted is up to your imagination. Your own body is the only energy source you can use. Make a sketch of your method. Show the applied force and the other forces with arrows.

Devise a technique to move the parked car.

Alternative Procedure

Step 1: Pick two (strong) students to hold each end of the chain. Have the students pull on the chain hard so that it is as level as possible.

Step 2: Successively add a 1-kg, then a 2-kg, and finally a 5-kg mass—having the students attempt to pull the chain as level as possible each time. Have the students compare the force on the chain to the masses you hang on the chain.

Fig. A

Analysis

1. Look at Figure A. Suppose a force F_3 is applied to a chain at right angles to the horizontal. Tension in the chain can then be shown as vectors F_1 and F_2. Since the system is not accelerating, all forces must add up to zero. The force F_1 is the tension in the chain and the force on whatever it is attached to, in this case, the right hand. The same is true for F_2. The force F_3, in this case the weight of the book, is small, while F_1 and F_2 are large. As the angle A becomes smaller, the forces F_1 and F_2 become larger. This idea is explained further in Section 2.5 of your text. Use a vector diagram to explain how a small sideways force can result in a large pull on the car.

2. List other situations that could use this technique for "force multiplication."

   _____

   _____

3. This method for making a large force is used to fell trees, pull stumps, straighten dents in car fenders, and pull loose teeth! Explain how this might be possible.

   _____

   _____

   _____

4 Sail with the Wind

Purpose

To investigate the relationship between the components of the force that propels a sailboat

Required Equipment/Supplies

dynamics cart fitted with an aluminum or cardboard sail
protractor
electric fan
ruler pulley
mass hangers
set of slotted masses
string

Discussion

In this experiment, you will use a small model sailboat and an electric fan. The physics of sailing involves vectors—quantities that have both magnitude and direction. Such directed quantities include force, velocity, acceleration, and momentum. In this lab, you will be concerned with force vectors.

In Figure A, a crate is being pulled across a floor. The vector F represents the applied force. This force causes motion in the horizontal direction, and it also tends to lift the crate from the floor. The vector can be "resolved" into two vectors—one horizontal and the other vertical. The horizontal and vertical vectors are *components* of the original vector. The components form two sides of a rectangle. The vector F is the diagonal of this rectangle. When a vector is represented as the diagonal of a rectangle, its components are the two sides of the rectangle.

Whatever the direction of wind impact on a sail, the direction of the resulting force is always perpendicular to the sail surface. The magnitude of the force is smallest when the wind blows parallel to the sail—when it goes right on by without making any impact. The force is largest when the sail is perpendicular to the wind—when the wind makes full impact. Even if the wind hits the sail at another angle, the resulting force is always directed *perpendicular* to the sail.

The keel of a sailboat is a sort of fin on the bottom of the boat. It helps prevent the boat from moving sideways in the water. The wind force on the sail can be resolved into two components. One component, K (for *keel*), is parallel to the keel. The other component, T (for *tip*), is perpendicular to the keel, as shown in Figure B. Only the component K contributes to the motion of the boat. The component T tends to move the boat sideways and tip it over.

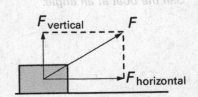

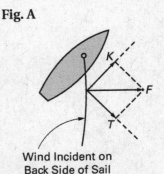

$F_{vertical}$ F

$F_{horizontal}$

Fig. A

K F T

Wind Incident on
Back Side of Sail

Fig. B

Any boat with a sail can sail downwind, that is, in the same direction as the wind. As the boat goes faster, the wind force on the sail decreases. If the boat is going as fast as the wind, then the sail simply sags. The wind force becomes zero. The fastest speed downwind is the speed of the wind.

A boat pointed directly into the wind with its sail at right angles to the keel is blown straight backward. No boat can sail *directly* into the wind. But a boat can *angle* into the wind so that a component of force *K* points in the forward direction. The procedure of going upwind is called *tacking*.

CAUTION: In the following procedure, you will be working with an electric fan. *Do not let hair or fingers get in the blades of the fan.*

Procedure

Step 1: Position the cart with its wheels (the keel) parallel to the wind from the fan. Position the sail perpendicular to the wheels. Start the fan blowing on the *front* of the cart with the wind parallel to the wheels.

Try to sail the boat directly upwind.

1. What happens to the cart?

_____

_____

Sail the boat directly downwind.

Step 2: Direct the wind from *behind* the cart and parallel to the wheels, keeping the sail perpendicular to the wheels, as shown in Figure C.

2. How does the cart move?

_____

_____

Fig. C

Sail the boat at an angle.

Step 3: Reposition the sail at a 45° angle to the wheels. Direct the wind behind, parallel to the wheels.

3. What happens to the cart?

_____

_____

Step 4: Use a ruler to draw a vector that represents the wind force perpendicular to the sail. Remember that the *length* of the vector you draw represents the size of the force. Split the vector into its *T* and *K* components. Label the forces and each component on the diagram.

Change the wind direction.

Step 5: Repeat Step 3 with the fan perpendicular to the wheels. Make a vector diagram for this case.

Change the wind direction.

Step 6: Repeat Step 3 but direct the wind at a 60° angle to the wheels from the front, as shown in Figure D.

4. Does the cart sail against or with the wind?

_____

_____

_____

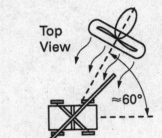

Top
View

≈60°

Fig. D

Draw a vector representing the wind force, and split it into its *T* and *K* components.

Step 7: Set up a pulley on the edge of the table, as shown in Figure E. Attach one end of a piece of lightweight string to the cart and thread the other end over the pulley. Attach a mass hanger to the string. Set the sail perpendicular to the direction of the cart. Place the fan directly between the pulley and the cart so that the full force of the wind strikes the sail at 90°. Holding the cart, turn the fan on its highest speed setting. The wind force depends on how close the fan is to the sail. Place the fan close to the sail. *Slowly* add very small masses to the mass hanger. Continue adding them until the weight of the masses (including the mass hanger) just balances the wind force on the cart. The wind force is balanced when adding the smallest mass you have causes the cart to move toward the pulley and removing the smallest mass causes the cart to move away from the pulley. Record the mass required to balance the cart.

Fig. E

mass = _____

Calculate the weight of this mass, using the approximation that a mass of 1 kg has a weight of 10 N.

weight = _____

5. What is the amount of wind force acting on the sail in this configuration?

_____

_____

Step 8: Repeat Step 7, but this time orient the sail at a 45° angle to the wind. Record the mass and calculate the weight required to balance the cart.

mass = _____

weight = _____

6. What is the amount of wind force acting on the sail in this configuration?

_____

_____

_____

Analysis

7. Which orientation of the sail with respect to the wind provided the greatest wind force?

_____

_____

8. When the sail is oriented at 45° to the wind, is the wind force less than half, equal to half, or greater than half the wind force at 90°? Justify your answer with a vector diagram.

_____

_____

5 Weight of a Sign

Purpose

To resolve a force vector into horizontal and vertical components

Required Equipment/Supplies

2 spring balances
strong cord or heavy string
ring stand or vertical rod with table clamp
5/8-inch dowel, 0.4 m long with screw eyehook
1-kg mass
graph paper
protractor

Discussion

Let's consider the forces that act on a sign on the side of a building. Look at where the cable connects with the boom on the sign. When we label all the forces acting *on* a body, it's referred to as a *free-body diagram*. Whereas a sketch of the problem helps us visualize the problem, a free-body diagram helps us analyze the forces that act *on the body*. Since the sign is at *equilibrium*, the *net force* on the sign is *zero*. This means the magnitude of the forces on the sign *upward* equal those *downward*, and the magnitude of the forces to the *left* equal those to the *right*. Now let's draw a free-body diagram and label forces acting on the sign at that point.

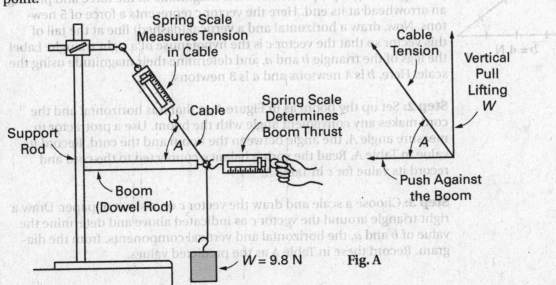

Spring Scale Measures Tension in Cable

Cable Tension

Vertical Pull Lifting *W*

Support Rod

Cable

A

Spring Scale Determines Boom Thrust

A

Push Against the Boom

Boom (Dowel Rod)

W = 9.8 N   **Fig. A**

Remember to label the forces acting *on the sign—not* the forces *the sign exerts on something else*. First, there is gravity, which acts down on the sign, or *weight*. The second is the *cable* pulling up at an angle. The third is the *boom* pushing sideways (away from the wall). To help visualize the boom force, consider what would happen if only the weight and the cable force acted on the sign—the sign would fall down and go (boom!) right into the wall!

Figure A illustrates a boom arrangement similar to the one we've discussed. It consists of a cable connected to a firm support and tied to a horizontal rod or *boom* at its other end. The *load* or weight is suspended from the junction of the cable and the boom represents the weight of the sign. In this apparatus a dowel rod with a screw eye serves as the boom.

The upper spring balance measures the tension in the cord used as a cable. The tension in the cable can be resolved into *components*. Its vertical component supports the load or weight and its horizontal component pushes against the boom, as shown in the vector diagram of Figure A, compressing it. Whereas *tension* stretches an object, *compression* squishes or presses inwards on it.

In this experiment, you will predict the value of the horizontal and vertical components of the cable tension by constructing a vector diagram similar to the one you've just drawn, using the measured values for the force and a protractor to measure the angle. You will then compare these predicted values with the values you obtain by direct measurement.

Procedure

Step 1: As a warm-up activity, let's *resolve* a force vector into horizontal and vertical components. One method is the so-called parallelogram method, where the *resultant* vector is the diagonal of two sides or *components* of a parallelogram. We use arrows to represent vectors and draw them from the tail, or beginning of the vector, to the end, or the *tip* of the vector. The tip of the arrow points in the *direction* of the vector and the length represents the *magnitude* when drawn to scale.

First, to represent the force as a vector as shown in Figure B, choose a scale that will give a large diagram (that fills most of the graph paper). Then, draw a line in the direction of the force at 37° to the horizontal, making its length proportional to the magnitude of the force and placing an arrowhead at its end. Here the vector *c* represents a force of 5 newtons. Now, draw a horizontal and a vertical (dashed) line at the tail of this vector so that the vector *c* is the hypotenuse of a right triangle. Label the legs of the triangle *b* and *a*, and determine their magnitude using the scale. Here, *b* is 4 newtons and *a* is 3 newtons.

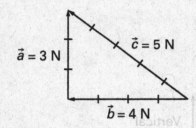

$\vec{a} = 3$ N $\vec{c} = 5$ N

$\vec{b} = 4$ N

Fig. B

Step 2: Set up the boom as in Figure A so that it is horizontal and the cord makes any convenient angle with the boom. Use a protractor to measure angle *A*, the angle between the boom and the cord. Record its value in Table A. Read the spring balance connected to the cord and record its value for *c* in Table A.

Step 3: Choose a scale and draw the vector *c* on a sheet of paper. Draw a right triangle around the vector *c* as indicated above and determine the value of *b* and *a*, the horizontal and vertical components, from the diagram. Record these in Table A as the predicted values.

Step 4: Measure the horizontal component b of the tension by connecting a second spring balance to the screw eye on the boom as shown in Figure A. Pull slowly in the horizontal direction *until the boom just falls away from the vertical support rod.* Record the spring balance reading at this instant. This is the measured value of the component of b. Record the magnitude of b in Table A.

Step 5: Now measure the vertical component of the tension, vector a. Again attach the spring balance to the screw eye and pull upward (vertically) until the spring balance completely supports the weight W and the boom. The reading of the balance is the measured value of the vertical component a. Record it in the table.

Step 6: Compare the predicted value of the components with the measured value in each case. Repeat the experiment using a different angle for the cable and a different weight W.

Data Table A

Trial	Given Force c (N)	Angle A (°)	Predicted Value of a (N)	Predicted Value of b (N)	Measured Value of a (N)	Measured Value of b (N)
1						
2						
3						

Analysis

1. Under what circumstances is the tension in the cable equal to the load?

   _____

   _____

2. If angle A is made smaller, what will happen to the tension in the cable? Why?

   _____

   _____

   _____

3. How was the weight of the boom taken into account in this experiment?

_____

_____

Going Further

Set up the derrick arrangement shown in Figure C. Design an experiment to discover (a) how the tension in the cable varies as angle A increases from 20° to 60° and (b) how the force of the boom varies as angle A increases from 20° to 60°.

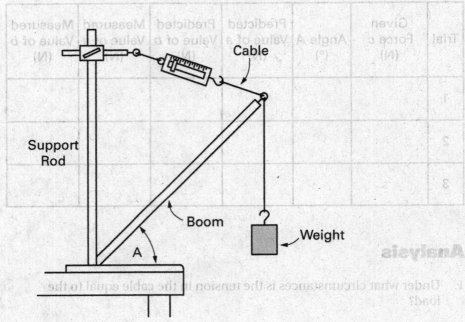

Fig. C

_____

_____

_____

_____

6   Going Nuts

Purpose

To explore the concept of inertia

Required Equipment/Supplies

8-, 10-, and 12-inch wooden embroidery hoops
narrow-mouth bottle
12 1/4-inch nuts
12 3/8-inch nuts

Discussion

Have you ever seen magicians on TV whip a tablecloth out from underneath an entire place setting? Can that really be done, or is there some trick to it?

Procedure

The game is simple. Carefully balance an embroidery hoop vertically on the mouth of a narrow-mouth bottle. Stack the nuts on the top of the hoop. The idea is to get as many nuts as possible into the bottle by touching the hoop with only one hand.

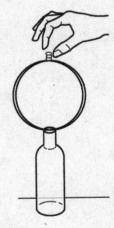

Analysis

1. Describe the winner's technique.

_____

_____

_____

_____

_____

_____

_____

2. Explain why the winner's technique was successful.

_____

_____

_____

_____

_____

_____

Going Further

Try again, this time using different sizes of hoops, nuts, and bottles.

Analysis

1. Is it easier for the nuts to land in the bottle with

   a. larger or smaller hoops? _____

   b. larger or smaller nuts? _____

   c. bottles with larger or smaller mouths? _____

2. Formulate a conclusion as to what combination of hoop size, nut size, and bottle–mouth size is easiest to land nuts in the bottle.

   _____

   _____

_____

_____

_____

_____

_____

_____

7 Buckle Up!

Purpose

To investigate how Newton's law of inertia is involved in collisions

Required Equipment/Supplies

4 m of string
2 dynamics carts
4 100-g slot masses
rubber band
2 small dolls
2 pulleys
2 wood blocks
masking tape

Discussion

Newton's first law of motion states that an object in motion keeps moving with constant velocity until a force is applied to that object. Seat belts in automobiles and other vehicles are a practical response to Newton's first law of motion. This activity demonstrates in miniature what happens when that important law is ignored.

Procedure

Step 1: Attach 2 m of string to each of two small dynamics carts. Attach a 200-g mass to the other end of each of the strings. Attach the pulleys to the table edge and hang the masses over them with the masses on the floor and the carts on the table. Place a wood block on the table in front of each pulley.

Step 2: Place one doll on each cart. Use a rubber band to serve as a seat belt for one of them.

Step 3: Pull the carts back side by side and release them so they accelerate toward the table's edge.

Crash doll on cart with and without "seat belts."

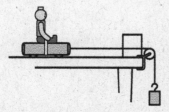

Analysis

1. What stopped the motion of the doll without a seat belt when the cart crashed to a stop?

   _____

   _____

   _____

2. Was there any difference for the doll with a seat belt?

   _____

   _____

   _____

Going Further

Step 4: Tape a 100-g mass to the doll.

3. Before repeating the experiment, predict the results with increased mass. Does the increased mass affect the movement of the doll after it crashes?

   _____

Going Even Further

Design a bumper for the cart so that when the cart collides with the solid barrier, a minimum of force is required to stop the doll. Sketch a few different designs on a separate sheet of paper. Then test each design and identify the one that provides maximum protection to the doll.

8 The Physics 500

Purpose

To compute the average speed of at least three different races and to participate in at least one race

Required Equipment/Supplies

meterstick
stopwatch
string
equipment brought by students for their races

Discussion

In this activity, you will need to think about what measurements are necessary to make in order to compute the average speed of an object. How does the average speed you compute compare with the maximum speed? How could you find the maximum speed of a runner or a car between stoplights?

Procedure

Step 1: Work in groups of about three students. Select instruments to measure distance and time. Develop a plan that will enable you to determine speed. Two students race each other in races such as hopping on one foot, rolling on the lawn, or walking backward. The third student collects and organizes data to determine the average speed of each racer. Repeat this process until each member of your group has a chance to be the timer. For the race in which you are the timer, record your plan and the type of race.

Measure average speed.

_____

_____

_____

When measurements are to be made in an experiment, a good experimenter organizes a table showing *all* data, not just the data that "seem to be right." Record your data in Data Table A. Show the units you used as well as the quantities. For each measurement, record as many digits as you can read directly from the measuring instrument, plus one estimated digit. Then calculate the average speed for each student.

Activity	Distance	Time	Speed

Data Table A

Compute unknown distance.

Step 2: Upon completing Step 1, report to your teacher. Your teacher will then ask you to perform one of your events over an unknown distance. Then, compute the distance covered (such as the distance across the amphitheater or the length of a corridor), using the average speed from Step 1.

event: _____

average speed = _____

distance = _____

Analysis

1. How does average speed relate to the distance covered and the time taken for travel?

   _____

2. Should the recorded average speed represent the maximum speed for each event? Explain.

   _____

3. Which event had the greatest average speed in the class in miles per hour (1.00 m/s $= 2.24$ mi/h)?

   _____

   _____

4. Does your measurement technique for speed enable you to measure the fastest speed attained during an event?

   _____

   _____

9 The Domino Effect

Purpose

To maximize the speed of falling dominoes

Required Equipment/Supplies

approximately 50 dominoes
stopwatch
meterstick

Discussion

A central property of motion is *speed*—the rate at which distance is covered. By rate, we mean how much or how many of something per unit of time: how many kilometers traveled in an hour, how many feet moved in a second, how many raindrops hitting a roof in a minute, how much interest earned on a bank account in a year. When we measure the speed of an automobile, we measure the rate at which this easily seen physical thing moves over the ground—for instance, how many kilometers per hour. But when we measure the speed of sound or the speed of light, we measure the rate at which energy moves. We cannot see this energy. We can, however, see and measure the speed of the energy pulse that makes a row of dominoes fall.

Procedure

Step 1: Set up 50 dominoes in a straight row, with equal spacing between them. The dominoes must be spaced at *least* the thickness of one domino apart. Your goal is to maximize the speed at which a row of dominoes falls down. Set the dominoes in a way you think will give the greatest speed.

Set up string of dominoes.

Step 2: Measure the total length of your row of dominoes.

length = _____

Step 3: Compute the average spacing distance between dominoes by measuring the length from the middle of the first domino to the middle of the last one, and divide this by the number of domino spacings.

average distance between dominoes = _____

Step 4: Measure the length of a domino.

length of domino = _____

spacing distance = _____ domino lengths

Step 5: Measure the time it takes for your row of dominoes to fall down.

time = _____

Compute average toppling speed.

Step 6: Compute the average toppling speed for your row of dominoes.

average speed = _____

Repeat for different spacings.

Step 7: Repeat Steps 5 and 6 for at least three more spacings. Include a spacing that is about as small as you can make it and still produce toppling and a spacing that is about as large as you can make it and still produce toppling. Record your data (including data for the first trial) in Data Table A.

Graph data.

Step 8: Using a separate piece of graph paper, make a graph of your data by sketching a smooth curve through your data points. Identify the point on the curve where the speed is maximum or minimum (this need not be exactly at one of your measured points).

Trial	Length	Average Spacing	Time	Speed

Data Table A

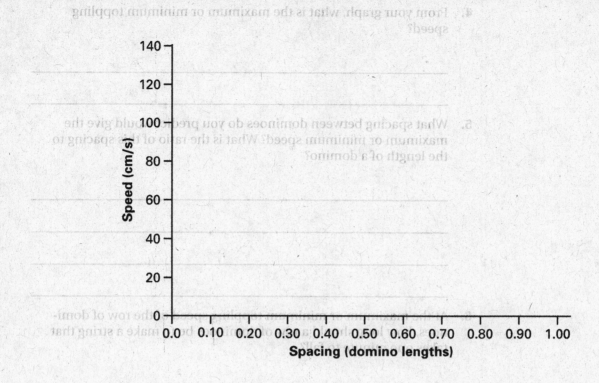

Analysis

1. What is a definition of average speed?

    _____

    _____

2. What are the factors that affect the speed of falling dominoes?

    _____

    _____

3. Why do we use *average speed* for the pulse running down the dominoes rather than *instantaneous speed*?

    _____

    _____

    _____

    _____

    _____

4. From your graph, what is the maximum or minimum toppling speed?

_____

_____

5. What spacing between dominoes do you predict would give the maximum or minimum speed? What is the ratio of this spacing to the length of a domino?

_____

_____

_____

_____

6. At the maximum or minimum toppling speed of the row of dominoes, how long should a row of dominoes be to make a string that takes one minute to fall?

_____

_____

10 Reaction Time

Purpose

To measure your reaction time

Required Equipment/Supplies

dollar bill
centimeter ruler

Discussion

Reaction time is the time interval between receiving a signal and acting on it—for example, the time between when a frog sees a fly land on
an adjacent leaf and the flick of the frog's tongue to capture the tasty
morsel.

   Reaction time often affects the making of measurements, such as
when using a stopwatch to measure the time for a 100-m dash. The
watch is started after the gun sounds and is stopped after the tape is
broken. Both actions involve the reaction time.

Procedure

Step 1: Hold a dollar bill so that the mid-point hangs between your partner's fingers. Challenge your partner to catch it by snapping his or her
fingers shut, without moving the rest of the hand, when you release it.
Also, have your partner hold the bill in the same way and see if you can
catch it when it is released. What do you discover?

Now try it using a ruler as shown to the right. The distance the ruler will
fall is found using

$$d = \frac{1}{2} g t^2$$

Simple rearrangement gives the time of fall in seconds.

$$t^2 = \frac{2d}{g}$$

$$t = \sqrt{\tfrac{2}{980}} \sqrt{d}$$

$$t = 0.045 \sqrt{d}$$

(For d in cm and t in s, we use $g = 980$ cm/s^2.)

Step 2: You and your partner will now take turns dropping a centimeter ruler between each other's fingers. Catch it and record the number of centimeters that passed during the reaction time it took each of you to catch the ruler each time. Each of you should drop the ruler three times. Then calculate your reaction time using the formula $t = 0.045\sqrt{d}$, where d is the average distance in centimeters.

Data Table A: Reaction Time Measured in Ruler-Catching Distance

Trial #	Starting Point (cm)	Ending Point (cm)	Distance Traveled (cm)
1			
2			
3			
Average			

Calculate your reaction time using the average for your three trials. Show your calculations.

your reaction time = _____

Analysis

1. Do you think your reaction time is always the same? Is your reaction time different for different stimuli?

   _____

   _____

2. Suggest possible explanations why reaction times are different for different people.

   _____

   _____

   _____

3. Do you think reaction time significantly affects measurements you might make when using timers for this course? How could you minimize its role?

_____

_____

_____

_____

4. What role does reaction time play in applying the brakes to your car in an emergency situation? Estimate the distance a car travels at 100 km/h due to your reaction time in braking.

_____

_____

_____

_____

5. List some examples where reaction time is important in sports.

_____

_____

_____

11   Merrily We Roll Along!

Purpose

To investigate the relationship between distance and time for a ball rolling down an incline

Required Equipment/Supplies

2-meter ramp
steel ball bearing or marble
wood block
stopwatch
tape
meterstick
protractor
overhead transparencies

Optional Equipment/Supplies

3 photogates with timing system
6 ring stands with clamps

Discussion

Measurement of the motion of a freely falling object is difficult because the speed increases rapidly. In fact, it increases by nearly 10 m/s every second. The distance that the object falls becomes very large, very quickly. Galileo slowed down the motion by using inclined planes. The component of gravity acting along the direction of the inclined plane is less than the full force of gravity that acts straight down—so the change of speed happens more slowly and is easier to measure. The less steep the incline, the smaller the acceleration. The physics of free fall can be understood by first considering the motion of a ball on an inclined plane.

This experiment will require you to make many timing measurements using a stopwatch or, if available, a computer. If you use a stopwatch, develop good timing techniques so as to minimize errors due to reaction time. The computer-photogate system is a powerful stopwatch because it not only eliminates reaction time, but can be used in a variety of timing modes. Since the diameter of the ball can be measured directly, its *speed* can be found by dividing the diameter by the amount of time it takes to pass through the beam striking the light probe. Strictly speaking, since the ball's speed is increasing as it rolls through the light beam, it exits the beam *slightly* faster than it enters the beam. The width of the ball divided by the time the ball eclipses the light beam gives the *average* speed of the ball through the light beam, not the *instantaneous* speed. But once the ball has picked up speed partway down the incline, its percentage change in speed is small during the short time that it eclipses the light. Then its measured average speed is practically the same as its instantaneous speed.

Procedure

Set up ramp.

Step 1: Set up a ramp with the angle of the incline at about 10° to the horizontal, as shown in Figure A.

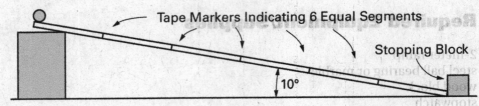

Tape Markers Indicating 6 Equal Segments

Stopping Block

10°

Fig. A

Divide ramp into equal parts.

Step 2: Divide the ramp's length into six equal parts and mark the six positions on the board with pieces of tape. These positions will be your release points. Suppose your ramp is 200 cm long. Divide 200 cm by 6 to get 33.33 cm per section. Mark your release points every 33.33 cm from the bottom. Place a stopping block at the bottom of the ramp to allow you to hear when the ball reaches the bottom.

Distance (cm)	Time (s)			
	Trial 1	Trial 2	Trial 3	Average

Data Table A

Time the ball down the incline.

Step 3: Use either a stopwatch or a photogate to measure the time it takes the ball to roll down the ramp from each of the six points. (If you use the computer, position one photogate at the release point and the other at the bottom of the ramp.) Use a ruler or a pencil to hold the ball at its starting position, and then pull it away quickly parallel to the incline to release the ball uniformly. Do several practice runs with the help of your partners to minimize error. Make at least three timings from each position, and record each time and the average of the three times in Data Table A.

Graph data.

Step 4: Graph your data, plotting distance (vertical axis) vs. average time (horizontal axis) on an overhead transparency. Use the same scales on the coordinate axes as the other groups in your class so that you can compare results.

Step 5: Repeat Steps 2–4 with the incline set at an angle 5° steeper. Record your data in Data Table B. Graph your data as in Step 4.

Change the tilt of the ramp and repeat.

Distance (cm)	Time (s)			
	Trial 1	Trial 2	Trial 3	Average

Data Table B

1. What is acceleration?

_____

2. Does the ball accelerate down the ramp? Cite evidence to defend your answer.

_____

_____

3. What happens to the acceleration if the angle of the ramp is increased?

_____

_____

Step 6: Remove the tape marks and place them at 10 cm, 40 cm, 90 cm, and 160 cm from the stopping block, as in Figure B. Set the incline of the ramp to be about 10°.

Reposition the tape markers on ramp.

Fig. B

160 cm

90 cm

10°

40 cm

10 cm

t_4

t_3

t_2

t_1

0 cm

Time the ball down the ramp.

Step 7: Measure the time it takes for the ball to roll down the ramp from each of the four release positions. Make at least three timings from each of the four positions and record each average of the three times in Column 2 of Data Table C.

Column 1	Column 2				Column 3	Column 4
Distance Traveled (cm)	Rolling Time (s)				Time Differences Between Successive Intervals (s)	Time in "Natural Units"
	Trial 1	Trial 2	Trial 3	Average		
10				$t_1 =$		1
40				$t_2 =$	$t_2 - t_1 =$	
90				$t_3 =$	$t_3 - t_2 =$	
160				$t_4 =$	$t_4 - t_3 =$	

Data Table C

Graph data.

Step 8: Graph your data, plotting distance (vertical axis) vs. time (horizontal axis) on an overhead transparency. Use the same coordinate axes as the other groups in your class so that you can compare results.

Study your data.

Step 9: Look at the data in Column 2 a little more closely. Notice that the *difference* between t_2 and t_1 is approximately the same as t_1 itself. The difference between t_3 and t_2 is also nearly the same as t_1. What about the difference between t_4 and t_3? Record these three time intervals in Column 3 of Data Table C.

Step 10: If your values in Column 3 are slightly different from one another, find their average by adding the four values and dividing by 4. Do as Galileo did in his famous experiments with inclined planes and call this average time interval one "natural" unit of time. Note that t_1 is already listed as one "natural" unit in Column 4 of Table C. Do you see that t_2 will equal—more or less—two units in Column 4? Record this, and also t_3 and t_4 in "natural" units, rounded to the nearest integer. Column 4 now contains the rolling times as multiples of the "natural" unit of time.

4. What happens to the *speed* of the ball as it rolls down the ramp? Does it increase, decrease, or remain constant? What evidence can you cite to support your answer?

_____

_____

Step 11: Overlay your transparency graph with other groups in your class and compare them.

5. Do balls of different mass have different accelerations?

_____

_____

Step 12: Investigate more carefully the distances traveled by the rolling ball in Table D. Fill in the blanks of Columns 2 and 3 to see the pattern.

Column 1	Column 2	Column 3
Distance Traveled (cm)	First Four Integers	Squares of First Four Integers
10	1	1
40	2	4
90	3	9
160		

Data Table D

6. What is the relation between the distances traveled and the squares of the first four integers?

_____

_____

Step 13: You are now about to make a very big discovery—so big, in fact, that Galileo is still famous for making it first! Compare the distances with the times in the fourth column of Data Table C. For example, t_2 is two "natural" time units and the distance rolled in time t_2 is 2^2, or 4, times as great as the distance rolled in time t_1.

7. Is the distance the ball rolls proportional to the square of the "natural" unit of time?

_____

The sizes of your experimental errors may help you appreciate Galileo's genius as an experimenter. Remember, there were no stopwatches 400 years ago! He used a "water clock," in which the amount of water that drips through a small opening serves to measure the time. Galileo concluded that the distance d is proportional to the square of the time t.

$$d \sim t^2$$

Step 14: Repeat Steps 6–10 with the incline set at an angle 5° steeper. Record your data in Data Table E.

Increase tilt of ramp.

8. What happens to the acceleration of the ball as the angle of the ramp is increased?

_____

_____

Column 1	Column 2				Column 3	Column 4
Distance Traveled (cm)	Rolling Time (s)				Time Differences Between Successive Intervals (s)	Time in "Natural Units"
	Trial 1	Trial 2	Trial 3	Average		
10				$t_1 =$		1
40				$t_2 =$	$t_2 - t_1 =$	
90				$t_3 =$	$t_3 - t_2 =$	
160				$t_4 =$	$t_4 - t_3 =$	

Data Table E

9. Instead of releasing the ball along the ramp, suppose you simply dropped it. It would fall about 5 meters during the first second. How far would it freely fall in 2 seconds? 5 seconds? 10 seconds?

_____

_____

_____

_____

Going Further: Investigating the Speed of the Ball Down the Ramp

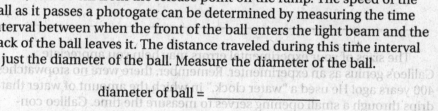

Set up computer with photogates.

You can use the computer to investigate the speed the ball acquires rolling down the ramp. This can be accomplished several different ways using light probes. One way is to position three photogates 10 cm, 40 cm, and 90 cm from the release point on the ramp. The speed of the ball as it passes a photogate can be determined by measuring the time interval between when the front of the ball enters the light beam and the back of the ball leaves it. The distance traveled during this time interval is just the diameter of the ball. Measure the diameter of the ball.

diameter of ball = _____

With the incline set at an angle of about 10°, measure the respective eclipse times for each photogate, and record your timings in Data Table F. To approximate the instantaneous speed of the ball at the three positions, divide the diameter of the ball by the eclipse time. Record the speeds in the table. Also record the average rolling time it took for the ball to travel each distance from the release point, from the information recorded in Data Table C.

Make a plot of instantaneous speed (vertical axis) vs. rolling time (horizontal axis).

Repeat with the ramp at an angle 5° steeper. Use the rolling times recorded in Data Table E.

	Total Distance Traveled (cm)	Eclipse Time (s)	Instantaneous Speed (cm/s)	Average Rolling Time (s)
First Angle	10			
	40			
	90			
Second Angle	10			
	40			
	90			

Data Table F

10. How do the slopes of the lines in your graphs of speed vs. time relate to the acceleration of the ball down the ramp?

_____

_____

_____

11. When you determined the speed of the ball with the photogates, were you really determining instantaneous speed? Explain.

_____

_____

_____

_____

12. As the angle of the ramp increased, the acceleration of the ball increased. Do you think there is an upper limit to the acceleration of the ball down the ramp? What is it?

_____

_____

_____

_____

_____

_____

_____

_____

_____

_____

12 Blind as a Bat

Purpose

To produce and compare graphs of different motions

Required Equipment/Supplies

computer, sonic ranger and sonic ranging software
masking tape
marking pen
can of soup (such as bean with bacon)
board
printer (optional)

Discussion

A bat can fly around in the dark without bumping into things by sensing the echoes of squeaks it emits. These squeaks reflect off walls and objects, return to the bat's head, and are processed in its brain to provide the location of nearby objects. The automatic focus on some cameras works on very much the same principle. The sonic ranger is a device that measures the time it takes for ultra-high frequency sound waves to go to and return from a target object. The data are fed to a computer where they are graphically displayed. The program can display the data in three ways: distance vs. time, velocity vs. time, and acceleration vs. time. Imagine how Galileo would marvel at such technology!

Procedure

Step 1: Your instructor will install the sonic ranger software on the computer for you. Familiarize yourself with the operation of the sonic ranger. Place the sonic ranger on a desk or table so that its beam is about chest high. (Note: Sometimes sonic rangers do not operate reliably on top of computer monitors.)

Select the option that plots distance vs. time. Adjust the sonic ranger so it graphs continuously. Depending on the ranging device you're using, readings at distances closer than 15 cm may be erratic. Test and see. Make small pencil marks or affix a piece of string to the floor in a straight line from the sonic ranger. Point the sonic ranger at a student standing at the 5-meter mark. Mark where the computer registers 0 m, 1 m, 2 m, etc. Set the maximum range approximately between 4 to 6 meters.

Part A: Analyzing Motion Plots

Step 2: Stand on the 1-meter mark. Face the sonic ranger and watch the monitor. Back away from the sonic ranger slowly and observe the real-time plot. Repeat, backing away from the sonic ranger more quickly, and observe the graph.

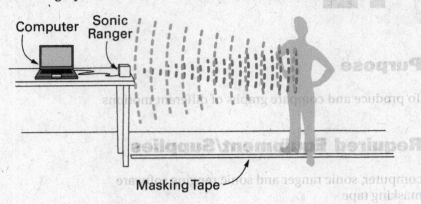

1. Make a sketch (or printout, if a printer is available) of each graph. How do the graphs compare?

_____

_____

_____

Step 3: Stand at the far end of the string. Slowly approach the sonic ranger and observe the graph plotted. Repeat, walking faster, and observe the graph plotted.

2. Make a sketch of each graph. How do the graphs compare?

_____

_____

_____

Step 4: Walk away from the sonic ranger slowly; stop, then approach the sonic ranger quickly.

3. Sketch the shape of the resulting graph. How do the slopes change?

_____

_____

_____

Step 5: Repeat Step 2, but select the option to display a plot of velocity vs. time.

4. Make a sketch of the graph. How do the distance-vs.-time and velocity-vs.-time graphs compare?

_____

_____

_____

Step 6: Repeat Step 3, but select the option to display a plot of velocity vs. time.

5. Make a sketch of the graph. How do the two new graphs compare?

_____

_____

_____

Step 7: Repeat Step 4, but select the option to display a plot of velocity vs. time.

6. Sketch the shape of the resulting graph. How do the slopes change?

_____

_____

_____

Part B: Move to Match the Graph

Generate a real-time plot of each motion depicted below and write a description of each. *Do not use the term "acceleration" in any of your descriptions.* Instead, use terms and phrases such as "rest," "constant speed," "speed up," "slow down," "toward the sonic ranger," "away from the sonic ranger." Generate each graph below. When you are ready, initiate the sonic ranger and move so that your motion generates a similar graph. Then describe the motion in words.

Example: Position-vs.-Time Graph

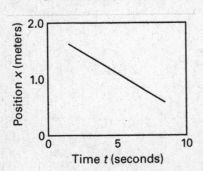

Description

Move toward the sensor (sonic ranger) at constant speed.

Make sure each person in the group can move to match this graph before moving onto the next graph.

1. Position-vs.-Time Graph   **Description**

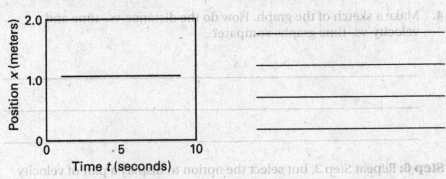

2. Position-vs.-Time Graph   **Description**

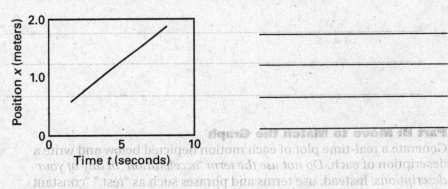

3. Position-vs.-Time Graph   **Description**

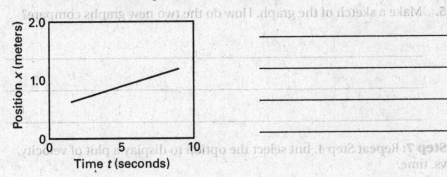

4. Position-vs.-Time Graph   **Description**

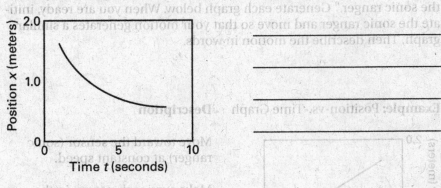

Example: Position-vs.-Time Graph   **Description**

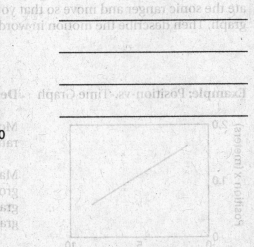

Part C: Move to Match the Words

Walk to match each description of motion. Draw the resulting position-vs.-time graph.

5. Description   **Position-vs.-Time Graph**

Move toward the sensor (sonic ranger) at constant speed, stop and remain still for a second, and then walk away from the sensor at constant speed.

6. Description   **Position-vs.-Time Graph**

Move toward the sensor at decreasing speed, and then, just as you come to rest, move away from the sensor with increasing speed.

7. Description   **Position-vs.-Time Graph**

Move away from the sensor with decreasing speed until you come to a stop. Then move toward the sensor with decreasing speed until you come to a stop.

Going Further: Analyzing Motion on an Incline

Set up the sonic ranger as shown in Figure A to analyze the motion of a can of soup, dynamics cart, or a large steel ball that is rolled up an incline and allowed to roll back. Practice rolling the can up the incline. Make sure the can is always at least 0.2 meter away from the sonic ranger. Predict what the shapes of distance-vs.-time and velocity-vs.-time graphs will look like for the can, cart, or ball as it rolls up and down the incline.

1. Make a sketch of your predicted graphs.

_____

_____

_____

Select the option so that both distance vs. time and velocity vs. time are displayed simultaneously.

2. Sketch the shape of the distance-vs.-time graph and velocity-vs.-time graphs.

_____

_____

_____

3. Is the velocity-vs.-time graph a straight line? Is the slope positive or negative?

_____

_____

_____

Chapter 4: Linear Motion

13 Bring Home the Bacon

Purpose

To investigate the motion of an object as it rolls down an incline

Required Equipment/Supplies

sonic ranger
computer and printer or graph paper
1–2 meter incline
can of soup with solid, nonsloshing contents (such as bean with bacon)
     or large ball
meterstick

Note: For best results, use an incline that is as smooth and flat as possible. If you are using wood, laminated shelving is preferred to solid boards because boards tend to warp. Using an undented can of soup works well; balls have a tendency to roll to one side. If you use a ball instead of a can, a smooth, massive ball such as a billiard ball is recommended.

Discussion

By sensing the echoes of squeaks it emits, a bat can fly in complete darkness without bumping into things. These squeaks reflect off walls and objects, return to the bat's head, and are processed in its brain to provide the location of nearby objects. The automatic focus on some cameras works on very much the same principle, as does the *sonic ranger.*

     The sonic ranger is a device that measures the time it takes for ultra high-frequency sound waves to go to and return from a target object. The computer processes the data from the sonic ranger and the graphs in real time. The program can display the data in three ways: distance vs. time, velocity vs. time, and acceleration vs. time.

     In this experiment, you will use a sonic ranger to compare the motion graphs of an object accelerating down an incline.

Procedure

Step 1: Set up an incline and adjust it to about 5–10 degrees above the horizontal. Set your sonic ranger to collect data. Your teacher will assist you with the setup and operation of the sonic ranger. Position the sonic ranger at the *top* of the incline. Mark a release point on the incline *no closer than 15 cm* from the ranger (its minimum range) with a piece of masking tape or small pencil mark. Practice releasing the can and allowing it to roll down the incline several times.

Release the can as soon as your lab partner activates the sonic ranger. Remember that the can must be released at least 15 cm from the sonic ranger. After successfully collecting data, plot the distance-vs.-time data.

Step 2: After you have plotted the data, describe the shape and character (positive or negative slope, steep or not steep) of the distance-vs.-time graph. Does the slope increase, decrease, or remain constant as time increases? If a printer is available, make a printout of the graph. If not, draw the graph on a piece of graph paper. Be sure to label the axes with both quantities and units.

Step 3: Now plot the data as a velocity-vs.-time graph. Describe the graph. Is the slope of the graph constant? Does the slope increase, decrease, or remain constant as time increases? Make a printout or draw this graph. Be sure to label the axes completely.

Step 4: Repeat the experiment but this time roll the can up the incline to the point where you released it in Step 1. This may require some practice to roll the can and coordinate activating the sonic ranger with your lab partner. Try to keep your hand flat and straight as you roll the can so that it goes straight up the incline. Take care *not* to overshoot the 15-cm mark on the incline.

Step 5: Repeat Steps 2 and 3 to collect and analyze the data.

Step 6: If the slope is constant (or nearly so), select the coordinates of two points on the velocity-vs.-time graph and use them to calculate the slope. Pick two points that represent a good average of your data (the straight portion of the graph). Label these two points as P_1 and P_2 on the velocity-vs.-time graph in your lab book. Make a right triangle formed by the velocity-vs.-time graph and the horizontal and vertical lines passing through P_1 and P_2. Use the sides of the triangle to calculate the slope (rise/run) of the graph, $\Delta v / \Delta t$.

Analysis

1. How are the distance-vs.-time and velocity-vs.-time graphs related for objects undergoing constant acceleration?

_____

_____

_____

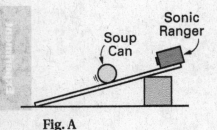

Fig. A

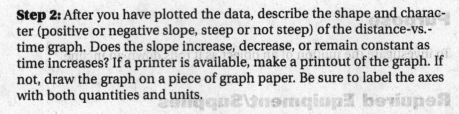

Fig. B

2. How would your results differ if the sonic ranger were positioned at the bottom of the incline instead of at the top? Try it and see if you are correct.

_____

_____

_____

_____

_____

3. How are your results comparable to the distance-vs.-time and velocity-vs.-time graphs for a ball thrown in the air?

_____

_____

_____

_____

_____

Going Further

Step 7: Manipulate the power of the x- and y-values of the distance-vs.-time data on the computer until the graph is linear. Ask your teacher for assistance on how to go about doing this.

4. What combination of powers of distance and time graph as a straight line? How are distance and time related?

_____

_____

Step 8: Your software can calculate the area under a velocity-vs.-time graph by calculating the area of the trapezoids formed by the data. Select this option for your velocity-vs.-time graph. Record the calculation displayed by the computer.

area under the graph = _____ m

5. How does this compare with the distance traveled by the can as measured by a meterstick?

_____

Chapter 4: Linear Motion

14 What a Drag!

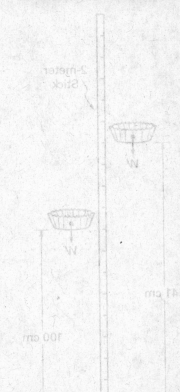

Purpose

To investigate how the terminal speed and weight of an object are related

Required Equipment/Supplies

coffee filters (basket type—not V-shaped), large and small
meterstick
2-m stick or two single metersticks taped together

Discussion

Drop a feather. It accelerates, but its large area-to-weight ratio causes it to quickly reach *terminal speed*. Common paper coffee filters also demonstrate this nicely, since they have a large area-to-weight ratio. Drop a couple of filters simultaneously from the same height and they fall together. Drop a single filter and a double-weight filter—two nested together—and the heavier one hits the floor first. When things are falling at or near their terminal speed, is air resistance proportional to *speed* or to the *square of the speed*? We can find out by seeing how much higher a twice-as-heavy filter should be dropped to reach the floor at the same time as a dropped single filter.

At terminal speed, v_T, the air resistance equals the weight of the falling object, and the distance fallen is

$$d = v_T t$$

Procedure

First Model
Air resistance is proportional to the speed (Resistance ~ v).

If resistance ~ v, then v_T ~ W. Then the falling distance

$$d \sim Wt$$

It follows that the double filter of weight $2W$ will fall $2d$ in the same time, a triple filter of weight $3W$ will fall $3d$ in the same time, etc.

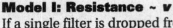

Model I: Resistance ~ v

If a single filter is dropped from rest 1 meter above the floor and at the same time a double filter is dropped 2 meters above the floor, and they land at the same time, then the hypothesis *Resistance ~ v* is confirmed.

Step 1: Drop the filters and see. Do they hit the floor at the same time? Record your observations.

_____

_____

Second Model

Air resistance is proportional to the speed squared (Resistance ~ v².).

If *Resistance ~ v²*, then *Resistance ~ W ~ v²*. Then $v \sim \sqrt{W}$, and

$$d \sim \sqrt{W}\, t$$

whereas for two filters and the weight *2W*

$$d \sim \sqrt{2W}\, t \sim \sqrt{2} \sqrt{W}\, t \sim 1.41d$$

Step 2: Now drop a single filter from 1 meter above the floor and at the same time drop the double filter 1.41 meters from the floor. If they land at the same time, the hypothesis *Resistance ~ v²* is confirmed.

Model II: Resistance ~ v²

Step 3: Simultaneously drop the single and the double filter. From what heights will they hit the floor at the same time? What is your conclusion? Test it by simultaneously dropping four nested filters 2 meters high and a single filter 1 meter high.

Analysis

1. What model of friction is confirmed by your experiment?

   _____

   _____

2. How does air friction vary with speed?

   _____

   _____

3. How does this experiment help explain how a parachute works?

   _____

   _____

2-meter Stick

W

W

141 cm

100 cm

Going Further

Predict what height three filters nested together should be dropped from so that they hit the floor at the same time as a single filter dropped from a height of 1 meter. Try it and see! Record your results.

_____

_____

_____

15 Impact Speed

Purpose

To estimate the speed of a falling object as it strikes the ground

Required Equipment/Supplies

stopwatch
string with a rock tied to one end
object with a large drag coefficient, such as a leaf or feather
plastic foam ball or table-tennis ball

Discussion

The area of a rectangle is its height multiplied by its base. The area of a triangle is its height multiplied by half its base. If the height and base are measured in meters, the area is measured in square meters. Consider the area under a graph of speed vs. time. The height represents the speed measured in meters per second, m/s, and the base represents time measured in seconds, s. The area of this patch is the speed times the time, expressed in units of m/s times s, which equals m. The speed times the time is the distance traveled. *The area under a graph of speed vs. time represents the distance traveled.* This very powerful idea underlies the advanced mathematics called integral calculus. You will investigate the idea that the area under a graph of speed vs. time can be used to predict the behavior of objects falling in the presence of air resistance.

If there were no air friction, a falling table-tennis ball or plastic foam ball would fall at a constant acceleration g so that its change of speed would be

$$v_f - v_i = gt$$

where v_f = final speed

v_i = initial speed

g = acceleration of gravity

t = time of fall

A graph of speed vs. time of fall is shown in Figure A, where $v_i = 0$. The y-axis represents the speed v_f of the freely falling object at the end of any time t. The area under the graph line is a triangle of base t and height v_f, so the area equals $\frac{1}{2}v_f t$.

To check that this does equal the distance traveled, note the following. The *average* speed $\bar{v}$ is half of v_f. The distance d traveled by a con-

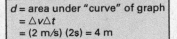

d = area under "curve" of graph
= $\triangle v \triangle t$
= (2 m/s) (2s) = 4 m

Effect of Air Friction
on Falling Bodies

Chapter 4: Linear Motion

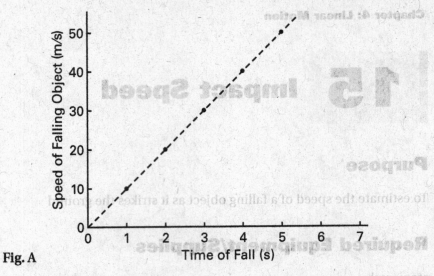

Fig. A

stantly accelerating body is its average speed $\bar{v}$ multiplied by the duration t of travel.

$$d = \bar{v}t \text{ or } d = \frac{1}{2}v_{\mathrm{f}}t$$

If you time a table-tennis ball falling from rest a distance of 43.0 m in air (say, from the twelfth floor of a building), the fall takes 3.5 s, *longer* than the theoretical time of 2.96 s. Air friction is *not negligible* for most objects, including table-tennis balls. A graph of the actual speed vs. the time of fall looks like the curve in Figure B.

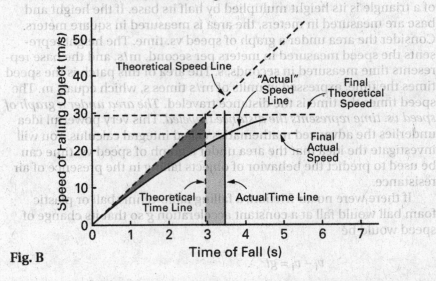

Fig. B

Since air resistance reduces the acceleration to below the theoretical value of 9.8 m/s², the falling speed is less than the theoretical speed. The difference is small at first, but grows as air resistance becomes greater and greater with the increasing speed. The graph of actual speed vs. time curves away from the theoretical straight line.

Is there a way to sketch the actual speed-vs.-time curve from only the distance fallen and the time of fall? Calculate the theoretical time of fall for no air resistance. The *height* from which the object is dropped is the same with or without air resistance. *The area under the actual speed-vs.-time curve must be the same as the area under the theoretical speed-vs.-time line.* It is the distance fallen. On a graph of theoretical speed vs. time, draw a vertical line from the theoretical time of fall on the horizontal axis up to the theoretical speed-vs.-time line. (In Figure B, this line is labeled "theoretical time line.") Draw another vertical line upward from the *actual* time of fall on the horizontal axis. (This line is labeled "actual time line" in Figure B.) Sketch a curve of actual speed vs. time that crosses the second vertical line below the theoretical speed-vs.-time line. Sketch this curve so that the area added below it due to increased time of fall (stippled area) equals the area subtracted from below the theoretical speed-vs.-time line due to decreased speed (cross-hatched area). *The areas under the two graphs are then equal.* This is a fair approximation to the actual speed-vs.-time curve. The point where this curve crosses the vertical line of the actual time gives the probable impact speed of the table-tennis ball.

Procedure

Step 1: Your group should choose a strategy to drop a table-tennis ball or plastic foam ball and clock its time of fall within 0.1 s or better. Consider a long-fall drop site, various releasing techniques, and reaction times associated with the timer you use.

Devise dropping strategy.

Step 2: Devise a method that eliminates as much error as possible to measure the distance the object falls.

Measure falling height.

Step 3: Submit your plan to your teacher for approval.

Submit proposal to teacher.

Step 4: Measure the height and the falling times for your object using the approved methods of Steps 1 and 2.

Measure height and falling times.

height = _____

actual time of fall = _____

Step 5: Using your measured value for the height, calculate the theoretical time of fall for your ball. Remember, this is the time it would take the ball to reach the ground if there were no air resistance.

Compute theoretical falling time.

theoretical time = _____

Step 6: Using an overhead transparency or graph paper, trace Figure B, leaving out the actual speed-vs.-time curve. Draw one vertical line from the *theoretical* time of fall for your height up to the theoretical speed-vs.-time line. Draw the other vertical line from the *actual* time of fall up to the theoretical speed-vs.-time line.

Draw theoretical and actual speed lines.

Step 7: Starting from the origin, sketch your approximation for the actual speed-vs.-time curve out to the point where it crosses the actual time line, using the example mentioned in the discussion. The area of your stippled region should be the same as that of the cross-hatched region.

Sketch curve on graph.

One possible way to do this is to tape a piece of cardboard to the wall and project your transparency onto it. Trace your two regions onto the cardboard and cut them out. Then measure the mass of the two regions. If their masses are not the same, adjust your actual speed curve and try again. Your approximation is done when the two regions have the same mass.

Step 8: Draw a horizontal line from the upper right corner of your stippled region over to the speed axis. Where it intersects the speed axis is the object's probable impact speed.

Predict probable impact speed.

Analysis

1. Have your teacher overlap your graph with those of others. How does your actual speed-vs.-time curve compare with theirs?

_____

2. What can you say about objects whose speed-vs.-time curves are close to the theoretical speed-vs.-time line?

_____

_____

3. What does the area under your speed-vs.-time graph represent?

_____

_____

4. The equation for distance traveled is $d = \bar{v}t$. In this lab, the distance fallen is the same with or without air friction. How do the average speeds and times compare with and without air friction? Try to use different-sized symbols such as those used on page 66 of your text.

_____

5. If you dropped a large leaf from the Empire State Building, what would its speed-vs.-time graph look like? How might it differ from that of a baseball?

_____

_____

_____

6. The *terminal* speed of a falling object is the speed at which it stops accelerating. How could you tell whether an object had reached its terminal speed by glancing at an actual speed-vs.-time graph?

_____

_____

16 Bull's Eye

Purpose

To predict the landing point of a projectile

Required Equipment/Supplies

ramp or toy car track
1/2-inch (or larger) steel ball
empty soup can
meterstick
plumb line
computer
photogate timing system

Discussion

Imagine a universe without gravity. In this universe, if you tossed a rock where there was no air, it would just keep going—forever. Because the rock would be going at a constant speed, it would cover the same amount of distance in each second. The equation for distance traveled when motion is uniform is

$$x = vt$$

The speed is

$$v = \frac{x}{t}$$

Coming back to earth, what happens when you drop a rock? It falls to the ground and the distance it covers in each second increases. Gravity is constantly increasing its speed. The equation of the vertical distance y fallen after any time t is

$$y = \frac{1}{2}gt^2$$

where g is the acceleration of gravity. The falling speed v after time t is

$$v = gt$$

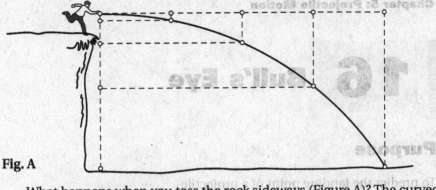

Fig. A

What happens when you toss the rock sideways (Figure A)? The curved motion that results can be described as the combination of two straight-line motions: one vertical and the other horizontal. The vertical motion undergoes the acceleration due to gravity, while the horizontal motion does not. The secret to analyzing projectile motion is to keep two separate sets of "books": one that treats the horizontal motion according to

$$x = vt$$

and the other that treats the vertical motion according to

$$y = \frac{1}{2} gt^2$$

Horizontal motion
- When thinking about how *far*, think about $x = vt$.
- When thinking about how *fast*, think about $v = x/t$.

Vertical motion
- When thinking about how *far*, think about $y = (1/2) gt^2$.
- When thinking about how *fast*, think about $v = gt$.

Your goal in this experiment is to predict where a steel ball will land when released from a certain height on an incline. The final test of your measurements and computations will be to position an empty soup can so that the ball lands in the can the *first* time!

Procedure

Step 1: Assemble your ramp. Make it as sturdy as possible so the steel balls roll smoothly and reproducibly, as shown in Figure D. The ramp should not sway or bend. The ball must leave the table *horizontally*. Make the horizontal part of the ramp at least 20 cm long. The vertical height of the ramp should be at least 30 cm.

Step 2: Use a stopwatch or photogate to measure the time it takes the ball to travel, from the first moment it reaches the level of the tabletop (point A in Figure B) to the time it leaves the tabletop (point B in Figure B). Divide this time interval into the horizontal distance on the ramp (from point A to point B) to find the horizontal speed. Release the ball from the same point (marked with tape) on the ramp for each of three runs.

Do *not* permit the ball to strike the floor! Record the average horizontal speed of the three runs.

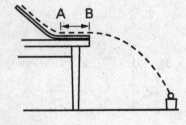

Fig. B

Compute the horizontal speed.

horizontal speed = _____

Step 3: Using a plumb line and a string, measure the vertical distance h the ball must drop from the bottom end of the ramp in order to land in an empty soup can on the floor.

1. Should the height of the can be taken into account when measuring the vertical distance h? If so, make your measurements accordingly.

_____

_____

_____

_____

_____

_____

_____

$h =$ _____

Step 4: Using the appropriate equation from the discussion, find the time t it takes the ball to fall from the bottom end of the ramp and land in the can. Write the equation that relates h and t.

equation for vertical distance: _____

Show your work in the following space.

$t =$ _____

Step 5: The range is the horizontal distance of travel for a projectile. Predict the range of the ball. Write the equation you used and your predicted range.

equation for range: _____

predicted range $R =$ _____

Place the can on the floor where you predict it will catch the ball.

Analysis

2. Compare the actual range of the ball with your predicted range. Compute the percentage error. (See Appendix 1 on how to compute percentage error.)

_____

_____

_____

3. What may cause the ball to miss the target?

_____

_____

_____

4. You probably noticed that the range of the ball increased in direct proportion to the speed at which it left the ramp. The speed depends on the release point of the ball on the ramp. What role do you think air resistance had in this experiment?

_____

_____

_____

_____

_____

Going Further

Horizontally launch ball.

Suppose you don't know the firing speed of the steel ball. If you go ahead and fire it, and then measure its range rather than predicting it, you can work backward and calculate the ball's initial speed. This is a good way to calculate speeds in general! Do this for one or two fired balls whose initial speeds you don't know.

_____

_____

_____

_____

17 Anatomy of a Homer

Purpose

To understand the principles of projectile motion by analyzing the physics of home runs

Required Equipment/Supplies

graph paper, pencil, protractor
colored pencils
coffee filters

Optional Equipment/Supplies

Conceptual Physics Alive! The San Francisco Years DVD set
squeeze foam rockets
video camera and monitor
computer with video capturing software
spreadsheet software
VideoPoint software or equivalent

Discussion

Baseball is not only a game that's fun to play and watch, it also illustrates some simple and complex physics principles *beautifully*, including force, velocity, acceleration, vectors, projectile motion, air friction, and rotational and fluid mechanics.

A home run is one of the most dramatic and exciting things in all of sports—partly because it's so difficult to do, but also because of the speed of the hit ball and its trajectory. Some home runs arch high into the sky, while others are nearly line drives, almost parallel to the field. What makes each home run so different? Fortunately, comprehending the basic physics of a home run is not nearly as difficult as it is to hit one! Understanding the underlying physics of baseball adds to the beauty and appreciation of the game.

In the lab Bull's Eye, the range of a projectile is calculated by measuring the *speed* of the ball at the top as it left the ramp using the formula v_x/t and the *time* (t_{top}) it took to reach the bottom from the formula $\frac{1}{2}gt^2$. Thus, the distance to the top of the can was simply the product of the speed and the time, $v_x t$. A home run is the "mirror image" of a Bull's-Eye—it's simply two Bull's-Eye trajectories put back to back.

Activity

There's no practical way to measure the speed of the home-run ball at the top of its path. Instead, we'll look at the initial speed of the *ball* off the bat (not to be confused with the speed of the *bat* as it hits the ball). We will separate this speed into its horizontal and vertical components. Since the horizontal and vertical motions of the ball are independent of each other, we can perform the calculations on each component separately to figure out the maximum height of the ball and where it's going to land (that is, its *range*).

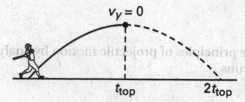

If you toss a ball straight up into the air, it reaches its maximum height when its speed is zero. So the time it takes to get to the top is simply the initial speed divided by the acceleration of gravity, g (since $v_y = gt$ then $t_{top} = v_y /g$). For a ball hit at an angle, we use the *vertical component* of the initial velocity to find the time it takes to reach the top (t_{top}). The time to reach the maximum height (t_{top}) is computed by dividing the initial vertical velocity by the acceleration of gravity, g. Assuming the trajectory of the ball is symmetric (which happens when there's no air resistance), the total time (t_{total}) the ball is in the air (the ball's *hang time*) is simply *twice* the time it takes to get to the top ($2t_{top}$). The range of the ball is the product of the horizontal component of the initial speed v_x and the hang time ($2t_{top}$).

Part A: Resolving Velocity Vectors Into Components

Procedure

Step 1: To get an idea about the relative importance of the initial speed and the direction the ball is struck, draw velocity vectors that represent the ball's speed just as it leaves the bat at various angles. Suppose a slugger strikes a ball so that it leaves the bat at 180 ft/s. Use the scale 1 cm = 10 ft/s to make velocity vectors. Draw all the vectors so they all have their tails on the same point, the first vector at 0°, the second vector at 15°, etc., up to 90°. To help make each vector clearly visible, draw each vector using a different colored pencil.

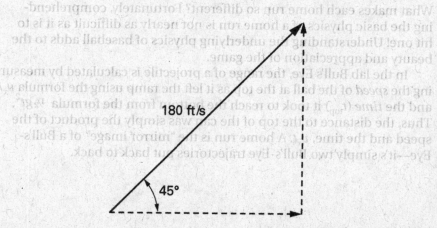

Step 2: Now sketch the components of each velocity vector using dashed lines. Remember, this velocity vector represents the *initial* velocity of the ball. Remember, just as in the lab Bull's Eye, the vertical components will decrease due to the acceleration of gravity whereas the horizontal ones won't.

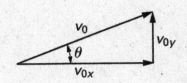

Step 3: Make a table of v_x and v_y for the various angles.

Analysis

1. Which ball goes the highest?

_____

_____

2. At what angle is the ball going fastest horizontally?

_____

_____

3. At what angle is the horizontal component the same as the vertical component?

_____

_____

4. At what angle does the ball go farthest? Why?

_____

_____

Part B: Dissecting a Homer

Procedure

Let's analyze some of the physics involved when a batter hits a homer. First, we need to make some assumptions. To keep things simple, we will neglect the effects of air friction or drag. Suppose the batter hits a 95-mi/h fastball at 120 mi/h at an angle of 38°. Let's do some calculations and see how high the ball goes and where it lands. To make this problem more familiar, we'll use units of feet and feet/second instead of meters and meters/second. To convert mi/h to ft/s, recall that there are 5280 feet in a mile and 3600 seconds in an hour. Therefore, 1 mi/h = 5280 ft/3600 s or approximately 1.47 ft/s.

Step 4: Convert the 120 mi/h into ft/s. Use the conversion factor of 1 mi/h = 1.47 ft/s. Show your conversion and record your result.

$$120 \text{ mi/h} = (120 \text{ mi/h}) \times \frac{(1.47 \text{ ft/s})}{(\text{mi/h})} = \underline{\hspace{2cm}} \text{ ft/s}$$

Step 5: Choose a scale (such as a 1 cm = 10 ft/s) so that your velocity vector will occupy a large portion of your graph paper. Write down the scale you choose.

scale: _____

Then use your scale to calculate the length of the velocity vector that represents the initial velocity of the ball. Record your calculations.

length of velocity vector = _____

Step 6: Use a protractor to draw the initial velocity vector on your graph paper. Then carefully sketch the horizontal and vertical components of the initial velocity using dashed lines.

Step 7: Measure the length of the horizontal components v_x of the ball's initial velocity. Then convert this measurement into ft/s. Record your measurement and calculation.

$v_x = $ _____ ft/s

Step 8: Repeat this procedure to find the ball vertical component of the ball's initial velocity.

$v_y = $ _____ ft/s

Analysis

Now that we know the ball's initial horizontal and vertical velocities for both the pitch and the hit, we can calculate some interesting things about the ball's trajectory.

The Pitch:

5. How long does it take a ball going 95 mi/h to reach home plate? The distance from the pitcher's mound to home plate is 60.5 ft. Show your calculations.

_____

6. Assuming the ball is pitched parallel to the ground, how *far* does it fall due to gravity by the time it reaches the plate? Show your calculations.

_____

_____

The Homer:

7. How long does it take for the ball hit at 120 mi/h at the 38° angle to reach its maximum height (t_{top})?

_____

8. How long is the ball in the air? (That is, what is the *hang time*? Remember, hang time = $2t_{top}$.)

_____

9. What is the maximum height of the ball?

_____

10. How far does the ball travel?

_____

11. What are the two most important factors that determine how far a batted ball will go?

_____

_____

12. Do your answers seem reasonable? Can the effects of air friction be neglected?

_____

_____

13. Why do baseballs travel farther at Coors Field in Denver, Colorado (which is at an altitude of 5000 ft)?

_____

_____

14. Why are most homers not hit at angles greater than 50°?

_____

_____

Going Further: The Effects of Friction

Step 9: Try to launch the foam rocket with the same force each time. This may take several trials to become a consistent "launcher." Launch a foam pop rocket at various angles. Devise a technique for estimating the angle the rocket was launched.

Step 10: Using a video or camcorder, make a recording of the rocket's trajectory when launched at the angle that results in the maximum range. Position a meterstick vertically in the background to give you a way to measure the height of the rocket in the video. It is helpful to choose a plain background to make viewing the rocket's path easier.

Step 11: After obtaining a video of the rocket, import the video clip into a computer program using video capturing software. Play it back onto a monitor frame by frame. Most video cameras take a frame every $1/30^{th}$ of a second. If available use _VideoPoint_ software; it will make analyzing the trajectory very easy.

Step 12: Construct a data table of the rocket's height vs. time. Record the data collected from the video analysis of the rocket launch. Plot your data as a line graph on graph paper, or alternatively, use spreadsheet software on a computer to produce the data table and graph. Print your data table and graph. You should be able to produce a smooth curve of the trajectory of the ball.

15. What angle results in the greatest horizontal range?

_____

16. Is the trajectory of the rocket a symmetric parabola?

_____

_____

17. What is causing the trajectory to diverge from a parabola?

_____

Step 13: View the video of a professional baseball player hitting home runs. Observe the angle of the ball as it leaves the bat. In the absence of friction, the maximum range of a projectile is when it is hit at 45°.

Name_____ Period_____ Date_____

Analysis

18. Are most of the homers hit at or near 45°?

_____

_____

19. You'll notice that most of the homers hit are at 45° to the horizontal or *less*—sometimes much less. Some are barely 25°. Explain.

_____

_____

_____

_____

20. In the lab What a Drag, you tested two models of friction: one in which the friction varies as the *speed* and another in which the friction varies as the *square of the speed*. What were your results from the lab? (If you have not done the lab, this would be an *excellent* time to do so!) Summarize your results below.

_____

_____

© Pearson Education, Inc., or its affiliates. All rights reserved.

Chapter 5 Projectile Motion **65**

Analysis

18. Are most of the homers hit at or near 45°?

_____

19. You'll notice that most of the homers hit are at 45° to the horizontal or less—sometimes much less. Some are barely 25°. Explain.

_____

_____

_____

20. In the lab What a Drag, you tested two models of friction: one in which the friction varies as the speed and another in which the friction varies as the square of the speed. What were your results from the lab? (If you have not done the lab, this would be an excellent time to do so.) Summarize your results below.

_____

_____

18 Getting Pushy

Purpose

To investigate the relationship among mass, force, and acceleration

Required Equipment/Supplies

roller skates, skateboard, or student dynamics cart
spring balance
stopwatch
meterstick
tape

Discussion

Most of us have felt the acceleration of a car as it leaves a stop sign or the negative acceleration when it comes to a stop. We hear sportscasters describe a running back as accelerating through the defensive line. In this activity, you will investigate some variables that influence acceleration.

Procedure 🏃

Step 1: With pieces of tape, mark positions on the floor at intervals of 0 m, 5 m, 10 m, and 15 m. The path along the floor should be smooth, straight, and level. Gym areas or hallways work well.

Mark off distances.

Step 2: A student must put on the skates (or sit on the cart) and stand on the 0-m mark. Another student must stand behind the 0-m mark and hold the skater. The skater holds a spring balance by its hook.

Step 3: A third student must grasp the other end of the spring balance and exert a constant pulling force on the skater when the skater is released.

Pull on skater . . . catch skater.

The puller must maintain a constant force throughout the distance the skater is pulled. Do not pull harder to "get going." Time how long it takes to get to the 5-m, 10-m, and 15-m marks, and record this data in Data Table A along with the readings on the spring balance.

Trial	Distance (m)	Force (N)	Time (s)
	5		
1	10		
	15		
	5		
2	10		
	15		
	5		
3	10		
	15		

Data Table A

Step 4: Repeat the experiment twice, using different skaters to vary the mass, but keeping the force the same. If the results are inconsistent, the skater may not be holding the skates parallel or may be trying to change directions slightly during the trial.

Step 5: Repeat with the puller maintaining a *different* constant force throughout the distance the skater is pulled, but using the same three skaters as before. Record your results in Data Table B.

Trial	Distance (m)	Force (N)	Time (s)
	5		
1	10		
	15		
	5		
2	10		
	15		
	5		
3	10		
	15		

Data Table B

Analysis

1. Until the time of Galileo, people believed that a constant force is required to produce a constant speed. Do your observations confirm or reject this notion?

   _____

   _____

   _____

2. What happens to the speed as you proceed farther and farther along the measured distances?

   _____

   _____

   _____

3. What happens to the rate of increase in speed—the acceleration—as you proceed farther and farther along the measured distances?

   _____

   _____

   _____

4. When the force is the same, how does the acceleration depend upon the mass?

   _____

   _____

   _____

5. When the mass of the skater is the same, how does the acceleration depend upon the force?

   _____

   _____

   _____

6. Suppose a 3-N force is applied to the skater and no movement results. How can this be explained?

   _____

   _____

Chapter 6: Newton's Second Law of Motion—
Force and Acceleration

19 Constant Force and Changing Mass

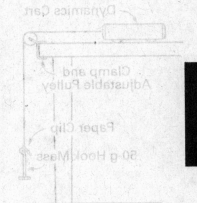

Purpose

To investigate the effect of increases in mass on an accelerating system

Required Equipment/Supplies

meterstick
2 Pasco dynamics carts and track
4 500-g masses (2 masses come with Pasco carts)
1 50-g hook mass
pulley with table clamp
triple-beam balance
string
paper clips or small weights
masking tape
graph paper or overhead transparencies
stopwatch or photogate timing system

Discussion

Airplanes accelerate from rest on the runway until they reach their takeoff speed. Cars accelerate from a stop sign until they reach cruising speed. And when they come to a stop, they decelerate. How does mass affect these accelerations?

In Activity 11, Getting Pushy, you discovered that less massive people undergo greater acceleration than more massive people when the same force is applied to each. In this experiment you will accelerate a dynamics cart. You will apply the same force to carts of different masses. You will apply the force by suspending a weight over a pulley. The cart and the hanging weight comprise a *system* and accelerate together. A relationship between mass and acceleration should become evident.

Set up pulley-and-cart system.

Procedure

Step 1: Fasten a pulley over the edge of the table. The pulley will change the direction of the force from a downward pull on the mass into a sideways pull on the cart.

Step 2: Mark off a distance on the tabletop slightly shorter than the distance the mass can fall from the table to the floor.

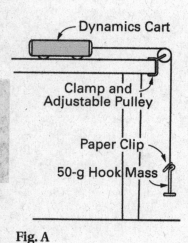

Fig. A

Set up timing system.

Step 3: Use a triple-beam balance to determine the mass of the carts. Record the total mass of the cart(s) and the four additional masses in Data Table A. Do not include the 50-g hanging mass or the mass of the paper clip counterweight.

Step 4: Nest the two dynamics carts on top of one another, and stack the 500-g masses on the top cart. It may be necessary to secure the masses and carts with masking tape. Tie one end of the string to the cart and thread it over the pulley, as shown in Figure A. To offset frictional effects, add enough paper clips or small weights to the other end of the string so that when the cart is pushed slightly it moves at a *constant speed*. (Give your teacher a break! Stop the cart before it crashes into the pulley during the experiment by adjusting the stop bar on the dynamics track.)

Step 5: Practice accelerating the cart a few times to ensure proper alignment. Add a 50-g hook mass to the paper clip counterweight. Keep this falling weight the same at all times during the experiment.

Step 6: There are a variety of ways to time the motion of the cart and the falling weight. You could use a stopwatch or a photogate timing system. The distance is the distance between two photogates. Position the cart so that, as it is released, it passes the first photogates and starts the timer. The timer stops when the second photogate is passed.

Repeat three times, recording the times in Data Table A. Compute and record the average time.

Mass of Cart	Time to Cover Same Distance				Acceleration (m/s²)
	Trial 1	Trial 2	Trial 3	Avg	

Data Table A

Remove masses from the cart and repeat.

Step 7: Repeat Step 5 five times, removing a 500-g mass from the cart each time (the last time removing the top cart). Record the times in Data Table A, along with the average time for each mass.

Compute the acceleration.

Step 8: Use the average times for each mass from Steps 5 and 6 to compute the accelerations of the system. To do this, use the equation for an accelerating system that relates distance d, acceleration a, and time t.

$$d = \frac{1}{2}at^2$$

Rearrange this equation to obtain the acceleration.

$$a = \frac{2d}{t^2}$$

The cart always accelerates through the same distance d. Calculate the acceleration a. Provided you express your distance in meters and your time in seconds, your units of acceleration will be m/s^2.

Record your accelerations in Data Table A.

Graph your data.

Step 9: Using an overhead transparency or graph paper, make a graph of acceleration (vertical axis) vs. mass (horizontal axis).

Analysis

1. Describe your graph of acceleration vs. mass. Is it a straight-line graph or a curve?

   _____

   _____

   _____

   _____

2. Share your results with other class members. For a constant applied force, how does increasing the mass of an object affect its acceleration?

   _____

   _____

   _____

20 Constant Mass and Changing Force

Purpose

To investigate how increasing the applied force affects the acceleration of a system

Required Equipment/Supplies

Pasco dynamics cart and track
masking tape
pulley with table clamp
6 20-g hook masses
string
paper clips
graph paper or overhead transparency
stopwatch or photogate timing system

Discussion

Have you ever noticed when an elevator cage at a construction site goes *up* that a large counterweight (usually made of concrete) comes *down*? The elevator and the counterweight are connected by a strong cable. Thus, the elevator doesn't move without the counterweight moving the same amount. Since the electric motor can't move one without moving the other, the two so connected together form a *system*.

In Experiment 19, Constant Force and Changing Mass, you learned how the acceleration of a dynamics cart was affected by increasing the mass of the cart. But the cart is really part of a *system* consisting of the *cart and the falling weight*—just as the elevator and the counterweight together form a system. The cart doesn't move without the falling weight moving exactly the same amount. By adding mass to the cart, you were actually adding mass to the *cart-and-falling-weight system*.

Adding mass to the cart rather than to the falling weight was *not* accidental, however. In doing so, you changed only one variable— mass—to see how it affects the acceleration of the entire system.

In this experiment, you will investigate how increasing the applied force on a cart-and-falling-weight system affects its acceleration while keeping the mass of the system constant. The applied force is increased without changing the mass *by removing mass from the cart and placing it on the hanging weight.*

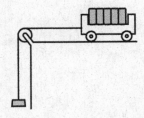

Only the weight of the falling mass accelerates the system, but the total mass of both the falling weight and the loaded cart resist acceleration.

The same general procedure used in Experiment 19 will be used here. In Experiment 19, you measured the total time the cart accelerated to compute the acceleration using the formula below:

$$a = \frac{2d}{t^2}$$

Procedure

Set up cart-and-hanging-weight system.

Step 1: Set up your apparatus much the same as you did in Experiment 19, except that you should load the dynamics cart with six 20-g masses. Masking tape may be required to hold the masses in position.

Step 2: Attach one end of the string to the cart, pass the other over the pulley, and tie a large paper clip to the end of the string. To offset frictional effects, place just enough paper clips or other small weights on the end of the string so that when the cart is moved by a small tap, it rolls on the track or table with constant speed. Do not remove this counterweight at any time during the experiment.

Set up timing system.

Step 3: You can time the system in a variety of ways. You could use a stopwatch or a photogate timing system. The distance is the distance between two photogates. Position the cart so that as it is released, it eclipses the first photogate and starts the timer. The timer stops when the second photogate is passed.

Step 4: For the first trial, remove one of the hooked 20-g masses from the cart and hang it on the end of the string.

Measure the acceleration time.

Step 5: With your timing system all set, release the cart and measure the time it takes to accelerate your cart toward the pulley. Catch the cart *before* it crashes into the pulley, spews your masses all over the floor, and damages the pulley! Repeat each trial at least twice. Record your data and compute the average of your three trials in Data Table A.

Mass of Falling Weight	Time to Cover Same Distance				Acceleration (m/s²)
	Trial 1	Trial 2	Trial 3	Avg	
20 g					
40 g					
60 g					
80 g					
100 g					

Data Table A

Increase the applied force.

Step 6: Remove another 20-g mass from the cart and place it on the end of the string with the other 20-g mass. Make several runs and record your data in Data Table A.

Step 7: Repeat Step 5 five times, increasing the mass of the falling weight by 20 grams each time. Make several runs and record your data in Data Table A.

Step 8: With the help of your teacher, calculate the accelerations and use an overhead transparency to make a graph of acceleration (vertical axis) vs. force (horizontal axis). Since the cart always accelerates through the same distance d, the acceleration equals $2d/t^2$. Express your distance in meters and your acceleration will have units of m/s^2. Call the force caused by the single 20-g mass "F," the force caused by two 20-g masses "$2F$," and so on.

Graph your data.

Analysis

1. Describe your graph of acceleration vs. force. Do your data points produce a straight-line graph or a curved graph?

   _____

   _____

2. Does the acceleration of the cart increase or decrease as the force increases?

   _____

   _____

3. Was the mass of the accelerating system (cart + falling weight) the same in each case?

   _____

   _____

4. In Experiment 19, you learned (or should have!) that when a constant force is applied, the acceleration of the system *decreases* as its mass increases. The acceleration is *inversely proportional* to the mass of the system. Here in Experiment 20, the acceleration of the system increases as the force applied to it (the weights of the falling masses) increases. That is, the acceleration is *directly proportional* to the applied force. Combine the results of Experiments 19 and 20 to come up with a general relationship between force, mass, and acceleration.

   _____

   _____

   _____

   _____

Experiment

21 Tension

Purpose

To introduce the concept of tension in a string

Required Equipment/Supplies

3 large paper clips
3 large identical rubber bands
1 m of strong string
500-g hook mass
ring stand
spring scale
ruler
marking pen

Discussion

When you put bananas on a hanging scale at the supermarket, a spring is stretched. The greater the weight of the bananas (the force that is exerted), the more the spring is stretched. Rubber bands act in a similar way when stretched. For stretches that are not too great, the amount of the stretch is directly proportional to the force.

If you hang a load from a string, you produce a tension in the string and stretch it a small amount. The amount of tension can be measured by attaching the top end of the string to the hook of a spring scale hanging from a support. The scale will register the tension as the sum of the weights of the load and the string. The string's weight is usually small enough to be neglected, so the tension is simply the weight of the load.

Is this tension the same all along the string? To find the tension at the lower end of the string you could place a second scale there, but the weight of the added scale would increase the tension in the top scale. You need a scale with a tiny mass. Since a rubber band stretches proportionally with the force, you could use it to measure the tension at the lower end of the string. Its tiny weight will not noticeably affect the reading in the top scale. In this activity, you will use rubber bands to investigate the tensions at different places along short and long strings supporting the same load.

Procedure

Step 1: Without stretching them, place three identical large rubber bands flat on a table. Carefully mark two ink dots 1 cm apart on each of the rubber bands.

Mark rubber bands.

Cut string.

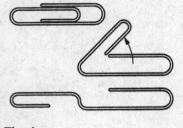

Fig. A

Step 2: Cut a 1-meter string into 2 lengths of 25 cm each, and 1 length of 50 cm. Tie each end of each string into a loop.

Step 3: Bend the paper clips into double hooks, as shown in Figure A.

Step 4: Suspend the spring scale from the top of a ring stand such that it extends over the edge of the table. Place one end of a rubber band over the scale hook. Suspend the 500-g load from the lower end of the rubber band as shown in Figure B. Note that the weight of the load stretches both the rubber band and the spring inside the spring scale.

While the load is suspended, measure and record the distance between the ink marks on the rubber band. Also record the reading on the spring scale.

distance between marks = _____

tension (scale reading) = _____

3-rubber-band stretch

Step 5: With the use of paper-clip hooks, repeat the previous step using three rubber bands connected as shown in Figure C. Measure the stretch of the three bands. Record your results.

distance between marks of top band = _____

distance between marks of middle band = _____

distance between marks of bottom band = _____

tension (spring-scale reading) = _____

Hang load from one band and string.

Step 6: Disconnect the load and two of the rubber bands. Using a paper-clip hook, connect one end of a 25-cm length of string to the remaining rubber band. Suspend the load on the other end of the string, as shown in Figure D. Record the spring-scale reading and the distance between the marks of the rubber band.

tension (spring-scale reading) = _____

distance between marks of band = _____

Hang load from string and two bands.

Step 7: Using a paper-clip hook, insert a rubber band between the lower end of the string and the load, as shown in Figure E. While you are attaching the bottom rubber band, mentally predict the amount of stretch of the added band. Compare the tensions at the top and the bottom of the string by measuring the stretches of the two rubber bands. Record your findings.

distance between marks of top band = _____

distance between marks of bottom band = _____

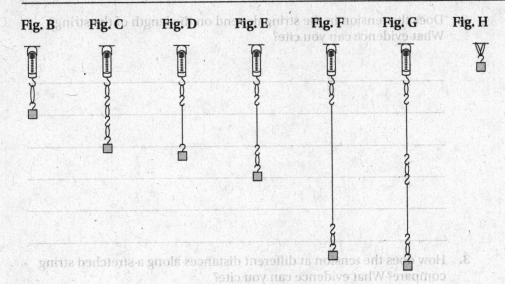

Fig. B   Fig. C   Fig. D   Fig. E   Fig. F   Fig. G   Fig. H

Step 8: Repeat Step 7 using the 50-cm piece of string, as shown in Figure F, to see whether the tension in the string depends on the length of the string. Make a mental prediction before you measure and record your findings.

Repeat using longer string.

distance between marks of top band = _____

distance between marks of bottom band = _____

Step 9: Repeat the previous step, substituting two 25-cm pieces of string joined by paper-clip hooks with a rubber band in the middle (as shown in Figure G) for the 50-cm string. This arrangement is to compare the tension at the middle of a string with the tension at its ends. While you are substituting, mentally predict how far apart the ink marks will be. After your prediction, measure and record your findings.

Add rubber band between two strings.

distance between marks of top band = _____

distance between marks of middle band = _____

distance between marks of bottom band = _____

Analysis

1. Does the length of the string have any effect on the reading of the spring scale? What evidence can you cite?

_____

_____

_____

_____

_____

2. Does the tension in the string depend on the length of the string? What evidence can you cite?

_____

_____

_____

_____

_____

_____

3. How does the tension at different distances along a stretched string compare? What evidence can you cite?

_____

_____

4. How much would each rubber band stretch if the 500-g load were suspended by two side-by-side bands as shown in Figure H? Make your prediction, and then set up the experiment. Explain your result.

predicted stretch = _____

actual stretch = _____

_____

_____

_____

_____

_____

_____

_____

_____

22 Tug-of-War

Purpose

To investigate the tension in a string, the function of a simple pulley, and a simple "tug-of-war."

Required Equipment/Supplies

5 large paper clips
2 large identical rubber bands
2 m of strong string
2 500-g hook masses

2 low-friction pulleys
2 ring stands
spring scale
measuring rule

Discussion

Suppose you push on the back of a stalled car. You are certainly aware that you are exerting a force on the car. Are you equally aware that the car is exerting a force on you? And that the magnitudes of the car's force on you and your force on the car are the same? A force cannot exist alone. Forces are always the result of interactions between two things, and they come in balanced pairs.

Now suppose you get a friend to tie a rope to the front of the car and pull on it. The rope will be pulling back on your friend with exactly the same magnitude of force that she is exerting on the rope. The other end of the rope will be pulling on the car and the car will be pulling equally back on it. There are two interaction pairs, one where your friend grasps the rope and one where the rope is attached to the car.

A rope or string is a transmitter of force. If it is not moving or it is moving but has a negligible mass, the forces at its two ends will also be equal. In this activity, you will learn about balanced pairs of interaction forces and about the way a string transmits forces.

Procedure

Step 1: Suspend a 500-g load from a string that is held by a spring scale as shown in Figure A.

1. What does the scale reading tell you about the tension in the string?

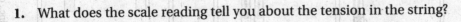

Fig. A

Put tension on a string.

Hang weight over pulley.

Step 2: Drape the string over a pulley such that both ends of the string hang vertically, as shown in Figure B. Hold the scale steady so that it supports the hanging load.

2. What does the scale read, and how does this force compare with the weight of the load?

_____

_____

_____

3. How does it compare with the tension in the string?

_____

_____

_____

Move spring scale to different positions along vertical.

Step 3: Move the spring scale first to a higher, then to a lower position, keeping the strings on each side of the pulley vertical.

4. Does the reading at the higher position change?

_____

_____

_____

5. Move the scale to a lower position. Does the reading at the lower position change? Briefly explain these results.

_____

_____

_____

_____

Fig. B Fig. C Fig. D Fig. E Fig. F

Step 4: Move the spring scale to various angles to the vertical, until the scale is horizontal, as shown in Figure C.

Move spring scale to different positions away from vertical.

6. Does the reading on the scale ever deviate from what you measured in the previous steps? Briefly explain your result.

_____

_____

_____

_____

Step 5: Remove the string from the pulley and drape it over a horizontal rod. Repeat Step 4, as shown in Figure D.

Hang weight over rod.

7. Do you find a difference between the results of Steps 4 and 5? Explain.

_____

_____

_____

_____

_____

_____

_____

_____

Step 6: Attach a spring scale to each end of the string. Drape the string over the pulley and attach equal masses to each end, as shown in Figure E.

Pull on both ends of string over pulley.

8. What do the scales read?

_____

_____

_____

_____

_____

9. What role does friction play in the function of a pulley?

_____

_____

Step 7: Have your partner hold one end of a spring scale stationary while you pull horizontally on the other end. Pull until the scale reads the same force as it did when suspending the mass. Record the following observations.

force you exert on the scale = _____

force the scale exerts on you = _____

force your partner exerts on the scale = _____

force the scale exerts on your partner = _____

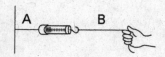

Step 8: Attach strings on both ends of the spring scale. Fasten one end to the wall or a steady support. Call this String A. Pull horizontally on the other string, String B, until the scale reads the same as in the previous step. Record the following observations.

force you exert on String A = _____

force String A exerts on scale = _____

force the scale exerts on String B = _____

force String B exerts on the wall = _____

force the wall exerts on String B = _____

10. What is the essential difference between the situations in Step 7 and Step 8?

_____

_____

_____

11. From a microscopic point of view, how does the spring or string transmit the force you are exerting on your partner or the wall?

_____

_____

_____

Step 9: Study Figure F and predict the reading on the scale when two 500-g loads are supported at each end of the strings. Then assemble the apparatus and check your prediction.

predicted scale reading = _____

actual scale reading = _____

23 Egg Toss

Purpose

To investigate the effect that stopping time has on stopping force

Required Equipment/Supplies

raw egg
garbage bag(s)
masking tape
safety goggles
football field or other playing field with distance measurements

Discussion

Drop an egg on a couch and chances are it won't break. Drop it on the carpet and it might. Drop an egg on a concrete floor and it will break for sure. You might say the couch and the carpet have more "give" than the concrete floor. In all three cases the egg comes to a complete stop, but what's different is the amount of time required to stop the egg in each case. The *change in momentum* or *impulse* stopping the egg is exactly the same in all three cases. What's different is the amount of *force and the time of impact*. More time results in less force. If the egg is dropped from the same height, it hits each surface with the same speed and the same momentum. However, as the time of impact is increased, the resulting force of impact is reduced in the same proportion.

Procedure

Divide the class up into teams of 3 or 4 members. The thrower will throw a raw egg to the catcher on their team. The catcher must catch the egg without letting it break. When the thrower and catcher are close, it's fairly easy. But as the distance increases, it becomes more challenging!

Step 1: The team must get prepared by first selecting their thrower, catcher, and one or two designated runners to retrieve and distribute eggs. Both the thrower and the catcher must only use their bare hands to handle the egg.

Step 2: The catcher must wear safety goggles and a plastic poncho. Use the garbage bag and masking tape to construct a plastic poncho. When the egg breaks, it can make a mess. Make sure the poncho covers any part of your clothes so that they are protected from raw egg.

Step 3: Go to the playing field and line up according to your teacher's instructions. The throwers and catchers should be facing each other and should start about 3 meters apart from each other.

Step 4: When the teacher gives the signal, the thrower throws the egg to the catcher. If the catcher catches the egg and the egg remains intact, the team may proceed onto the next toss. If the egg breaks, the catcher must remove the poncho and use it to clean up the egg and a runner records the distance to last clean catch.

The runners retrieve the eggs from the catchers. The catchers move back 3 meters for each successive throw, while the throwers return to their original throwing line.

Step 5: Repeat until the last group breaks their egg.

Analysis

1. How far did your thrower and catcher get from each other before the egg broke? What was the longest distance achieved in the class?

   _____

   _____

   _____

2. What techniques were employed when making a successful catch? What do they have to do with stopping force and the time of impact?

   _____

   _____

   _____

   _____

3. Compare a sudden-stop catch with a gradual-stop catch.

   a. In which case is the mass of the egg greater? Or is it the same either way?

   _____

   b. In which case is the change in velocity of the egg greater? Or is it the same either way?

   _____

c. In which case is the change in momentum ($\Delta mv = m\Delta v$) of the egg greater? Or is it the same either way?

_____

d. In which case is the stopping time greater? Or is it the same either way?

_____

e. In which case is the stopping force greater? Or is it the same either way?

_____

4. How do your findings explain the purpose of airbags in cars? Refrain from using words like "cushion" or "absorb." Do use words like "stopping time," "stopping force," or "changes in momentum."

_____

_____

_____

_____

5. Suppose a baseball pitcher throws the ball to his catcher.

a. In the change in the speed of the ball thrown by the pitcher different than the change in the speed of the ball caught by the catcher? Or is it the same?

_____

b. Is the magnitude of the change in momentum greater for the ball thrown by the pitcher or the ball caught by the catcher? Or is it the same?

_____

c. In which case is the impulse greater? Or is it the same?

_____

d. Does it take longer to throw the ball or to catch it?

_____

_____

e. Does it take more force to throw the ball or to catch it?

_____

_____

24 Conserving Your Momentum

Purpose

To investigate the momentum changes when two balls collide

Required Equipment/Supplies

collision in two dimensions apparatus or equivalent
one half-inch steel ball
one half-inch glass marble
plumb bob with string
C-clamp
carbon paper
blank paper, tape
meterstick
balance, preferably electronic
protractor
graph paper

Discussion

When you're playing pool, you strike the cue ball to hit the 8-ball. The cue ball comes to a stop and the 8-ball moves with the same speed and momentum the cue ball had. When a bowling ball strikes the pins, the ball slows down and the pins go flying. When one atom collides with a stationary one, the incoming atom bounces off in one direction while the target atom bounces in another direction. All these collisions have *changes of momentum*. A quantity is conserved when the amount before equals the amount after. In this experiment, you're going to investigate the momentum (*mv*) of two balls: one that rolls down a ramp and collides with the other, a stationary "target" ball. To keep things simple at first, you'll adjust the apparatus so that the collisions are along a straight line (one dimension). Then if time permits, you'll investigate what happens when the balls collide and fly off in different directions (two dimensions).

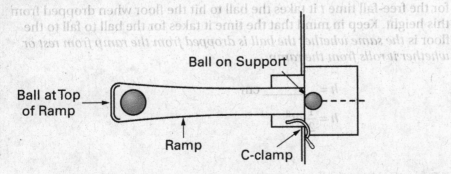

Ball on Support

Ball at Top of Ramp →

Ramp

C-clamp

In this experiment, you're going to use similar techniques to those you learned in the lab Bull's Eye. You will compute the speeds of the first ball. In Bull's Eye you measured the horizontal speed of a ball to figure out its horizontal range (where it would land). In this lab, you're going to backtrack and use the horizontal range where the ball lands and the time of fall to figure out the speed of the ball as it leaves the ramp. Since the horizontal and vertical motions are independent of each other, the ball's horizontal speed does not change (at these low velocities air friction can be ignored). As in Bull's Eye, the time it takes the ball to fall is found by measuring the vertical distance, equating it to $\frac{1}{2}gt^2$, and solving for t. Therefore, the horizontal speed of the ball is simply the horizontal distance divided by the time it takes the ball to fall, (v_x/t).

Part A: Collisions in One Dimension

Procedure

Step 1: Clamp the ramp so that the lower end hangs just off the lab table. Make sure the ramp is horizontal at the table edge where the ball leaves the ramp. Arrange the apparatus as shown in Figure A. Notice that the set-screw at the bottom of the ramp has a depression at its top. This is the resting place for the target ball for each collision. Position the set-screw directly in front of the ramp and about one ball-radius away from the groove.

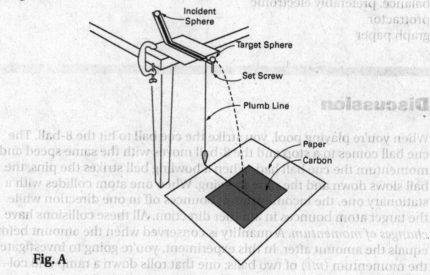

Fig. A

Step 2: Adjust the set-screw so that, when a ball is released from the ramp, it *just* misses it.

Step 3: Measure the height h the ball falls to the floor in centimeters. Solve for the free-fall time t it takes the ball to hit the floor when dropped from this height. Keep in mind that the time it takes for the ball to fall to the floor is *the same whether the ball is dropped from the ramp from rest or whether it rolls from the ramp.*

$$h = \underline{\hspace{2cm}} \text{ cm}$$

$$h = \frac{1}{2}gt^2$$

Since your measurements for h are in centimeters, use $g = 980$ cm/s^2, so that the cm units cancel. Show your calculations.

$$t = \text{_____} \text{ s}$$

Step 4: As accurately as you can, measure the mass of the steel ball, m_b, and the glass marble, m_m.

$$m_b = \text{_____} \text{ g} \qquad m_m = \text{_____} \text{ g}$$

Step 5: Use the plumb bob to find the point right on the floor directly underneath the end of the ramp. Hold the string against the end of the ramp so that the weight on the end of the string just touches the floor. Tape a piece of paper on the floor and then mark a small "X" on the paper directly underneath the end of the ramp. All your distance measurements will be made from this point on the paper.

Step 6: You're almost ready to start taking data. First, make certain that the balls move horizontally after leaving the ramp. You can tell if the bottom portion of the ramp is level if the ball doesn't tend to roll when placed there. It may be necessary to adjust the set-screw slightly so that the glass marble is not too high or too low.

Step 7: Now, place the steel ball on the top of the ramp. Release it and observe where it lands. Tape another piece of paper to the floor so that the ball lands near the middle of the paper. Place a piece of carbon paper on top of the paper (carbon side down). Release the ball several times. Remove the carbon paper and mark the average position where the ball lands on the paper. Measure the distance in centimeters from the plumb bob mark to the average landing point. Record your measurement.

$$d_{ball} = \text{_____} \text{ cm}$$

Step 8: Use the time you calculated in Step 3 and the distance you measured in Step 7 to calculate the horizontal speed of the ball as it left the ramp.

$$v_x = \text{_____} \text{ cm/s}$$

Step 9: Calculate the momentum of the ball as it left the ramp.

$$mv_x = \text{_____} \text{ g·cm/s}$$

Step 10: Place the glass marble on the set-screw so that its center is along the path of the center of the steel ball as the ball rolls down the ramp. Release the steel ball from the top of the ramp as you did in Step 8. The objective is to cause both the steel ball and the marble to move along the same line after they collide. It may take several trials to adjust the height and position of the marble to accomplish this. Once you're certain the balls land in a straight line, tape a piece of paper where each ball lands. Get ready to take data. As you did in Step 7, place a piece of carbon paper (carbon side down) on top of the sheets of paper to mark your landing points.

Step 11: Place the glass marble on the set-screw. Release the ball from the top of the ramp as you did in Step 8, allowing the ball and the marble to collide and land on the floor. Make certain that the ball and the marble always move along a straight line. Remove the carbon paper and mark the average landing point of the ball and the marble. Measure the distances, and then calculate the speeds and corresponding momenta as you did in Steps 8 and 9. Show your calculations.

_____

$d_{ball} =$ _____ cm $d_{marble} =$ _____ cm

$v_{ball} =$ _____ cm/s $v_{marble} =$ _____ cm/s

Analysis

1. What was the momentum of the steel ball as it left the ramp?

2. What was the momentum of the steel ball after the collision with the marble?

_____

3. What was the momentum of the marble after the collision with the steel ball?

_____

4. How does the sum of the momenta of the steel ball and the marble compare to the steel ball before it left the ramp? Calculate the percent difference between them.

5. Write down the equation for momentum conservation for the collision. Label what each variable represents in your equation.

equation: _____

variables: _____

Going Further

Choose an appropriate scale and draw a momentum vector to represent the momentum of the ball as it leaves the ramp. Appropriate means that the vector is at least half a page long or more.

Now draw momentum vectors for the steel ball and marble after the collision.

Part B: Collisions in Two Dimensions

Procedure

In Part A, we took great care to assure the balls moved in a straight line after the collision. The motivation for doing this was to keep the calculations relatively simple: the momentum of the steel ball as it left the ramp was simply the sum of the momentum of the steel ball and the marble after the collision.

$$m_x v_x = m_b v_b + m_m v_m$$

This time we will modify the experiment so the marble is off-center with the path of the steel ball. When they collide, they will move at different angles relative to the straight line after the collision. Let's call the direction parallel to the ramp the x-direction, and perpendicular to the ramp will be the y-direction.

Before proceeding, remember that momentum is a *vector* quantity. That means, *the sum of the components* equals *the resultant momentum vector.*

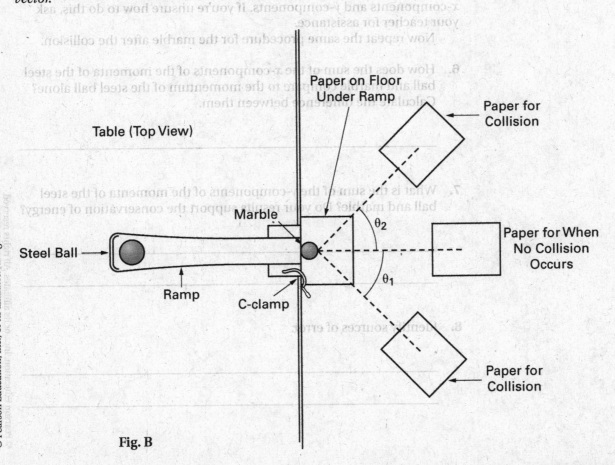

Table (Top View)

Paper on Floor Under Ramp

Paper for Collision

Steel Ball

Marble

Ramp

C-clamp

θ_2

θ_1

Paper for When No Collision Occurs

Paper for Collision

Fig. B

Since the steel ball and marble have no momentum in the y-direction before the collision, the momentum in the y-direction must also be zero after the collision in order to conserve momentum. Therefore, the y-component of the steel ball has the same magnitude (or length) as the y-component of the marble after the collision.

Employ the same procedure as in Part A except this time adjust the set-screw so that the steel ball and marble collide so that they move at an angle relative to the straight line the steel ball had by itself. Be sure to release the steel ball from the same position each time. Tape pieces of paper where the steel ball and the marble land. Place a piece of carbon paper on top of each paper. Release the ball several times and mark the average landing point. Measure the distances and the angles where the steel ball and marble land relative to the straight line the steel ball had alone. Calculate their corresponding velocities and momenta.

$d_{ball} = $ _____ cm $d_{marble} = $ _____ cm

$\theta_{ball} = $ _____ degrees $\theta_{marble} = $ _____ degrees

$v_{ball} = $ _____ cm/s $v_{marble} = $ _____ cm/s

$mv_{ball} = $ _____ g·cm/s $mv_{marble} = $ _____ g·cm/s

Analysis

Draw vectors on a piece of graph paper to represent the momentum of the steel ball after the collision. Resolve the momentum vector into x-components and y-components. If you're unsure how to do this, ask your teacher for assistance.

Now repeat the same procedure for the marble after the collision.

6. How does the sum of the x-components of the momenta of the steel ball and marble compare to the momentum of the steel ball alone? Calculate the difference between them.

_____

7. What is the sum of the y-components of the momenta of the steel ball and marble? Do your results support the conservation of energy?

_____

_____

8. Identify sources of error.

_____

_____

25 Go Cart

Purpose

To investigate the momentum imparted during elastic and inelastic collisions

Required Equipment/Supplies

"bouncing dart" from Arbor Scientific
ring stand with ring
dynamics cart (with a mass of 1 kg or more)
string
pendulum clamp
C-clamp
meterstick
brick or heavy weight

Discussion

If you fell from a tree limb onto a trampoline, you'd bounce. If you fell into a large pile of leaves, you'd come to rest without bouncing. In which case, if either, is the change in your momentum greater? This activity will help you answer that question. You'll compare the changes in momentum in the collision of a "bouncing dart" when bouncing does take place and when it doesn't.

The dart consists of a thick wooden dowel with a rubber tip on *each* end. Although the tips look and feel the same, the tips are made of different kinds of rubber. One end acts somewhat like a very bouncy ball. The other end acts somewhat like a lump of clay. They have different *elasticities*. Bounce each end of the dart on the table and you'll easily see which end is more elastic. In the activity, you'll do the same against the dynamics cart using the dart as a pendulum.

Procedure

Step 1: Attach the dart to the ring stand as a pendulum, using a heavy weight to secure the base of the ring stand. To prevent the dart from swinging into the weight, position the ring on the stand so that it faces the opposite direction. Adjust the string so that the dart strikes the middle of one end of the cart when the dart is at the lowest point of its swing.

Step 2: Elevate the dart so that, when impact is made, the cart will roll forward a foot or so on a level table or floor when struck by the inelastic end of the dart. Use a meterstick to measure the vertical distance

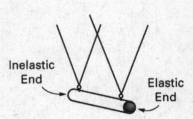

Fig. A

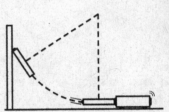

Inelastic End

Elastic End

Observe collision without bouncing.

between the release point of the dart and the bottom of its swing. Repeat several times. Record the average stopping distance of the cart.

vertical distance = _____

stopping distance (no bouncing) = _____

Observe collision with bouncing.

Step 3: Repeat using the elastic end of the dart. Be sure to release the dart from the *same position* as in Step 2. Note what happens to the dart after it hits the cart. Make sure to release the dart from the same height each time. Repeat several more times to see whether your results are consistent. Record the average stopping distance of the cart.

stopping distance (with bouncing) = _____

Write down your observations.

_____

_____

_____

_____

_____

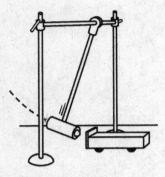

Alternate setup

Analysis

1. Define the momentum of the swinging dart before it hits the cart to be positive, so that momentum in the opposite direction is negative. After the dart bounces off the cart, is its momentum negative or positive?

_____

_____

_____

_____

_____

2. When does the dart acquire the greater momentum—when it bounces off the cart or when it doesn't? Explain.

_____

_____

_____

3. When does the *cart* undergo the greater change in momentum—
    when struck by the end of the dart that bounces or by the end of the
    dart that doesn't bounce? Explain.

    _____

    _____

    _____

    _____

4. How do the stopping distances of the cart compare?

    _____

    _____

    _____

    _____

5. How would you account for the difference in stopping distances?

    _____

    _____

    _____

    _____

    _____

Chapter 9: Energy

Mechanical Energy

26 Making the Grade

Purpose

To investigate the force and the distance involved in moving an object up an incline

Required Equipment/Supplies

board for inclined plane
spring scale
meterstick
ring stand
clamp
cart

Discussion

One of the simplest machines that makes doing work easier is the inclined plane, or ramp. It is much easier to push a heavy load up a ramp than it is to lift it vertically to the same height. When it is lifted vertically, a greater lifting force is required, but the distance moved is less. When it is pushed up a ramp, the distance moved is greater, but the force required is less. This fact illustrates one of the most powerful laws of physics, the law of energy conservation.

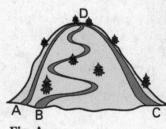

Fig. A

1. A hill has three paths up its sides to a flat summit area, point *D*, as shown in Figure A. The three path lengths *AD*, *BD*, and *CD* are all different, but the vertical height is the same. Not including the energy used to overcome the internal friction of a car, which path requires the most energy (gasoline) for a car driving up it? Explain your answer.

   _____

   _____

   _____

   _____

   _____

Procedure

Step 1: Place a clamp on a ring stand. Clamp the board in place at an angle of 45°, as shown in Figure B. Pull the cart up the inclined plane with a spring scale kept parallel to the plane to measure the force. Measure the distance s from the bottom of the incline to the ring stand clamp. Record the force and distance in Data Table A.

Fig. B

Raise the cart.

	10°	30°	45°	60°
Force (N)				
Distance (cm)				

Data Table A

Change the angle of the incline.

Step 2: Vary the angle while keeping the height h the same by sliding the board up or down inside the clamp to make angles of 10°, 30°, and 60°. For each of the different angles (and distances), pull the cart parallel to the board. Record your force and distance data in Data Table A.

Analysis

2. What pattern or relationship do you find between the forces and the distances?

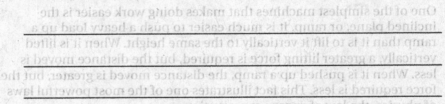

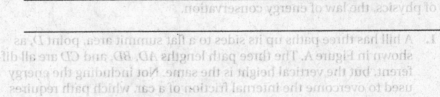

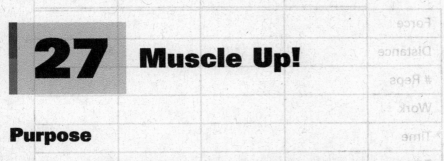

27 Muscle Up!

Purpose

To determine the power that can be produced by various muscles of the human body

Required Equipment/Supplies

bleachers and/or stairs
stopwatch
meterstick
weights
rope

Discussion

Power is usually associated with mechanical engines or electric motors. Many other devices also consume power to make light or heat. A lighted incandescent bulb may dissipate 100 watts of power. The human body also dissipates power as it converts the energy of food to heat and work. The human body is subject to the same laws of physics that govern mechanical and electrical devices.

The different muscle groups of the body are capable of producing forces that can act through distances. Work is the product of the force and the distance, provided they both act in the same direction. When a person runs up stairs, the force lifted is the person's weight, and the distance is the vertical distance moved—not the distance along the stairs. If the time it takes to do work is measured, the power output of the body, which is the work divided by the time, can be determined in watts.

Procedure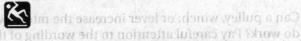

Step 1: Select five different activities from the following list: *Measure force and distance.*

Possible Activities
- Lift a mass with your wrist only, forearm only, arm only, foot only, or leg only.
- Do push-ups, sit-ups, or some other exercise.
- Run up stairs or bleachers.
- Pull a weight with a rope.
- Jump with or without weights attached.

Perform these activities, and record in Data Table A the *force* in newtons that acted, the *distance* in meters moved against the force, the number of repetitions (or "reps"), and the *time* in seconds required. Then calculate the *power* in watts. (One hundred seconds is a convenient time interval.)

Count the number of reps and measure the time.

	1	2	3	4
Force				
Distance				
# Reps				
Work				
Time				
Power				

Data Table A

Step 2: Complete the table by recording the results of four other activities performed by other class members.

Analysis

1. What name is given to the rate at which work is done? What are the units of this rate?

_____

_____

2. In which activity done by your class was the largest power produced? Which muscle groups were used in this activity?

_____

_____

3. Did the activity that used the largest force result in the largest power produced? Explain how a large force can result in a relatively small power.

_____

_____

4. Can a pulley, winch, or lever increase the rate at which a person can do work? Pay careful attention to the wording of this question, and explain your answer.

_____

_____

_____

_____

28 Cut Short

Purpose

To illustrate the principle of conservation of energy with a pendulum

Required Equipment/Supplies

3 ring stands
pendulum clamp
string
steel ball
rod
clamp

Discussion

A pendulum swinging to and fro illustrates the conservation of energy. Raise the pendulum bob to give it potential energy. Release it and the potential energy is converted to kinetic energy as the bob approaches its lowest point. Then, as the bob swings up on the other side, kinetic energy is converted to potential energy. Back and forth, the forms of energy change while their sum is constant. Energy is conserved. What happens if the length of the pendulum is suddenly changed? How does the resulting motion illustrate energy conservation?

Procedure

Step 1: Attach a pendulum clamp to the top of a ring stand set between two other ring stands, as shown in Figure A. Attach a steel ball to a piece of string that is nearly as long as the ring stand is tall.

Make a pendulum.

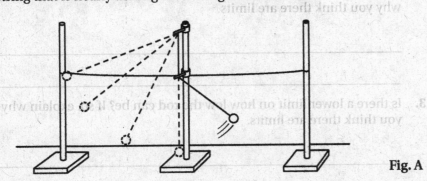

Fig. A

Step 2: Tie a string horizontally from one empty ring stand to the other, as shown in Figure A. The string should be about two-thirds as high as the pendulum clamp.

Set up level string.

Step 3: Attach a rod to the central ring stand at the same height as the horizontal string (Figure A). The rod should touch the pendulum string when the string is vertical.

Predict height.

Step 4: Predict what height the ball will reach if the ball is released at the same height as the horizontal string and the pendulum string is stopped by the rod. Check one:

Prediction   Observation

☐   ☐   **a.** The ball will go higher than the horizontal string.

☐   ☐   **b.** The ball will go just as high as the horizontal string.

☐   ☐   **c.** The ball will not go as high as the horizontal string.

Release pendulum.

Step 5: Release the pendulum! Record whether you observe a, b, or c.

Raise rod.

Step 6: Predict what would happen if the rod were attached higher than the string. Perform the experiment to confirm or deny your prediction.

Prediction: _____

Observation: _____

Lower rod.

Step 7: Predict what would happen if the rod were attached lower than the string. Perform the experiment to confirm or deny your prediction.

Prediction: _____

Observation: _____

Analysis

1. Explain your observations in terms of potential and kinetic energy and the conservation of energy.

   _____

   _____

2. Is there an upper limit on how high the rod can be? If so, explain why you think there are limits.

   _____

   _____

3. Is there a lower limit on how low the rod can be? If so, explain why you think there are limits.

   _____

   _____

29 Conserving Your Energy

Purpose

To measure the potential and kinetic energies of a pendulum in order to see whether energy is conserved

Required Equipment/Supplies

ring stand
pendulum clamp
pendulum bob
balance
string
meterstick
photogate timing system

Discussion

In Activity 28, Cut Short, you saw that the height to which a pendulum swings is related to its initial height. The work done to elevate it to its initial height (the force times the distance) becomes stored as potential energy with respect to the bottom of the swing. At the top of the swing, all the energy of the pendulum is in the form of potential energy. At the bottom of the swing, all the energy of the pendulum is in the form of kinetic energy.

    The *total energy* of a system is the sum of its kinetic and potential energies. If energy is conserved, the sum of the kinetic energy and potential energy at one moment will equal their sum at any other moment. For a pendulum, the kinetic energy is zero at the top, and the potential energy is minimum at the bottom. Thus, if the energy of a pendulum is conserved, the extra potential energy at the top must equal the kinetic energy at the bottom. For convenience, potential energy at the bottom can be defined to be zero. In this experiment, you will measure kinetic and potential energy and see if their sum is conserved.

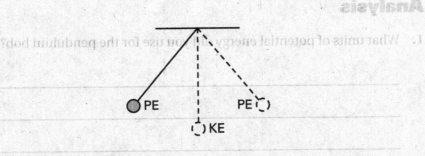

Procedure

Step 1: Devise an experiment with the equipment listed to test the conservation of energy. Write down your procedure in the space following. Include a diagram of your pendulum and label it with all the quantities, such as the height, potential energy, kinetic energy, speed, and so on.

Step 2: Perform your experiment. Record your data below in the form of a table.

Analysis

1. What units of potential energy did you use for the pendulum bob?

   _____

   _____

   _____

   _____

2. What units of kinetic energy did you use for the pendulum bob?

_____

_____

_____

_____

3. List the sources of error in your experiment. Which one do you think is the most significant?

_____

_____

_____

_____

_____

_____

_____

_____

4. Based on your data, does the total energy of the pendulum remain the same throughout its swing?

_____

_____

_____

_____

_____

_____

_____

_____

30   Wrap Your Energy in a Bow

Purpose

To determine the energy transferred into an archer's bow

Required Equipment/Supplies

toy bow and arrow (with rubber suction cup tips)
large-capacity spring scale
meterstick
clamp
graph paper

Discussion

The kinetic energy of an arrow is obtained from the potential energy of the drawn bow, which in turn is obtained from the work done in drawing the bow. This work is equal to the average force acting on the bowstring multiplied by the distance it is drawn.

In this experiment, you will measure the amounts of force required to hold the center of a bowstring at various distances from its position of rest, and plot these data on a force-vs.-distance graph. The force is relatively small for small deflections, but it becomes progressively larger as the bow is bent further. The area under the force-vs.-distance curve out to some final deflection is equal to the average force multiplied by the total distance. This equals the work done in drawing the bow to that distance. Therefore, your graph will show not only the relationship of the force to the distance stretched, but also the potential energy possessed by the fully drawn bow.

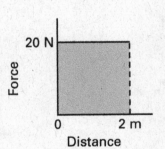

Fig. A

The effect of a constant force of 10 N acting over a distance of 2 m is represented in the graph of Figure A. The work done equals the area of the rectangle.

$$\text{work} = F \times d = (20 \text{ N}) \times (2 \text{ m}) = 40 \text{ N·m} = 40 \text{ J}$$

When the force is not constant, as in Figure B, the work done on the system still equals the area under the graph (between the graph and the horizontal axis). In this case, the total area under the graph equals the area of the triangle plus the area of the rectangle.

$$\text{work} = \text{total area} = \text{area of triangle} + \text{area of rectangle}$$
$$= [(1/2) (\text{base}) \times (\text{height})] + [(\text{base}) \times (\text{height})]$$
$$= [(1/2) (2 \text{ m}) \times (20 \text{ N})] + [(3 \text{ m}) \times (20 \text{ N})]$$
$$= (20 \text{ N·m}) + (60 \text{ N·m})$$
$$= 80 \text{ N·m}$$
$$= 80 \text{ J}$$

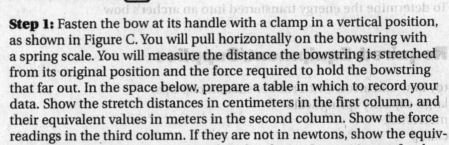

Fig. B

Procedure

Step 1: Fasten the bow at its handle with a clamp in a vertical position, as shown in Figure C. You will pull horizontally on the bowstring with a spring scale. You will measure the distance the bowstring is stretched from its original position and the force required to hold the bowstring that far out. In the space below, prepare a table in which to record your data. Show the stretch distances in centimeters in the first column, and their equivalent values in meters in the second column. Show the force readings in the third column. If they are not in newtons, show the equivalent force values in newtons in a fourth column. Leave 10 rows for data in your table.

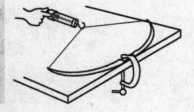

Fig. C

Draw data table.

Stretch bowstring and measure forces.

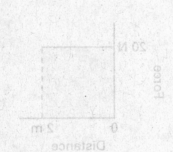

Make a graph.

Compute area.

Step 2: Stretch the bowstring by 1.0 cm, and record the stretch distance and force reading. Continue to stretch the bowstring in 1.0-cm increments, and record your data in the table. Compute the stretch distances in meters and the equivalent force values in newtons.

Step 3: Plot a graph of the force (vertical axis) vs. distance (horizontal axis). Use the units newtons and meters.

Step 4: Estimate the area under the graph in units of newtons times meters, N•m. Since 1 N•m = 1 J, this area is the total energy transferred to the bow. When the bow is drawn, this energy is in the form of elastic potential energy.

area = _____

Analysis

1. If a 50-g arrow were shot straight up with the bow stretched to the maximum displacement of your data, how high would it go? (To find the answer in meters, express 50 g as 0.05 kg.)

_____

_____

_____

_____

_____

_____

_____

_____

_____

2. How high would a 75-g arrow go?

_____

_____

_____

3. At what speed would the 50-g arrow leave the bow?

_____

_____

_____

4. List three other devices that transform potential energy into work on an object.

_____

_____

31 How Hot Are Your Wheels?

Purpose

To measure the efficiency of a toy car on an inclined track

Required Equipment/Supplies

toy car
3 m of toy car track
meterstick
tape
2 ring stands
2 clamps

Discussion

According to the law of energy conservation, energy is neither created nor destroyed. Instead, it *transforms* from one kind to another, finally ending up as heat energy. The potential energy of an elevated toy car on a track transforms into kinetic energy as the car rolls to the bottom of the track, but some energy becomes heat because of friction. The kinetic energy of the car at the bottom of the track is transformed back into potential energy as the car rolls to higher elevation, although again some of the energy becomes heat. The car does not reach its initial height when it moves back up the incline, because some of its energy has been transformed into heat.

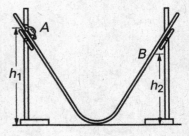

Fig. A

Procedure

Step 1: Set up a toy car track as shown in Figure A. Both ends of the track should be elevated to a height of 1 meter above the table or floor. Secure the track to the table or floor and supporting ring stands with tape to eliminate motion of the track.

Set up track.

Step 2: Mark starting point A with a piece of masking tape and record its height h_1. Release the car from starting point A. Record the height h_2 of point B to which the car rises on the other end of the track.

Measure the initial and final height of the car.

$$h_1 = \underline{\hspace{2cm}}$$

$$h_2 = \underline{\hspace{2cm}}$$

Step 3: Efficiency is defined as the useful energy out divided by the total energy in. It is a ratio or a percentage. In this activity, we can define the total energy *in* as the change in potential energy as the car rolls from its

Compute efficiency.

highest to its lowest point. This is energy supplied by earth's gravity. The useful energy out we can take to be the potential energy change as the car rolls from its lowest point until it stops at point B. This is energy that the car now possesses relative to the lowest point of its travel. Since the potential energy at any height h above a reference level is mgh, the ratio of the potential energy transferred back into the car at point B (the output energy) to the potential energy lost by the car in rolling down to point A (the input energy) is equal to the ratio of the final height h_2 to the initial height h_1. This ratio of h_2 to h_1 can be called the "efficiency" of the car-and-track system from point A to point B. It shows the fraction of the energy supplied by gravity in rolling down the track that is retained after it rolls up the track. Compute this efficiency.

$$\text{efficiency} = \frac{PE_{\text{point } B}}{PE_{\text{point } A}} = \frac{h_2}{h_1}$$

Analysis

1. Is the efficiency of the car-and-track system changed if the track is not taped?

   _____

   _____

2. In what units is efficiency measured?

   _____

   _____

   _____

3. Is the efficiency of the car-and-track system changed if the height of the track is altered?

   _____

   _____

32 Releasing Your Potential

Purpose

To find quantitative relationships among height, speed, mass, kinetic energy, and potential energy

Required Equipment/Supplies

pendulum apparatus as in Figure A
2 steel balls of different mass
graph paper or overhead transparencies
meterstick

Optional Equipment/Supplies

computer with graphing software
photogate timing system

Discussion

Drop two balls of different mass and they fall together. Tie them separately to two strings of the same length and they will swing together as pendulums. The speeds they achieve in falling or in swinging do not depend on their mass, but only on the vertical distance they have moved downward from rest. In this experiment, you will use a rigid pendulum (see Figure A) raised to a certain height. At the bottom of the pendulum's swing, a crossbar stops the pendulum, but the ball leaves the holder and keeps going.

How far downrange does the ball travel? The horizontal distance from the crossbar depends on *how fast* the ball is going and *how long* it remains in the air. How fast it is launched depends on *the launcher*. How long it remains in the air depends on how high it is above the floor or table.

Procedure

Step 1: Devise an appropriate method for measuring the vertical height *h* the pendulum ball falls. Record your method in the following space.

_____

_____

_____

Fig. A

Measure vertical height.

Launch ball with pendulum.

Step 2: Raise the pendulum to the desired vertical height, using your finger to hold the ball in place. Take your finger away in such a manner that you do not push the pendulum up or down. Both the ball and pendulum swing down together, and the ball is launched upon impact with the crossbar. Practice your technique until you get consistent landings of the ball downrange.

Measure the range.

Step 3: When your results have become consistent, release the ball three times from the same height. Use a meterstick to measure the downrange distance for each trial. Repeat the experiment for six different heights. Record each average distance and height in Data Table A.

Height	Distance			
	Trial 1	Trial 2	Trial 3	Average

Data Table A

Calculate minimum launch speed.

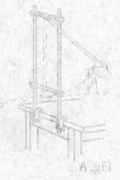

Step 4: Suppose the ball were attached to a lightweight string (as in a simple pendulum) that struck a razor mounted on the crossbar as shown in Figure A. If the ball is released from a sufficient height, its inertia will cause the string to be cut as it strikes the crossbar, projecting the ball horizontally. From the law of conservation of energy, the kinetic energy of the ball as it is launched from the low point of its swing is equal to the potential energy that it lost in swinging down, so $KE_{gained} = PE_{lost}$ or $\frac{1}{2}mv^2 = mgh$.

The launcher pictured in Figure A has its mass distributed along its length, so strictly speaking it isn't a *simple* pendulum. We'll see in Chapter 11 that it has less "rotational inertia" and swings a bit faster than if all its mass were concentrated at its bottom. For simplicity, we won't treat this complication here, and acknowledge that the speed calculated for a simple pendulum, $v = \sqrt{2gh}$, is a *lower limit*—the *minimum* launch speed. Record your computation of the minimum launch speed for each height from which the pendulum was released, in the second column of Data Table B.

Data Table B

Height	Launch Speed Computed	Launch Speed as Measured by Photogate

Step 5: (Optional) Use a photogate timer to measure the launch speed of the ball at each of the six heights. Record your results in the third column of Data Table B.

1. How do the minimum and measured speeds of the ball compare?

_____

_____

_____

_____

Step 6: In this step, you will investigate the relationship between the mass of the ball and its launch speed. Use a ball with a different mass, and release it from the same six heights as before. Record the downrange distances in Data Table C.

Use balls of different mass.

Height	Distance			
	Trial 1	Trial 2	Trial 3	Average

Data Table C

Graph data.

Step 7: You now have a tremendous amount of data. What does it mean? What is the pattern? You can often visualize a pattern by making a graph. Graph the pairs of variables suggested. You may want to graph other quantities instead. Use overhead transparencies or graph paper. Each member of your team should make one graph, and then all of you can pool your results. If a computer and data-plotting software are available, use them to make your graphs.

Suggested graphs
(a) Distance or range (vertical axis) vs. height from which the pendulum is released (horizontal axis) for the same mass
(b) Launch speed (vertical axis) vs. release height (horizontal axis) for the same mass
(c) Mass (vertical axis) vs. distance (horizontal axis) for the same height

If you are using data-plotting software, vary the powers of the *x*- and *y*-values until the graph is a straight line.

Analysis

2. Describe what happens to the kinetic energy of the ball as it swings from the release height to the launch position.

_____
_____
_____

3. Describe what happens to the potential energy of the ball as it swings from the release height to the launch position.

_____

4. Describe what happens to the total energy of the ball as it swings from the release height to the launch position.

_____
_____
_____
_____
_____

Going Further

Have your teacher assign you a specified distance downrange. Try to predict the angle from the vertical or height at which the pendulum must be released in order to score a bull's-eye.

33 Slip-Stick

Purpose

To investigate three types of friction and to measure the coefficient of friction for each type.

Required Equipment/Supplies

friction block (foot-long 2 × 4 with an eye hook)
spring scale with maximum capacity greater than
    the weight of the friction block
set of slotted masses
flat board
meterstick
shoe

Discussion

The force that presses an object against a surface is the entire weight of the object only when the supporting surface is horizontal. When the object is on an incline, the component of gravitational force pressing the object against the surface is *less* than the object's weight. This component that is perpendicular (normal) to the surface is the *normal force*. For a block on an incline, the normal force varies with the angle. Although an object presses with its full weight against a horizontal surface, it presses with only half its weight against a 60° incline. So the normal force is half the weight at this angle. The normal force is zero when the incline is vertical because then the surfaces do not press against each other at all.

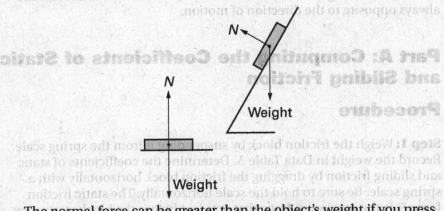

The normal force can be greater than the object's weight if you press down on the object. In general, the coefficient of friction is defined by replacing weight in the formula above by the normal force, whatever the

source of the force. So, in general, the force of friction F_f depends on the coefficient of friction μ and the normal force N:

$$F_f = \mu N$$

so that the coefficient of friction, μ, equals

$$\mu = \frac{\text{friction force}}{\text{weight}}$$

The coefficient of friction μ is greatest when the two surfaces are at rest, just before motion starts. (Then the ridges and valleys have had time to sink into each other and are meshed.) Once sliding begins, μ is slightly less. The coefficient of friction for sliding objects is called the *coefficient of sliding friction* (or coefficient of kinetic friction). When friction holds an object at rest, we define the *coefficient of static friction* as the greatest friction force than can act without motion divided by the normal force. A partial list of coefficients of both sliding and static friction is shown in Figure A.

Surfaces	μ_s (Static)	μ_k (Kinetic)
Steel on Steel, Dry	0.6	0.3
Steel on Wood, Dry	0.4	0.2
Steel on Ice	0.1	0.06
Wood on Wood, Dry	0.35	0.15
Metal on Metal, Greased	0.15	0.08

Fig. A

Friction also occurs for objects moving through fluids. This friction, known as *fluid friction*, does not follow laws as simple as those that govern sliding friction for solids. Air is a fluid, and the motion of a leaf falling to the ground is quite complicated! In this experiment, you will be concerned only with the friction between two solid surfaces in contact.

Friction always acts in a direction to oppose motion. For a ball moving upward in the air, the friction force is downward. When the ball moves downward, the friction force is upward. For a block sliding along a surface to the right, the friction force is to the left. Friction forces are always opposite to the direction of motion.

Part A: Computing the Coefficients of Static and Sliding Friction

Procedure

Step 1: Weigh the friction block by suspending it from the spring scale. Record the weight in Data Table A. Determine the coefficients of static and sliding friction by dragging the friction block horizontally with a spring scale. Be sure to hold the scale horizontally. The static friction force F_f is the maximum force that acts just before the block starts moving. The sliding friction force F_f' is the force it takes to keep the block moving at *constant velocity*. Your scale will vibrate around some average

Drag friction block.

value; make the best judgment you can of the values of the static and sliding friction forces. Record your data in Data Table A.

F_f Force to Just Get Going	F_f' Drag Force at Constant Velocity	W Weight of Cart	μ static $= \dfrac{F_f}{W}$	μ sliding $= \dfrac{F_f'}{W}$

Data Table A

Step 2: Drag the block at different speeds. Note any changes in the sliding friction force.

Change dragging speed.

1. Does the dragging speed have any effect on the coefficient of sliding friction, μ_{sliding}? Explain.

_____

_____

_____

Step 3: Increase the force pressing the surfaces together by adding slotted masses to the friction block. Record the weight of both the block and the added masses in Data Table A. Find both friction forces and coefficients of friction for at least six different weights and record in Data Table A.

Add weights to block.

Analysis

2. At each weight, how does μ_{static} compare with μ_{sliding}?

_____

Chapter 6   Newton's Second Law of Motion—Force and Acceleration   **123**

3. Does $\mu_{sliding}$ depend on the weight of the friction block? Explain.

_____

$\frac{F}{W}$ μ sliding =	$\frac{F}{W}$ μ static =	W Weight of Car	F Drag Force at Constant Velocity	F Force to Just Get Going

4. Tables in physics books rarely list coefficients of friction with more than two significant figures. From your experience, why are more than two significant figures not listed?

5. If you press down upon a sliding block, the force of friction increases but μ does not. Explain.

_____

_____

_____

6. Why are there no units for μ? _____

_____

Part B: The Effect of Surface Area on Friction

Procedure

Step 4: Drag a friction block of known weight at constant speed by means of a horizontal spring scale. Record the friction force and the weight of the block in Data Table B.

Drag friction block.

Configuration	F_f Force of Friction	W Normal Force	A Area of Contact	μ Coefficient Of Friction
1				
2				
Average				

Data Table B

Step 5: Repeat Step 4, but use a different side of the block (with a different area). Record the friction force in Data Table B.

Use different side of friction block.

Step 6: Compute $\mu_{sliding}$ for both steps and list it in Data Table B.

Compute μ.

7. Does the area make a difference in the coefficient of friction?

_____

_____

Going Further: Friction on an Incline

Place an object on an inclined plane and it may or may not slide. If friction is enough to hold it still, then tip the incline at a steeper angle until the object just begins to slide.

The coefficient of friction of a shoe is critical to its function. When will a shoe on an incline start to slip? Study Figure B. To make the geometry clearer, a cube can represent the shoe on the incline, as in Figure C. Triangle B shows the vector components of the shoe's weight. The component perpendicular to the incline is the normal force N; it acts to press the shoe to the surface. The component parallel to the incline, which points downward, tends to produce sliding. Before sliding starts, the friction force F_f is equal in magnitude but opposite in direction to this component. By tilting the incline, we can vary the normal force and the friction force on the shoe.

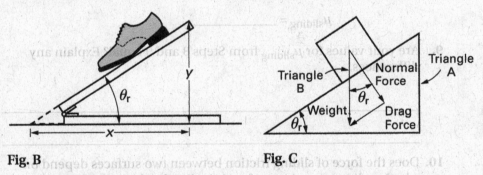

Fig. B   **Fig. C**

At the angle at which the shoe starts to slip (the *angle of repose*) θ_r, the component of weight parallel to the surface is just enough to overcome friction and the shoe breaks free. At that angle, the parallel weight component and the friction force are at their maximum. The ratio of this friction force to the normal force gives the coefficient of static friction.

In Figures B and C, the angle of incline has been set to be the angle of repose, θ_r. With the help of geometry, it can be proven that triangles A and B in Figure C are *similar triangles*—that is, they have the same angles—and triangle B is a shrunken version of triangle A. The importance of similar triangles is that the *ratios* of corresponding parts of the two triangles are *equal*. Thus, the ratio of the parallel component to the normal force equals the ratio of the height y to the horizontal distance x. The coefficient of static friction is the ratio of those sides.

$$\mu_{static} = \frac{F_f}{N} = \frac{y}{x}$$

Procedure

Step 7: Put your shoe on the board, and slowly tilt the board up until the shoe just begins to slip. Using a meterstick, measure the horizontal distance x and the vertical distance y. Compute the coefficient of static friction μ_{static} from the equation in the preceding paragraph.

$$\mu_{static} = \underline{\hspace{4cm}}$$

Tap the incline.

Step 8: Repeat Step 7, except have a partner tap the board constantly as you approach the angle of repose. Adjust the board angle so that the shoe slides at constant speed. Compute the coefficient of sliding (kinetic) friction, $\mu_{sliding}$, which equals the ratio of y to x at that board angle.

$$\mu_{sliding} = \underline{\hspace{4cm}}$$

8. Did you measure any difference between μ_{static} and $\mu_{sliding}$?

_____

_____

Drag shoe on level.

Step 9: With a spring scale, drag your shoe along the same board when it is level. Compute $\mu_{sliding}$ by dividing the force of friction (the scale reading) by the weight of the shoe. Compare your result with that of Step 8.

$$\mu_{sliding} = \underline{\hspace{4cm}}$$

9. Are your values for $\mu_{sliding}$ from Steps 8 and 9 equal? Explain any differences.

_____

_____

10. Does the force of sliding friction between two surfaces depend on whether the supporting surface is inclined or horizontal?

_____

11. Does the coefficient of sliding friction between two surfaces depend on whether the supporting surface is inclined or horizontal?

_____

12. Explain why Questions 10 and 11 are different from each other.

_____

_____

34 Going in Circles

Purpose

To determine the relative magnitude and direction of acceleration of an object at different positions on a rotating turntable

Required Equipment/Supplies

dynamics cart
accelerometer
mass
pulley
string
support for pulley and mass
rotating platform
masking tape

Discussion

How can a passenger in a smooth-riding train tell when the train undergoes an acceleration? The answer is easy: He or she can simply watch to see whether the surface of the liquid in a container is disturbed, or look for motion at the bottom of the hanging curtains. These are two simple accelerometers.

Procedure

Step 1: Attach the accelerometer securely to a cart, and place the cart on a smooth surface such as a table.

Observe accelerometer moving in straight line.

Step 2: Attach the cart to the mass with a string. Attach a pulley to the edge of the table and place the string on the pulley.

Step 3: Allow the liquid in the accelerometer to settle down (level) while holding it in position ready to release. Allow the mass to fall and cause the cart to accelerate. Observe and sketch the surface of the liquid in the accelerometer. Label the direction of the acceleration of the cart.

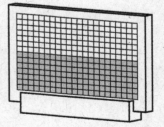

Activity

1. What happens to the surface as the cart continues to accelerate?

_____

_____

Repeat the experiment several times.

2. Does the surface behave the same way each time?

_____

_____

_____

Observe accelerometer on turntable.

Step 4: Remove the accelerometer from the cart, and securely attach the accelerometer to the turntable. Make sure that the accelerometer will not fly off.

Step 5: Place the center of the accelerometer at the center of the turn-table, and rotate the turntable at various speeds. Observe and sketch the surface of the liquid each time.

3. What do you conclude about the magnitude and direction of the acceleration on the rotating turntable?

_____

_____

_____

_____

Analysis

4. Figures A, B, C, and D show the surface of the liquid for a particular situation. What situation of the ones you observed most closely matches these figures?

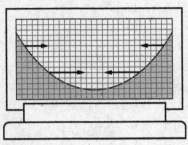

Fig. A

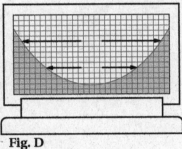

Fig. B

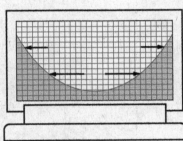

Fig. C

Fig. D

_____

_____

_____

5. The four figures show four possible sets of arrows representing the magnitude and direction of the acceleration at different points. Which figure is most correct? Explain the reason(s) for your choice.

_____

_____

_____

35 The Flying Pig

Purpose

To show that the net force for a conical pendulum is mv^2/r

Required Equipment/Supplies

flying pig apparatus (or equivalent) available from Arbor Scientific
vertical and horizontal rod
table clamp
stopwatch
meterstick

Discussion

When an object travels at constant speed along a circular path, we say it has uniform circular motion (if its speed were changing, then its motion would not be uniform). Any object moving in uniform circular motion is accelerated toward the center of its circular path. This acceleration is called *centripetal acceleration*, and equals v^2/r, where v is the speed of the object and r is the radius of the circular path. Although the net force on any object equals ma, during uniform circular motion, the net force, called *centripetal force*, equals mv^2/r and is directed *toward the center*. When an object suspended by a string moves in a circular path the centripetal force creates a *conical pendulum*. The string of a conical pendulum sweeps out a right-circular cone. In this experiment you will measure the speed of an object that produces a conical pendulum and show that the net force is mv^2/r.

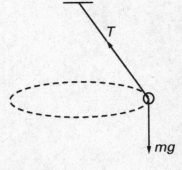

1. Draw the force vectors (a free-body diagram) that act on a conical pendulum. Ignoring air resistance, note that only two forces act on the pendulum bob—in this case, the pig. One is mg, the force due to gravity, and the other is string tension, T.

2. Resolve the tension into horizontal and vertical components. Represent the tension T with a solid line and its components with dashed lines. Also label the angle between the tension T and the vertical as θ.

3. Does the pig accelerate in the *vertical* direction? What does this tell you about the magnitude of the vertical component of T and mg?

$T_y =$ _____

4. Does the pig accelerate in the horizontal (radial) direction? Knowing that the net force in the radial direction for any object in uniform circular motion is the centripetal force, what does this tell you about the magnitude of the horizontal component of T and mv^2/r?

$T_x =$ _____

5. Write an equation that shows how the horizontal and vertical components of T are related to the weight and the centripetal force.

Hint: $\tan \theta = \dfrac{\text{opposite}}{\text{adjacent}} = \dfrac{T_x}{T_y} =$

6. Algebraically solve for the tangential speed of the pendulum from your equation in Question 5. Show your work.

$v =$ _____

Procedure

Set up the flying pig. (Note: Anything that "flies" in a circle works here—whether it be toy airplane, a toy flying pig or flying cow, etc.) Be careful not to damage their delicate wings as you click them into their fixed-wing position. Ask your instructor to check your pivot *before* switching on battery power. Carefully hold the pig by its body and give it a *slight* shove about 30° from the vertical, just enough so that the pig "flies" in a circle. The goal is to launch the pig *tangent* to the circle of flight. It's better to launch it too easy than too hard. If the pig does not fly in a stable circle in 10 seconds or so, carefully grab it and try launching it again.

Step 1: Once the pig is up and flying in a circle of constant radius, measure the radius of the circle as accurately as you can. Express your answer in meters.

$r =$ _____

Step 2: There are several ways to determine the angle the string makes with the vertical, θ. Using a protractor may not be as practical as other methods you may devise. Describe your method and then record your value for θ. Include a sketch.

Method: _____

_____

$\theta =$ _____

Step 3: Using the values for r and θ you determined in Steps 1 and 2, compute the theoretical speed of the pig using the formula you derived for the speed in Questions 5 and 6 from the Discussion section. (Remember, this speed is based on $F_{net} = mv^2/r$.)

$$v = \underline{\hspace{2cm}}$$

Step 4: In Step 3 you calculated the *theoretical* speed of the pig. Now, actually *measure* the speed of the pig and see how these two values for the speed compare. Since the pig flies in a circle, the speed is the circumference ($2\pi r$) divided by the time t for one complete revolution. To make your measurements of t more precise, measure the time it takes the pig to make 10 revolutions—then divide by 10.

$$10t = \underline{\hspace{2cm}} \text{ s (for ten revolutions)}$$

So for one revolution, $t = \underline{\hspace{2cm}}$ s.

Step 5: Using your measurement of r, compute the speed of the pig:

$$v = d/t = 2\pi r/t = \underline{\hspace{2cm}} \text{ m/s}$$

Step 6: Compute the percent difference between the value for the speed you computed in Step 3 and measured in Step 5. (Use the calculated speed as the known.)

$$\% \text{ difference} = \underline{\hspace{2cm}}$$

Analysis

7. What techniques for measuring r and θ would you recommend for best results?

_____

_____

8. What do you conclude about the magnitude of the string tension compared with the weight of the pig? Choose one: For uniform circular motion, the tension will always be (less than) (the same as) (greater than) the weight.

_____

_____

9. What do you conclude about the direction of the net force that keeps the flying pig in uniform circular motion?

_____

_____

10. Choose one: For uniform circular motion, the centripetal force will always be (less than) (the same as) (greater than) the tension in the string.

_____

11. How does the pig overcome air friction?

_____

_____

_____

12. List sources of error.

_____

_____

_____

_____

_____

_____

37 Where's Your CG?

Purpose

To locate your center of gravity.

Required Equipment/Supplies

2 bathroom scales
8' × 2" × 12" "reaction" board
meterstick
bricks or old books
2 large triangular supports (such as 1-inch angle iron or
    machine-shop files)

Discussion

For a symmetrical object such as a ball or donut, the center of gravity, or CG, is located in the geometric center of the object. For asymmetrical objects, such as a baseball bat or a person, the CG is located closer to the heavier end. When your arms are at your side, your center of gravity is near your navel, where your umbilical cord was attached. This is no coincidence—unborns sometimes rotate about their CG.

Your CG is a point that moves when you move. When you raise your hands above your head, your CG is a little higher than when your hands are by your sides. In this activity, you will locate your CG when your hands are by your sides.

Procedure

Step 1: Using a bathroom scale, weigh yourself and then a reaction board. Record these weights.

Weigh yourself.

weight of self = _____   weight of board = _____

Step 2: Measure your height in centimeters.

Measure your height.

height = _____

Step 3: Place one triangular support on each bathroom scale. You may need to add bricks or books between the scale and the support if the bubble on the scale causes the support to rock. Position the scales so that the tops of the triangular supports are separated by a distance equal to your height. Place the reaction board on the two supports. *The overhangs of the ends of the reaction board on each support should be equal.*

Position reaction board.

Read the weight reading on each bathroom scale. These readings should each be half the weight of the reaction board (plus the books or bricks, if any). If they are not, either adjust the calibration knob on one scale until the readings are equal or record the readings for future calculations.

Position yourself on reaction board.

Step 4: Lie down on the reaction board so that the tip of your head is over one support and the bottoms of your feet are over the other support, as in Figure A. Remain flat on the board with your hands by your sides. Have someone record the reading on each bathroom scale.

weight at head = _____   weight at feet = _____

Adjust your position.

Step 5: After you are informed of the weight readings, adjust your position along the length of the board until the two readings become equal. Have someone measure how far the bottoms of your feet are from the support near your feet.

distance from support to feet = _____

Fig. A

1. Did you have to move toward the foot end or toward the head end?

   _____

   _____

2. When the readings on the scales are equal, where is your CG in relation to the supports?

   _____

   _____

   _____

Determine your CG.

Step 6: Determine the location of your CG, in relation to the bottoms of your feet.

location of CG = _____ cm from the feet

Place your finger on your navel and have someone measure the distance from the bottom of your feet to your navel.

location of navel = _____ cm from the feet

Analysis

3. How close is your CG to your navel?

_____

_____

4. What would happen if the two weight readings of the board were not equal?

_____

_____

_____

_____

5. When an astronaut spins when doing acrobatics aboard an orbiting space vehicle, what point does the body spin about?

_____

_____

_____

Analysis

4. What would happen if the two weight readings of the board were not equal?

41 Rotational Derby

Purpose

To observe how round objects of various shapes and masses roll down an incline and how their rotational inertias affect their rate of rotation

Required Equipment/Supplies

smooth, flat board, 1 m in length
ring stand or metal support with clamp and rod
balance
meterstick
3 solid steel balls of different diameter (3/4" minimum)
3 empty cans of different diameter, with both the top and the bottom
    removed
3 unopened cans of different diameter, filled with nonsloshing contents
    (such as chili or ravioli)
2 unopened soup cans filled with different kinds of soup, one liquid
    (sloshing) and one solid (nonsloshing)

Discussion

Why is most of the mass of a flywheel, a gyroscope, or a Frisbee concentrated at its outer edge? Does this mass configuration give these objects a greater tendency to resist changes in rotation? How does their "rotational inertia" differ from the inertia you studied when you investigated linear motion? Keep these questions in mind as you do this activity.

The *rotational speed* of a rotating object is a measure of how fast the rotation is taking place. It is the angle turned per unit of time and may be measured in degrees per second or in radians per second. (A radian is a unit similar to a degree, only bigger; it is slightly larger than 57 degrees.) The *rotational acceleration*, on the other hand, is a measure of how quickly the rotational speed changes. (It is measured in degrees per second squared or in radians per second squared.) The rotational speed and the rotational acceleration are to rotational motion what speed and acceleration are to linear motion.

Procedure

Step 1: Make a ramp with the board and support. Place the board at an angle of about 10°.   *Set up ramp.*

Roll balls down ramp.

Step 2: Select two balls. Predict which ball will reach the bottom of the ramp in the shorter time.

predicted winner: _____

Place a meterstick across the ramp near the top, and rest the balls on the stick. Quickly remove the stick to allow the balls to roll down the ramp. Record your results.

actual winner: _____

Repeat the race for the other pair of balls.

1. What do you conclude about the time it takes for two solid steel balls with different diameters to roll down the same incline?

_____

_____

_____

Roll hollow cylinders.

Step 3: Repeat the race for two hollow cylinders (empty cans). Record your predictions and results.

predicted winner: _____

actual winner: _____

Repeat the race for the other pairs of hollow cylinders.

2. What do you conclude about the time it takes for two hollow cylinders with different diameters to roll down the same incline?

_____

_____

_____

Roll solid cylinders.

Step 4: Repeat the race for two solid cylinders (filled cans with non-sloshing contents). Record your predictions and results.

predicted winner: _____

actual winner: _____

Repeat the race for the other pairs of solid cylinders.

3. What do you conclude about the time it takes for two solid cylinders with different diameters to roll down the same incline?

_____

_____

Step 5: Repeat the race for a hollow cylinder and a solid one. Before trying it, predict which cylinder will reach the bottom of the ramp first.

Roll hollow and solid cylinders.

predicted winner: _____

Now try it, and record your results.

actual winner: _____

Repeat for other pairs of hollow vs. solid cylinders.

4. What can you conclude about the time it takes for a hollow and a
solid cylinder to roll down the same incline?

_____

_____

5. How do you explain the results you observed for the hollow and
solid cylinders?

_____

_____

_____

_____

_____

_____

Step 6: Repeat the race for a solid ball and a solid cylinder. Record your
prediction and result.

Roll balls and solid cylinders.

predicted winner: _____

actual winner: _____

6. What do you conclude about the time it takes for a solid ball and a
solid cylinder to roll down the same incline?

Step 7: Repeat the race for a solid ball and a hollow cylinder. Record
your prediction and result.

Roll balls and hollow cylinders.

predicted winner: _____

actual winner: _____

7. What can you conclude about the time it takes for a solid ball and a hollow cylinder to roll down the same incline?

_____

_____

_____

Roll cans of different kinds of soup.

Step 8: Repeat the race for two soup cans, one with liquid (sloshing) contents and the other with solid (nonsloshing) contents. Record your prediction and results.

predicted winner: _____

actual winner: _____

8. How can you explain the results you observed for the sloshing vs. nonsloshing kinds of soup?

_____

_____

_____

_____

_____

_____

_____

Analysis

9. Of all the objects you tested, which took the least time to roll down the incline?

_____

_____

10. Gravity caused the objects to turn faster and faster—that is, they had rotational acceleration. Of the objects you tested, what shape of objects had the greatest rotational inertia—that is, the greatest *resistance* to rotational acceleration?

_____

_____

42 On or Off the Mark?

Purpose

To explore conservation of energy for a rolling body

Required Equipment/Supplies

ramp
¾-inch-diameter steel ball
meterstick
balance
string, small piece of masking tape, marker
photogate (optional)

Discussion

When a pendulum swings back and forth, potential energy (PE) is converted into kinetic energy (KE) and vice versa. This is a beautiful example of conservation of energy. It's relatively simple because it involves little or no rotation. A small amount of energy is converted into heat due to air friction as the pendulum knocks air out of its way, so eventually the amplitude of the swings diminish. Nevertheless, energy is conserved if we take into account the heating of the room. Similarly, when a roller coaster rolls from the top to the bottom PE is converted into KE. Let's explore the principle of conservation of energy and see how it applies to a ball rolling down a hill.

Procedure

Step 1: Set up a ramp for a steel ball (the one you used for Bull's Eye is perfect). Your teacher will assign a position on the ramp from which you will release the ball. Without releasing the ball, have your lab partner measure the vertical height of the ball from the bottom of the ramp. Record the value for the height.

$$h = \underline{\hspace{2cm}} \text{ cm}$$

Step 2: Measure the mass of the ball.

$$m = \underline{\hspace{2cm}} \text{ g}$$

Step 3: Calculate the potential energy of the ball, *mgh*. Remember, $g = 9.8$ m/s^2 or 980 cm/s^2.

$$PE = \underline{\hspace{2cm}} \text{ cm}$$

Step 4: Using the formula for kinetic energy, $KE = \frac{1}{2}mv^2$, solve for the speed of the ball as it leaves the ramp.

$$v = \underline{\hspace{2cm}} \text{ cm/s}$$

Step 5: Assuming all the potential energy of the ball is converted into (translational) kinetic energy, predict the landing point of the ball (on the floor). Make a mark with an erasable marker where you think the ball will land.

$$\text{predicted distance, } d_x = \underline{\hspace{2cm}} \text{ cm}$$

Step 6: Before you release the ball, determine the point on the floor directly above where the ball leaves the ramp. Make a small mark with an erasable marker. Fasten one end of a piece of string there. Your lab partner should be prepared to record where the ball lands. Release the ball on the ramp and observe where it lands. Repeat several times until you're convinced you have a consistent value for the landing distance. Stretch out the string so that it forms a straight line through the landing point. Record your results.

$$\text{actual distance, } d_x = \underline{\hspace{2cm}} \text{ cm}$$

Analysis

1. Calculate the percent difference between the actual and the predicted landing points.

   _____

2. How far did the ball land from your predicted landing point? Is it short, long, or relatively close? Close would be within a few percent.

   _____

   _____

   _____

3. Compare your findings with those of the rest of the class. Is there a pattern to the results?

   _____

   _____

   _____

4. How would you account for the discrepancy between the predicted and actual landing points?

_____

_____

_____

_____

Going Further

To find out what's going on, let's make some more measurements. If a photogate is available, measure the speed of the ball just as it leaves the ramp. If a photogate is not available, you can compute the speed of the ball by simply taking the horizontal distance it traveled divided by the time it was in the air (measure the height of the ball and use $h = 1/2gt^2$ and solve for t). This is simply the reverse procedure used in Bull's Eye. Compare this to the predicted value in Step 4. Notice that the measured or computed value of v_x is consistently *less*. Why?

_____

_____

_____

_____

4. How would you account for the discrepancy between the predicted and actual landing points?

Going Further

To find out what's going on, let's make some more measurements. If a photogate is available, measure the speed of the ball just as it leaves the ramp. If a photogate is not available, you can compute the speed of the ball by simply taking the horizontal distance it traveled divided by the time it was in the air (measure the height of the ball and use $h = 1/2gt^2$ and solve for t). This is simply the reverse procedure used in Bull's Eye. Compare this to the predicted value in Step 4. Notice that the measured or computed value of v is consistently less. Why?

43 Apparent Weightlessness

Purpose

To observe the effects of gravity on objects in free fall

Required Equipment/Supplies

2 plastic foam or paper cups	masking tape
2 long rubber bands	large paper clip
2 washers or other small masses	water

Discussion

Some people believe that because astronauts aboard an orbiting space vehicle appear weightless, the pull of gravity upon them is zero. This condition is commonly referred to as "zero-*g*." While it is true that they *feel* weightless, gravity *is* acting upon them. It acts with almost the same magnitude as on Earth's surface.

The key to understanding this condition is realizing that both the astronauts and the space vehicle are in free fall. It is very similar to how you would feel inside an elevator with a snapped cable! The primary difference between the runaway elevator and the space vehicle is that the runaway elevator has no *horizontal velocity* (relative to the earth's surface) as it falls toward the earth, so it eventually hits the earth. The horizontal velocity of the space vehicle ensures that as it falls *toward* the earth, it also moves *around* the earth. It falls without getting closer to Earth's surface. Both cases involve free fall.

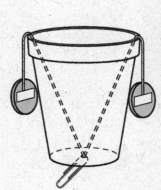

Fig. A

Procedure

Step 1: Knot together two rubber bands to make one long rubber band. Knot each end around a washer and tape the washers to the ends. Poke a small hole about the diameter of a pencil through the bottom of a plastic foam or paper cup. Fit the rubber bands through the hole from the inside. Use a paper clip to hold the rubber bands in place under the bottom of the cup (see Figure A). Hang the washers over the lip of the cup. The rubber bands should be taut.

Attach washers.

Step 2: Drop the cup from a height of about 2 m.

Drop cup.

1. What happens to the washers?

_____

Fill cup with water.

Step 3: Remove the rubber bands from the cup and fill the cup half full with water, using your finger as a stopper over the hole. Hold the cup directly over a sink. Drop the cup into the sink.

2.   What happens to the water as the cup falls?

_____

_____

Step 4: Repeat Step 3 for a second cup half filled with water, with two holes poked through its *sides* (Figure B). You may wish to place a piece of masking tape over the hole on the bottom of the cup.

3.   What happens to the water as the cup falls?

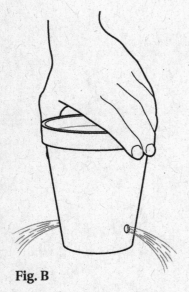

Fig. B

_____

Analysis

4.   Explain why the washers acted as they did in Step 2.

_____

_____

_____

5.   Explain why the draining water acted as it did in Steps 3 and 4.

_____

_____

6.   Suppose you were standing on a bathroom scale inside an elevator. Based on your observations in this activity, predict what would happen to your weight reading when the elevator

   a. accelerated upward.

_____

   b. accelerated downward at an acceleration less than *g*.

_____

   c. moved upward at a constant speed.

_____

   d. moved downward at a constant speed.

_____

   e. accelerated downward at an acceleration greater than *g*.

_____

44 Getting Eccentric

Purpose

To investigate the geometry of an ellipse

Required Equipment/Supplies

about 20 cm of string
2 pushpins
pencil and paper
a flat surface that will accept pushpin punctures (such as cardboard)

Discussion

An ellipse is an oval-like closed curve. Planets orbit the sun in elliptical paths, with the sun's center at one focus. Nothing in particular is located at the other focus.

Elliptical trajectories are not confined to "outer space." Toss a ball and the parabolic path it seems to trace is actually a small segment of an ellipse. If extended, its path would continue through Earth and swing about Earth's center and return to its starting point. In this case, the far focus is Earth's center. The near focus is somewhere inside Earth, close to the thrower. The ellipse is very stretched out—like a flattened circle—with its long axis considerably longer than its short axis. We say the ellipse is very *eccentric*. Toss the rock faster and the ellipse is wider—less eccentric. The far focus is still Earth's center, and the near focus is nearer to Earth's center than before. Toss the rock at 8 km/s and both foci will coincide at Earth's center. The elliptical path is now a circle—a special case of an ellipse. Toss the rock even faster, and it follows an ellipse external to Earth. Now we see the near focus is the center of Earth and the far focus is beyond—again, at no particular place. As the speed of the rock is increased the ellipse becomes more and more eccentric again, and the far focus is *outside* Earth's interior.

Constructing an ellipse with pencil, paper, string, and tacks is interesting. Let's do it!

Procedure

Step 1: Attach the end of the string to a pushpin, and pull the string taut with a pencil. Then slide the pencil along the string, keeping it taut. It helps to avoid twisting the string by making the top and bottom halves in separate operations. The location of each pushpin is a focus of the ellipse.

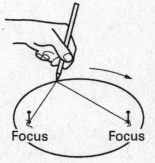

Focus   Focus

Step 2: Repeat twice, using a different distance between the foci. The greater the distance between foci, the more eccentric is the ellipse.

Step 3: Construct a circle by bringing both foci together. A circle is a special case of an ellipse. It is not eccentric—that is, the eccentricity is zero.

Step 4: Another special case of an ellipse is a straight line. Determine the positions of the foci that give you a straight line.

Analysis

1. Which of your drawings is closest to Earth's orbit around the sun?

   _____

   _____

2. Which of your drawings is closest to the orbit of Halley's comet around the sun?

   _____

   _____

3. An ellipse is defined as the locus of all points the sum of whose distances from a pair of foci (focal points) is a constant. What is your evidence that the figure you drew fits the definition of the ellipse—that the sum of the distances from the foci is constant?

   _____

   _____

45 Tracking Mars

Purpose

To employ the technique of Johannes Kepler in plotting the orbit of Mars, using data acquired by Tycho Brahe four centuries ago

Required Equipment/Supplies

4 sheets of graph paper
protractor
sharp pencil
compass
ruler
French curve (optional)

Discussion

In the early 1500s, the Polish astronomer Nicolaus Copernicus used observations and geometry to determine the orbital radius and orbital period for the planets known at the time. Copernicus based his work on the revolutionary assumption that the planets moved around the sun. In the late 1500s, before telescopes were invented, the Danish astronomer Tycho Brahe spent twenty years making extensive and accurate measurements of planets and bright stars. Near the end of Tycho's career, he hired a young German mathematician, Johannes Kepler, who was assigned the task of plotting the orbit of Mars using Tycho's data.

Kepler started by drawing a circle to represent Earth's orbit (a good beginning, even though Earth's orbit only approximates a circle). Since Mars takes 687 Earth days to orbit the sun once, Kepler made note of observations that were exactly 687 days apart. In this way, Mars would be in the same place when Earth would be in a different location. Two angular readings of Mars' location from the same location on Earth 687 days apart was all that was needed—where the two lines crossed was a point on the orbit of Mars. Plotting many such points did not trace out a circle, as Kepler expected—rather, the path was an ellipse. Kepler was the first to discover that if the planets orbit the sun, they do so in elliptical rather than circular paths. He then went on to plot a better orbit for Earth based on observations of the sun, and further refined the plotted orbit of Mars.

In this activity you will duplicate the work of Kepler, simplified somewhat by assuming a circular orbit for Earth—it turns out the difference is minor and the elliptical path of Mars is obvious. From Brahe's extensive tables, we'll use only the data shown in Table A.

Procedure

Step 1: Get a sheet of graph paper with about a 14 x 14-inch working area. If need be, tape two legal-sized sheets of borderless graph paper together, or four 8 × 11-inch sheets.

Step 2: Make a dot at the center of your paper to represent the sun. Place a compass there and draw a 10-cm-radius circle to represent the orbit of Earth around the sun. Draw a light line from the center to the right of the paper and mark the intersection with Earth's orbit at 0°. This is the position of Earth on March 21. All your plotting will be counter-clockwise around the circle from this reference point.

Brahe's data are grouped in 14 pairs of Mars' sightings. For the first nine pairs, the first line of data is for Mars in opposition—sun, Earth, Mars on the same line—when Mars was 90° from Earth's horizon (directly overhead) at midnight. The second line of data is for positions measured 687 days later, when Mars was again in the same place in its orbit, and Earth in a different place. A different angle was then measured. All angles given in Brahe's table read from a 0° reference line—the line from the sun to Earth at the vernal equinox, March 21. Points 10–14 are nonopposition sightings of Mars. The first line of point 10, for example, shows that when Earth was at 277°, Mars was seen not directly overhead, but at 208.5° with respect to the 0° reference line. Then 687 days later Earth was at 235°, and Mars was seen at 272.5°. The data are neatly arranged for plotting even though it took Kepler several years to produce the data.

Step 3: Locate the first point in Mars' orbit, point 1, from Table A. Do this by first marking with a protractor the position of Earth along the circle for the date November 28, 1580. This is 66.5° above the 0° reference line. Draw a dot to show Earth's position at this time.

Step 4: Mars at this time was in *opposition*—opposite to the sun in the sky. A line from the sun to Earth at this time extends radially outward to Mars. Draw a line from the center of your circle (the sun) to Earth's position at this time and beyond Earth through Mars. Where is Mars along this line? You'll need another sighting of Mars 687 days later when Mars is at the same place and Earth is at another.

Mars Orbit Point	Date			Earth Position (Ecliptic)	Mars Position (Ecliptic)
	Mo.	Day	Year		
1	11	28	1580	66.5	66.5
	10	16	1582	22.5	107
2	1	7	1583	107	107
	11	24	1584	62.5	144
3	2	10	1585	141.5	141.5
	12	29	1586	97.5	177
4	3	16	1587	175.5	175.5
	1	31	1589	132	212
5	4	24	1589	214.5	214.5
	3	12	1591	171.5	253.5
6	6	18	1591	266.5	266.5
	5	5	1593	225	311
7	9	5	1593	342.5	342.5
	7	24	1595	300.5	29.5
8	11	10	1595	47.5	47.5
	9	27	1597	4	90
9	12	24	1597	92.5	92.5
	11	11	1599	48	130.5
10	6	29	1589	277	208.5
	5	16	1591	235	272.5
11	8	1	1591	308	260.5
	6	18	1593	266.5	335
12	9	9	1591	345.5	273
	7	27	1593	304	347.5
13	10	3	1593	9.5	337.5
	8	20	1595	327	44.5
14	11	23	1593	60.5	350.5
	10	10	1595	17	56

Step 5: If you were to add 687 days to November 28, 1580, you'd get October 16, 1582. At that date, Mars was measured to be lower in the sky—107.0° with respect to the 0° reference line of March 21. Use a protractor and ruler to draw a line with respect to the reference line at 107.0°, as shown in Figure A. Where your two lines intersect is a point along Mars' orbit.

Step 6: Carefully plot the 13 other intersections that represent points along Mars' orbit, using the data in Table A.

Step 7: Connect your points, either very carefully freehand or with a French curve.

　　You have plotted the orbit of Mars using Kepler's method from four centuries ago.

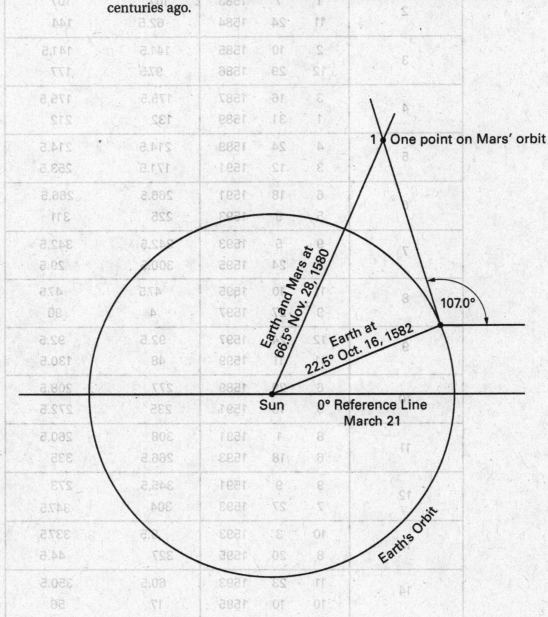

Figure A: Your plot should look like this for finding Mars' orbit point 1; data are in the first pair of lines of Table A. Angles from Earth to Mars are given with respect to the 0° reference line of March 21.

Analysis

1. Place the point of your compass on the position of the sun and place the pencil on the first point of the plotted orbit of Mars. Draw a circular orbit with that radius. Does that circle match the orbit of Mars? If not, describe the differences.

   _____

   _____

2. Does your plot agree with Kepler's finding that the orbit is an ellipse?

   _____

   _____

46 Trial and Error

Purpose

To discover Kepler's third law of planetary motion through a procedure of trial and error using a computer

Required Equipment/Supplies

computer
data-plotting software or spreadsheet

Discussion

Pretend you are a budding astronomer. In order to earn your Ph.D. degree, you are doing research on planetary motion. You are looking for a relationship between the time it takes a planet to orbit the sun (the *period*) and the average radius of the planet's orbit around the sun. Using a telescope, you have accumulated the planetary data shown in Table A.

You have access to a program that allows you to plot data easily on a computer. It can also plot many different relations between the variables. You can plot the period T vs. the radius R. You can also plot T vs. R^2, T vs. R^3, and so on. You can even plot R vs. T, R vs. T^2, and R vs. T^3, and so on, just as easily.

Planet	Period (years)	Average Radius (AU)
Mercury	0.241	0.39
Venus	0.615	0.72
Earth	1.00	1.00
Mars	1.88	1.52
Jupiter	11.8	5.20
Saturn	29.5	9.54
Uranus	84.0	19.18
Neptune	164.8	30.06

Table A

Procedure

Step 1: Using data-plotting software, try to make a graph involving T and R that is a straight line. A linear (straight-line) relationship shows that the two plotted variables are directly proportional to each other. Try plotting T vs. R, T vs. R^2, T vs. R^3, R vs. T, R vs. T^2, and R vs. T^3 to see whether any of these relationships form a straight line when graphed.

Step 2: If the relationship between T and R cannot be discovered by modifying the power of only one variable at a time, try modifying the power of both variables at the same time.

If you find the exact relationship between T and R during this lab period, feel *good*. It took Johannes Kepler (1571–1630) ten years of painstaking effort to discover the relationship. Computers were not around in the 1600s.

1. Did you discover a linear relationship between some power of T and some power of R using the program? What powers of T and R graph as a straight line?

_____

_____

_____

_____

2. Make a printout of the graph closest to a straight line and include it with your report.

47 Flat as a Pancake

Purpose

To estimate the diameter of a BB

Required Equipment/Supplies

75 mL of BB shot
100-mL graduated cylinder
tray
rulers
micrometer

Discussion

Consider 512 cubes, each with sides one centimeter long. If all the cubes are packed closely with no spaces between them to make a large cube with sides 8 cubes long, the volume of the large cube is 8 cm × 8 cm × 8 cm, or 512 cm^3. If the cubes are stacked to make a block 4 cm by 16 cm by 8 cm, the volume remains the same, but the outside surface area becomes greater. For a block 2 cm by 16 cm by 16 cm, the area of the surface is greater still. If the cubes are spread out so that the stack is only one cube high, the area of the surface is the greatest it can be.

The different configurations have different surface areas, but the volume remains constant. The volume of pancake batter is also the same whether it is in the mixing bowl or spread out on a surface (except that on a hot griddle the volume increases because of the expanding bubbles that form as the batter cooks). The volume of a pancake equals the surface area of one flat side multiplied by the thickness. If both the volume and the surface area are known, then the thickness can be calculated from the following equations.

$$volume = area \times thickness$$

$$thickness = \frac{volume}{area}$$

Instead of cubical blocks or pancake batter, consider a shoe box full of marbles. The total volume of the marbles equals the volume of the box (length times width times height). Suppose you computed the volume and then poured the marbles onto a large tray. Can you think of a way to *estimate* the diameter (or thickness) of a single marble without measuring the marble itself? Would the same procedure work for smaller size balls such as BB's? Try it in this activity and see. It will be simply another step smaller to consider the size of molecules.

Procedure

Step 1: Use a graduated cylinder to measure the volume of the BB's. (Note that 1 mL = 1 cm^3.)

volume = _____

Step 2: Spread the BB's to make a compact layer one pellet thick on the tray. If trays are not available, try taping three rulers together in a U-shape on your lab table. Determine the area covered by the BB's. Describe your procedure and show your computations.

area = _____ cm^2

Step 3: Using the area and volume of the BB's, estimate the diameter of a BB. Show your computations.

estimated diameter = _____ cm

Step 4: Check your estimate by using a micrometer to measure the diameter of a BB.

measured diameter = _____ cm

Analysis

1. What assumptions did you make when estimating the diameter of the BB?

   _____

   _____

   _____

   _____

   _____

2. How do the measured and estimated diameters of the BB compare?

   _____

   _____

3. Oleic acid is an organic substance that is insoluble in water. When a drop of oleic acid is placed on water, it usually spreads out over the water surface, creating a layer one molecule thick. Describe a method to estimate the size of an oleic acid molecule.

   _____

   _____

   _____

48 Extra Small

Purpose

To estimate the size of a molecule of oleic acid

Required Equipment/Supplies

chalk dust or lycopodium powder   tray
oleic acid solution   water
10-mL graduated cylinder   eyedropper

Discussion

An oleic acid molecule is not spherical, but elongated like a hot dog. One end is attracted to water, and the other end points away from the water surface.

During this investigation, you will estimate the length of a single molecule of oleic acid, to determine for yourself the extreme smallness of a molecule. The length can be calculated by dividing the volume of oleic acid used by the area of the *monolayer*, or layer one molecule thick. The length of the molecule is the depth of the monolayer.

$$\text{volume} = \text{area} \times \text{depth}$$

$$\text{depth} = \frac{\text{volume}}{\text{area}}$$

Procedure

Step 1: Pour water into the tray to a depth of about 1 cm. Spread chalk dust or lycopodium powder very lightly over the surface of the water; too much will hem in the oleic acid.

Set up tray.

Step 2: Using the eyedropper, gently add a single drop of the oleic acid solution to the surface of the water. When the drop touches the water, the alcohol in it will dissolve in the water, but the oleic acid will not. The oleic acid spreads out to make a circle on the water. Measure the diameter of the oleic acid circle in three places, and compute the average diameter of the circle. Also, compute the area of the circle.

Compute area of film.

$$\text{average diameter} = \underline{\hspace{2cm}} \text{ cm}$$

$$\text{area of circle} = \underline{\hspace{3cm}} \text{ cm}^2$$

Step 3: Count the number of drops of solution needed to occupy 3 mL (or 3 cm^3) in the graduated cylinder. Do this three times, and find the average number of drops in 3 cm^3 of solution.

number of drops in 3 cm^3 = _____

Divide 3 cm^3 by the number of drops in 3 cm^3 to determine the volume of a single drop.

volume of drop = _____ cm^3

Step 4: The volume of the oleic acid alone in the circular film is much less than the volume of a single drop of the solution. The concentration of oleic acid in the solution is 5 cm^3 per 1000 cm^3 of solution. Every cubic centimeter of the solution thus contains only 5/1000 cm^3 of oleic acid. The ratio of oleic acid to total solution is 0.005 for any volume. Multiply the volume of a drop by 0.005 to find the volume of oleic acid in the drop. This is the volume of the layer of oleic acid in the tray.

volume of oleic acid = _____ cm^3

Compute length of molecule.

Step 5: Estimate the length of an oleic acid molecule by dividing the volume of oleic acid by the area of the circle.

length of molecule = _____

Analysis

1. What is meant by a monolayer?

_____

_____

2. Why is it necessary to dilute the oleic acid?

_____

_____

3. Which substance forms the monolayer film—the oleic acid or the alcohol?

_____

4. The shape of oleic acid molecules is more like that of a rectangular hot dog than a cube or marble. Furthermore, one end is attracted to water so that the molecule actually "floats" vertically like a log with a heavy lead weight at one end. If each of these rectangular molecules is 10 times as long as it is wide, how would you compute the volume of one oleic acid molecule?

_____

_____

49 Stretch

Purpose

To verify Hooke's law and determine the spring constants for a spring and a rubber band

Required Equipment/Supplies

ring stand or other support with rod and clamp
3 springs
paper clip
masking tape
meterstick
set of slotted masses
large rubber band
graph paper
computer, printer, and data-plotting software (optional)

Discussion

When a force is applied, an object may be stretched, compressed, bent, or twisted. The internal forces between atoms in the object resist these changes. These forces become greater as the atoms are moved farther from their original positions. When the outside force is removed, these forces return the object to its original shape. Too large a force may overcome these resisting forces and cause the object to deform permanently. The minimum amount of stretch, compression, or torsion needed to do this is called the *elastic limit*.

Hooke's law applies to changes below the elastic limit. It states that the amount of stretch or compression is directly proportional to the applied force. The proportionality constant is called the *spring constant, k*. Hooke's law is written $F = kx$, where x is the displacement (stretch or compression). A stiff spring has a high spring constant and a weak spring has a small spring constant.

Procedure

Step 1: Hang a spring from a support. Attach a paper clip to the free end of the spring with masking tape. Clamp a meterstick in a vertical position next to the spring. Note the position of the bottom of the paper clip relative to the meterstick. Place a piece of masking tape on the meterstick with its lower edge at this position.

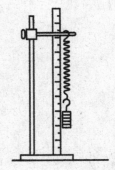

Set up apparatus.

Attach masses to spring.

Step 2: Attach different masses to the end of the spring. With your eye level with the bottom of the paper clip, note its position each time. The stretch in each case is the difference between the positions of the paper clip when a load is on the spring and when no load is on the spring. Be careful not to exceed the elastic limit of the spring. Record the mass and stretch of each trial in the first section of Data Table A.

Data Table A

	Mass	Force	Stretch	Spring Constant
Spring 1				
Spring 2				
Spring 3				
Rubber Band				
Springs In Series				

Repeat using different springs.

Step 3: Repeat Steps 1 and 2 for two more springs. Record the masses and strains in the next two sections of Data Table A.

Step 4: Repeat Steps 1 and 2 using a large rubber band. Record the masses and the corresponding stretches in the fourth section of Data Table A.

Repeat using rubber band.

Step 5: Calculate the forces and record them in Data Table A. On graph paper, make a graph of force (vertical axis) vs. stretch (horizontal axis) for each spring and the rubber band. If available, use data-plotting software to plot your data and print out your graph.

Graph data.

Step 6: For each graph that is an upward-sloping straight line, draw a horizontal line through one of the lowest points on the graph. Then draw a vertical line through one of the highest points on the graph. Now you have a triangle. The slope of the graph equals the vertical side of the triangle divided by the horizontal side. The slope of a force-vs.-stretch graph is equal to the spring constant. By finding the slope of each of your graphs, determine the spring constant k for each spring and record your values in Data Table A.

Measure slope of graphs.

1. How is the value of k related to the stiffness of the springs?

   _____

   _____

$$\text{Slope} = \frac{y}{x}$$

2. Are all your graphs straight lines? If they are not, can you think of a reason why?

   _____

   _____

   _____

   _____

   _____

Going Further

Step 7: Repeat Steps 1 and 2 for two springs connected in series (end to end). Record the masses and stretches in the last section of Data Table A.

Connect several springs in series.

Step 8: Repeat Steps 5 and 6 to determine the spring constant for the combination.

Graphically determine the spring constant.

3. How does the spring constant of two springs connected in a series compare with that of a single spring?

   _____

   _____

   _____

   _____

Repeat using rubber band.

Graph data.

Measure slope of graphs.

_____

_____

_____

_____

_____

_____

Connect several springs in series.

Graphically determine the spring constant.

_____

_____

_____

50 Geometric Physics

Purpose

To investigate ratios of surface area to volume

Required Equipment/Supplies

plastic foam balls of
    diameter 1 in., 2 in., 4 in., 8 in.
4 sheets of paper
stopwatch or clock with
    second hand
50-mL beaker
hot plate
2 200-mL beakers
400-mL beaker
800-mL beaker

water
10 g granulated salt
10 g rock salt
2 stirrers
thermometer or 2 temperature
    probes with computer interface
printer

Discussion

Why do elephants have big ears? Why does a chunk of coal burn, while coal dust explodes? Why are ants not the size of horses? This activity will give you insights into some secrets of nature that may at first appear to have no direct connection to physics.

Part A

Procedure

Step 1: Drop pairs of different-size plastic foam balls from a height of about 3 m. Drop the balls at the same moment with no push or retardation. Compare their falling times by observing when one ball strikes the ground relative to another. Summarize your observations in Data Table A.

Drop plastic foam balls.

Falling Time	Ball Diameter
Hits the Ground 1st	
Hits the Ground 2nd	
Hits the Ground 3rd	
Hits the Ground Last	

Data Table A

1. Describe any regularity you observe.

_____

_____

Analysis

2. Which size plastic foam ball had the greatest average speed when dropped?

_____

_____

_____

3. Which size plastic foam ball had the least average speed when dropped?

_____

_____

4. Which size plastic foam ball has the greatest surface area?

_____

_____

_____

5. Which size plastic foam ball has the greatest volume?

_____

_____

6. Which size plastic foam ball has the greatest ratio of surface area to volume?

_____

_____

_____

_____

7. Which size plastic foam ball has the smallest ratio of surface area to volume?

_____

_____

_____

_____

8. A plastic foam ball falling through the air has two forces acting on it. One is the downward force due to gravity—its weight. The weight of the ball is proportional to its volume. The other force is the upward force of air resistance—drag—which opposes the fall. Drag is proportional to the surface area of the ball.

a. To what is the upward force due to drag proportional?

_____

_____

_____

b. Which size plastic foam ball should have experienced the greatest upward force due to drag?

_____

_____

_____

c. Which size plastic foam ball should have experienced the greatest *net* downward force per unit mass (due to gravity *and* drag)—that is, which should show the greatest acceleration?

_____

_____

_____

_____

_____

d. Does your answer to (c) agree with your observations?

_____

_____

_____

_____

9. Predict which will fall to the ground faster—a heavier raindrop or a lighter one. Why?

_____

_____

_____

Dissolve salt in water.

Part B

Procedure

Step 2: Record the number of seconds it takes to dissolve 10 g of granulated salt at room temperature in 100 mL of water that is being stirred vigorously. Repeat, substituting 10 g of rock salt for the granulated salt.

time for granulated salt = _____

time for rock salt = _____

Analysis

10. Which salt dissolved more quickly—the granulated salt or the rock salt? Why?

_____

_____

11. Suggest a relationship for predicting dissolving times for salt granules of different size, such as rock salt and table salt.

_____

_____

_____

Part C

Procedure

Step 3: Make similar paper airplanes from whole, half, and quarter sheets of paper. Record which one flies the farthest.

airplane that flies farthest: _____

Analysis

12. Which paper airplane generally traveled farthest? Why?

_____

_____

_____

_____

_____

Part D

Procedure

Step 4: Heat 500 mL of water to 40°C. Then pour 50 mL into a 50-mL beaker and 400 mL into a 400-mL beaker. Allow the beakers to cool down by themselves on the lab table. Measure the temperature of both every 30 seconds, using either a thermometer or temperature probes connected to a computer. (If you are using the computer, use two temperature probes to monitor the temperatures of the two beakers of water. Save your data, and print a copy of your graph; include it with your lab report.) Record your findings in Data Table B.

Monitor cooling water.

Data Table B

Time (s)	Temperature (°C) 50 mL	Temperature (°C) 400 mL
0		
30		
60		
90		
120		
150		
180		
210		
240		
270		
300		

Analysis

13. Which beaker of warm water cooled faster?

_____

_____

14. Which beaker has more surface area?

_____

_____

15. Which beaker has the greater volume?

_____

_____

16. Which beaker has the larger ratio of surface area to volume?

_____

_____

17. Which beaker has the smaller ratio of surface area to volume?

_____

_____

_____

18. The cooling of a beaker of warm water takes place at the surface. The total amount of heat that must leave the water for it to cool to room temperature depends on the volume. Therefore, on what ratio does the rate of cooling (the temperature drop with time) depend?

_____

_____

_____

19. Suppose that a small wading pool is next to a swimming pool. Predict which pool will heat up faster during the day. Why?

_____

_____

_____

51 Eureka!

Purpose

To explore the displacement method of finding volumes of irregularly shaped objects and to compare their masses with their volumes

Required Equipment/Supplies

two 35-mm film canisters (prepared by the teacher), one of which is
    filled with lead shot, and the other with a bolt just large enough to
    cause the canister to sink when placed in water
triple-beam balance
string
graduated cylinder
water
masking tape
5 steel bolts of different size
irregularly shaped piece of scrap iron
1000-mL beaker

Discussion

The volume of a block is easy to compute. Simply measure its length, width, and height. Then, multiply length times width times height. But how would you go about computing the volume of an irregularly shaped object such as a bolt or rock? One way is by the displacement method. Submerge the object in water and measure the volume of water displaced, or moved elsewhere. This volume is also the volume of the object. Go two steps further and (1) measure the mass of the object; (2) divide the mass by the volume. The result is an important property of the object—its *density*.

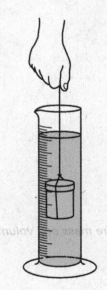

Fig. A

Part A
Procedure

Find the mass of each canister.

Step 1: Your teacher has prepared two film canisters for you. Each canister should have a piece of string attached to it. Use a triple-beam balance to find the mass of each one.

mass of lighter canister = _____

mass of heavier canister = _____

Observe rise in water level.

Step 2: Place a strip of masking tape vertically at the water level of a graduated cylinder about 2/3 full of water. Mark the water level on the tape. Submerge the lighter canister in the water, as shown in Figure A. Observe the rise in water level. Mark the new water level on the tape. Remove the canister.

Predict rise in water level.

Step 3: Predict what you think the rise in the water level for the heavier canister will be when it is submerged. Do you think it will be less than, the same as, or greater than the rise in water level for the lighter canister?

prediction: _____

Observe rise in water level.

Step 4: Test your prediction by submerging the heavier canister. Write down your findings.

findings: _____

Analysis

1. How do the amounts of water displaced by each canister compare?

_____

_____

_____

2. Does the amount of water displaced by a submerged canister depend on the mass of the canister? On the volume of the canister?

_____

_____

Part B
Procedure

Measure mass and volume of bolts.

Step 5: Measure the masses of five different-sized bolts and then measure their volumes using the displacement method. Record your data in Data Table A.

Bolt Number	Mass (g)	Volume (mL)	_ _ _ _ _ _ _ _ (g/mL or g/cm³)
1			
2			
3			
4			
5			

Data Table A

Step 6: For each bolt, divide its mass by its volume and enter the results in the last column of Data Table A.

Analysis

3. How do the ratios of mass to volume compare for each of the bolts?

   _____

   _____

4. Would you expect the ratio of mass to volume to be the same for bolts of different metals?

   _____

   _____

5. What name is given to the ratio of mass to volume? (Fill this name in at the top of the last column in Data Table A.)

   _____

   _____

Part C

Going Further

Pretend that you are living in ancient Greece during the time of Archimedes. The king has commissioned a new crown to be made of pure gold. The king is worried that the goldsmith may have cheated him by replacing some of the gold with less-precious metals. You are asked to devise a way to tell, without damaging the crown, whether the king was cheated or not.

Unfortunately, your school cannot supply you with an actual gold crown for this activity. A less valuable piece of scrap iron will simulate the crown.

Write down your procedure and any measurements you make.

   _____

   _____

   _____

   _____

   _____

   _____

   _____

Chapter 19: Liquids **Archimedes' Principle and Flotation**

52 Sink or Swim

Purpose

To introduce Archimedes' principle and the principle of flotation

Required Equipment/Supplies

spring scale
triple-beam balance
string
rock or hook mass
600-mL beaker
500-mL graduated cylinder
clear container

water
masking tape
chunk of wood
modeling clay
toy boat
50-g mass
2 100-g masses

Discussion

An object submerged in water takes up space and pushes water out of the way. The water is said to be displaced. Interestingly enough, the water that is pushed out of the way, in effect, pushes back on the submerged object. For example, if the object pushes a volume of water with a weight of 10 N out of its way, then the water reacts by pushing back on the object with a force of 10 N. We say that the object is buoyed upward with a force of 10 N. In this experiment, you will investigate what determines whether an object sinks or floats in water.

Procedure

Step 1: Use a spring scale to determine the weight of an object (rock or hook mass) first in air and then underwater. The difference in weights is the buoyant force. Record the weights and the buoyant force.

Weigh an object in air and submerged in water.

weight of object in air = _____

apparent weight of object in water = _____

buoyant force on object = _____

Step 2: Devise an experimental setup to find the volume of water displaced by the object. Record the volume of water displaced. Compute the mass and weight of this water.

Measure the water displaced.

volume of water displaced = _____

mass of water displaced = _____

weight of water displaced = _____

1. How does the buoyant force on the submerged object compare with the weight of the water displaced?

_____

_____

_____

Float a piece of wood.

Step 3: Find the mass of a piece of wood with a triple-beam balance, and record the mass in Data Table A.

NOTE: To keep the calculations simple, from here on in this experiment, you will measure and determine masses, without finding the equivalent weights. Keep in mind, however, that an object floats because of a buoyant force. This force is due to the *weight* of the water displaced.

Measure the volume of water displaced when the wood floats. Record the volume and mass of water displaced in Data Table A.

Object	Mass (g)	Volume of Water Displaced (mL)	Mass of Water Displaced (g)
Wood			
Wood and 50-g Mass			
Clay Ball			
Floating Clay			

Data Table A

2. What is the relation between the buoyant force on any floating object and the weight of the object?

_____

_____

3. How does the mass of the floating wood compare to the mass of water displaced?

_____

_____

4. How does the buoyant force on the wood compare with the weight of water displaced?

_____

_____

_____

Step 4: Add a 50-g mass to the wood so that the wood displaces more water *but still floats*. The 50-g mass needs to float on top of the wood. Measure the volume of water displaced and calculate its mass, recording them in Data Table A.

Float wood plus 50-g mass.

5. How does the combined buoyant force on the wood and the 50-g mass compare with the weight of water displaced?

   _____

   _____

   _____

Step 5: Find the mass of a ball of modeling clay. Measure the volume of water it displaces when it sinks to the bottom. Calculate the mass of water displaced and record all volumes and masses in Data Table A.

Measure dipslacement of clay.

6. How does the mass of water displaced by the clay compare to the mass of the clay?

7. Is the buoyant force on the submerged clay greater than, equal to, or less than its weight in air? Explain.

   _____

   _____

   _____

Step 6: Retrieve the clay from the bottom, and mold it into a shape that allows it to float. Sketch or describe this shape.

Mold the clay so that it floats.

   _____

   _____

   Measure the volume of water displaced by the floating clay. Calculate the mass of the water and record it in Data Table A.

8. Does the clay displace more, less, or the same amount of water when it floats as it did when it sank?

   _____

   _____

9. Is the buoyant force on the floating clay greater than, equal to, or less than its weight in air?

_____

10. What can you conclude about the weight of water displaced by a floating object compared with the weight in air of the object?

_____

_____

_____

Predict new water level in canal lock.

Step 7: Suppose you are on a ship in a canal lock. If you throw a ton of bricks overboard into the canal lock, will the water level in the canal lock go up, down, or stay the same? Write down your answer *before* you proceed to Step 8.

prediction for water level in canal lock: _____

Step 8: Float a toy boat loaded with "cargo" (such as one or two 100-g masses) in a container filled with water deeper than the height of the masses. Mark and label the water levels on masking tape placed on the container and on the sides of the boat. Remove the masses from the boat and put them in the water. Mark and label the new water levels.

11. What happens to the water level on the side of the boat when you place the cargo in the water?

_____

_____

_____

12. If a large freighter is riding high in the water, is it carrying a relatively light or heavy load of cargo?

_____

_____

13. What happens to the water level in the container when you place the cargo in the water? Explain why it happens.

_____

_____

14. What will happen to the water level in the canal lock when the bricks are thrown overboard?

_____

_____

53   Float a Big Stick

Purpose

To investigate how objects float by analyzing forces acting on a floating stick

Required Equipment/Supplies

vernier calipers
250-mL graduated cylinder
meterstick
triple-beam balance
stick, about 30.5 cm long and 2.54 cm square, or a cylinder of similar dimensions

Discussion

An object submerged in water takes up space and pushes water out of the way. The water that is moved is said to be *displaced*. Interestingly, the water that is pushed out of the way in effect pushes back on the submerged object. For example, if the object pushes a volume of water with a weight of 10 N out of its way, then the water reacts by pushing back on the object with a force of 10 N. We say that the object is *buoyed* upward with a force of 10 N. This is summed up in Archimedes' principle, which states that the buoyant force that acts on any completely or partially submerged object is equal to the *weight of the fluid it displaces.*

If the buoyant force is less than the weight of the submerged object, the object sinks. If the buoyant force is equal to the weight of a submerged object, as in the case of a fish, the object neither sinks nor floats. If the buoyant force is greater than the weight of a submerged object, the object rises until it floats. It will float at a level that makes the weight of water displaced exactly equal to the weight of the floating object. This is summed up by the *principle of flotation,* which states that the *weight of the fluid displaced by any floating object is equal to the weight of the object.*

We cannot forget the presence of air pressure. If you press your hand against a surface, and somebody else presses against your hand in the same direction, then the pressure against the surface is greater than if you pressed alone. Likewise with the atmospheric pressure that presses on the surface of a liquid. Therefore total pressure of a liquid is the density of the liquid × depth *plus* the pressure of the atmosphere. Therefore, the total fluid pressure, P, at a depth h in a fluid of density ρ is given by

$$P = P_0 + \rho g h$$

where P_0 is the atmospheric pressure and g is the acceleration of gravity.

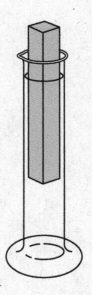

Fig. A

In this experiment, you will investigate the force and the pressure that a fluid exerts on objects under different conditions.

Procedure

Show your calculations. Be sure to express your data and subsequent calculations with the appropriate number of significant figures.

Step 1: Determine, in cubic centimeters, the volume of the stick. The volume is the area of the bottom of the stick times its length.

$$V = \underline{\hspace{2cm}} \text{ cm}^3$$

Step 2: Determine, in grams, the mass of the stick.

$$m = \underline{\hspace{2cm}} \text{ g}$$

Step 3: Calculate, in g/cm^3, the density of the stick.

$$\rho = \underline{\hspace{2cm}} \text{ g/cm}^3$$

Step 4: The definition of a newton is the force required to accelerate one kilogram one m/s^2 (in SI units). Calculate the weight of the stick in newtons.

$$W = \underline{\hspace{2cm}} \text{ N}$$

Step 5: Place the stick in the graduated cylinder. Fill the cylinder with enough water to float the stick. Determine the volume of the water displaced by the floating stick by measuring the volume of the water before and after you float the stick.

$$V = \underline{\hspace{2cm}} \text{ cm}^3$$

Step 6: Calculate the mass, in grams, of water displaced by the stick. Recall that 1 mL of water has a mass of 1 gram.

$$m = \underline{\hspace{2cm}} \text{ g}$$

Step 7: Calculate the weight, in newtons, of water displaced by the stick.

$$W = \underline{\hspace{2cm}} \text{ N}$$

Step 8: Calculate the *pressure*, in N/m^2, of the water pressing against the bottom of the stick at that depth. Convert your answer to pascals. Show your work.

$$P = \underline{\hspace{2cm}} \text{ N/m}^2 = \underline{\hspace{2cm}} \text{ Pa}$$

Step 9: Determine, in cm^2, the area of the bottom (or the top) of the stick. Convert your answer into m^2. Recall that 1 m = 100 cm.

$$A = \underline{\hspace{2cm}} \text{ cm}^2 = \underline{\hspace{2cm}} \text{ m}^2$$

Step 10: Calculate, in newtons, the *force* exerted by the stick at the bottom of the stick. Express your answer in newtons.

$$F_{bottom} = \underline{\hspace{2cm}} \text{ N}$$

Analysis

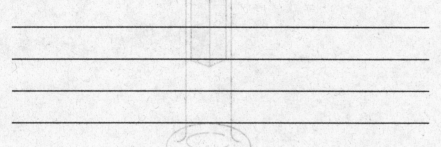

1. What is the *pressure* being exerted by air on the top of the stick? Does this pressure act to submerge the stick into the water or to buoy it up?

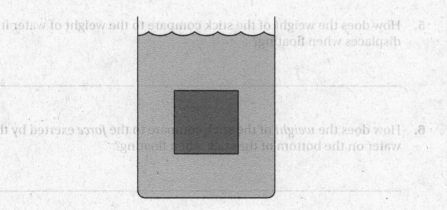

   _____

   _____

   _____

   _____

2. **a.** An object is completely submerged in water as shown in Figure B. Draw arrows, which represent the *force* of the water at that depth, at various locations on the top, bottom, and sides of the object.

   b. How does the force on one side of the object compare to the force on the other? How does the force on the top compare to the bottom?

Fig. B

   _____

   _____

   _____

   _____

3. A sketch of a stick floating in a graduated cylinder, much like yours, is shown below. Label all the forces acting on the stick. Make a vector diagram that represents your floating stick.

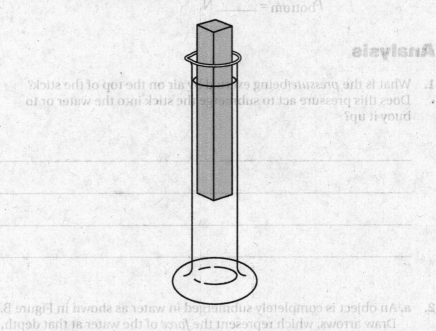

4. How does the mass of the stick compare to the mass of water it displaces when floating?

_____

_____

5. How does the weight of the stick compare to the weight of water it displaces when floating?

_____

_____

6. How does the *weight* of the stick compare to the *force* exerted by the water on the bottom of the stick when floating?

_____

_____

_____

_____

_____

7. How does the ratio of the density of the stick to that of water compare to the fraction of the stick immersed in the water when floating? Can you explain?

_____

_____

_____

_____

_____

_____

Going Further

Does the force the water exerts against the bottom of the stick change if you shove the stick deeper in the water? Does the attraction of the stick to Earth change if you shove the stick deeper in the water? Try it and see! Push the stick deeper in the water.

8. What happens when you release it?

_____

Does the force the water exerts against the bottom of the stick change if you lift the stick higher in the water? Does the attraction of the stick to Earth change if you lift the stick higher in the water? Try it and see! Lift the stick higher in the water.

9. What happens when you release it?

_____

54 Heat Mixes: Part I

Purpose

To predict the final temperature of a mixture of cups of water at different temperatures

Required Equipment/Supplies

3 plastic foam cups
liter container
thermometer (Celsius)
pail of cold water
pail of hot water

Discussion

If you mix a pail of cold water with a pail of hot water, the temperature of the mixture will be between the two initial temperatures. What information would you need to predict the final temperature? This lab investigates what factors are involved in changes of temperature.

Your goal is to find out what happens when you mix equal masses of water at different temperatures. Before actually doing this, imagine a cup of hot water at 60°C and a pail of room-temperature water at 20°C.

(circle one)

1. Which do you think is hotter—the cup or the pail? cup pail

2. Which do you think has more thermal energy? cup pail

3. Which would take longer to change its temperature by 10°C if the cup and pail were set outside on a winter day? cup pail

4. If you put the same amount of red-hot iron into the cup and the pail, which one would change temperature more? cup pail

Procedure

Step 1: Two pails filled with water are in your room, one with cold water and one with hot water. Fill one cup 3/4 full with water from the cold-water pail. Mark the water level along the inside of the cup. Pour the cup's water into a second cup. Mark it as you did the first one. Pour the cup's water into a third cup, and mark it as before. Now all three cups have marks that show nearly equal measures.

Mark cups.

5. Why don't the marks show exactly equal measures?

_____

Measure temperature of two cups.

Step 2: Fill the first cup to the mark with water from the hot-water pail. Measure and record the temperature of both cups of water.

temperature of cold water = _____°C

temperature of hot water = _____°C

Predict temperature of mixture.

Step 3: What will be the temperature if you mix the two cups of water in the liter container? Record your prediction.

predicted temperature of mixture = _____°C

Measure temperature of mixture.

Step 4: Pour the two cups of water into the liter container, stir the mixture, and measure and record its temperature.

actual temperature of mixture = _____°C

6. If there was a difference between your prediction and your observation, what might have caused it?

_____

Pour the mixture into the sink or waste pail. Do not pour it back into either the pail of cold or hot water!

Measure temperature of three cups.

Step 5: Fill one cup to its mark with water from the cold-water pail. Fill the other two cups to their marks with hot water from the hot-water pail. Measure and record their temperatures.

temperature of cold water = _____°C

temperature of hot water (cup 1) = _____°C

temperature of hot water (cup 2) = _____°C

Predict temperature of mixture.

Step 6: What will be the temperature when all three cups of water are mixed in one container? Record your prediction.

predicted temperature of mixture = _____°C

Measure temperature of mixture.

Step 7: Pour the three cups of water into the liter container, stir the mixture, and measure and record its temperature.

actual temperature of mixture = _____°C

7. How did your observation compare with your prediction?

_____

_____

8. Which of the water samples (cold or hot) changed more when it became part of the mixture? Why do you think this happened?

_____

_____

_____

Pour the mixture into the sink or waste pail. Do *not* pour it back into either the pail of cold or hot water!

Step 8: Fill one cup to its mark with *hot* water. Fill the other two cups to their marks with *cold* water. Measure and record their temperatures.

Reverse Step 5.

> temperature of hot water = _____°C
>
> temperature of cold water (cup 1) = _____°C
>
> temperature of cold water (cup 2) = _____°C

Step 9: Record your prediction of the temperature when these three cups of water are mixed in one container.

Predict temperature of mixture.

> predicted temperature of mixture = _____°C

Step 10: Pour the three cups of water into the liter container, stir the mixture, and measure and record its temperature.

> actual temperature of mixture = _____°C

9. How did this observation compare with your prediction?

_____

_____

10. Which of the water samples (cold or hot) changed more when it became part of the mixture? Why do you think this happened?

_____

_____

_____

 **Heat Mixes: Part II**

Purpose

To predict the final temperature of water and nails when mixed

Required Equipment/Supplies

balance
2 large insulated cups
bundle of short, stubby nails tied with string
thermometer (Celsius)
hot and cold water
paper towels

Discussion

If you throw a hot rock into a pail of cool water, you know that the temperature of the rock will go down. You also know that the temperature of the water will go up—but will its rise in temperature be more than, less than, or the same as the temperature drop of the rock? Will the temperature of the water go up as much as the temperature of the rock goes down? Will the changes of temperature instead depend on how much rock and how much water are present and how much energy is needed to change the temperature of water and rock by the same amount?

You are going to study what happens to the temperature of water when hot nails are added to it. Before doing this activity, think about the following questions.

1. Suppose that equal masses of water and iron are at the same temperature. Suppose you then add the same amount of heat to each of them. Would one change temperature more than the other?

   (circle one)   yes   no

   If you circled "yes," which one would warm more?

   (circle one)   water   iron

2. Again, suppose that equal masses of water and iron are at the same temperature. Suppose you then take the same amount of heat away from each of them. Would one cool more than the other?

   (circle one)   yes   no

   If you circled "yes," which one would cool more?

   (circle one)   water   iron

Procedure

Balance nails with cold water.

Step 1: Place a large cup on each pan of the balance. Drop the bundle of nails into one of the cups. Add cold water to the other cup until it balances the cup of nails. When the two cups are balanced, the same mass is in each cup—a mass of nails in one, and an equal mass of water in the other.

Step 2: Set the cup of cold water on your work table. Lift the bundle of nails out of its cup and place it beside the cup of cold water.

Warm nails in hot water.

Step 3: Fill the empty cup 3/4 full with hot water. Lower the bundle of nails into the hot water and leave it there for two minutes to allow the nails to come to the temperature of the hot water.

Measure temperature of cold and hot water.

Step 4: Measure and record the temperature of the cold water and the temperature of the hot water around the nails.

temperature of cold water = _____°C

temperature of hot water = _____°C

3. Is the temperature of the hot water equal to the temperature of the nails? Why do you think it is or is not? Can you think of a better way to heat the nails to a known temperature?

_____

_____

_____

_____

_____

Predict temperature of mixture.

Step 5: Predict what the temperature of the mixture will be when the hot nails are added to the cold water.

predicted temperature of mixture = _____°C

Measure temperature of mixture.

Step 6: Lift the nails from the hot water and put them quickly into the cold water. When the temperature of the mixture stops rising, record it.

actual temperature of mixture = _____°C

4. How close is your prediction to the observed value?

_____

_____

_____

Step 7: Now you will repeat Steps 1 through 6 for hot water and cold nails. First, dry the bundle of nails and place them in a cup. Then, balance the cup that holds the dry bundle of nails with a cup of *hot* water.

Balance nails with hot water.

Step 8: Remove the nails and fill the cup 3/4 full with *cold* water. Record the temperature of the hot water in the first cup.

Record temperature.

temperature of hot water = _____°C

Step 9: Lower the bundle of nails into the cup of cold water, wait one minute (why?), and then record the temperature of the water around the nails.

Cool nails in cold water.

temperature of cold water = _____°C

Step 10: Predict what the temperature of the mixture will be when the cold nails are added to the hot water.

Predict temperature of mixture.

predicted temperature of mixture = _____°C

Step 11: Lift the nails from the cold water and put them quickly into the hot water. When the temperature of the mixture stops changing, record it.

Measure temperature of mixture.

actual temperature of mixture = _____°C

5. How close is your prediction to the observed value? _____

_____

_____

_____

Analysis

6. Discuss your observations with the rest of your team, and write an explanation for what happened.

_____

_____

_____

_____

_____

_____

_____

7. Suppose you have equal masses of water and nails at the same temperature. Suppose you then light similar candles and place a candle under each of the masses, letting the candles burn for equal times. Would one of the materials change temperature more than the other?

(circle one)   yes   no

If your answer to the question is "yes," which one would reach a higher temperature?

(circle one)   water   nails

8. Suppose you have cold feet when you go to bed, and you want something to warm your feet. Would you prefer to have a hot-water bottle filled with hot water, or one filled with an equal mass of nails at the same temperature as the water? Explain.

_____

_____

_____

_____

_____

9. Why does the climate of a mid-ocean island stay nearly constant, getting neither very hot nor very cold?

_____

_____

_____

_____

_____

_____

_____

**Specific Heat and
Thermal Equilibrium**

56 Temperature of a Flame

Purpose

To indirectly measure the temperature of a flame

Required Equipment/Supplies

brass ball and ring apparatus (the ball needs to be removable)
fisher (preferred) or bunsen burner
400-mL beaker
100-mL graduated cylinder
balance
thermometer

Discussion

How hot is a typical flame? Certainly hot enough to shatter any thermometer placed in it, so don't! Instead, you can measure the temperature of a flame indirectly. If a brass ball is held in a flame and becomes
red-hot, at some point the ball and flame are in thermal equilibrium. If
we determine the temperature of the hot ball, then we'll know the temperature of the flame.

Procedure

Step 1: Unscrew the brass ball of a ball-and-ring apparatus and measure
its mass using a balance. Record the mass of the ball. Reattach the brass
ball to the handle.

mass of ball, m_b = _____

Step 2: Use a graduated cylinder to measure 250 mL of water into a
400-mL beaker. Warm the water until it is about 60°C. Measure and
record the temperature of the water. Record the mass of the water below.

initial temperature of water, T_i = _____

mass of water, m_w = _____

Step 3: Heat the brass ball until it is red-hot. CAUTION: *Do not touch
anything or anybody with the ball!* While it is still red-hot, *carefully* thrust
the ball into the beaker of water. Try to hold it steady in the middle of the
beaker. What do you observe?

_____

Step 4: After the ball has completely cooled down, record the final temperature of the water.

final temperature of the water, $T_f =$ _____

change in temperature of the water, $\Delta T_w =$ _____

Analysis

1. The quantity of heat in calories lost by the ball equals the quantity of heat gained by the water. Calculate this quantity of heat gained by the water using the equation $Q_{\text{gained by water}} = m_w c_w \Delta T_w$. Remember, the specific heat of water is 1 cal/g°C.

$Q_{\text{gained by water}} =$ _____ cal

2. The heat gained by the water equals the heat lost by the ball.

$Q_{\text{gained by water}} = Q_{\text{lost by ball}}$

$m_w c_w \Delta T_w = m_b c_b \Delta T_b$

The specific heat of brass is 0.09 cal/g°C. Calculate the change in temperature of the brass ball after it was cooled down by the water.

$\Delta T_b =$ _____ °C

3. What is temperature of the flame? Remember, the final temperature of the water and the ball is higher than room temperature.

_____

_____

4. What would have been your calculated flame temperature if the change in water temperature were 1°C greater than what you actually measured? Show your calculations.

_____

_____

_____

5. What are sources of error for this experiment? Considering your sources of error, does your calculation for the temperature of the flame more likely represent a minimum or maximum value?

_____

_____

_____

_____

_____

_____

_____

_____

57 Antifreeze in the Summer?

Purpose

To investigate what effect antifreeze (ethylene glycol) has on the cooling of a car radiator during the summer

Required Equipment/Supplies

400 mL (400 g) water
timer
380 mL (400 g) 50% mixture of antifreeze and water
500-mL graduated cylinder
2 600-mL beakers
single-element electric immersion heater
thermometer (Celsius) or
   temperature probe with computer interface

Part A

Discussion

Put an iron frying pan on a hot stove, and very quickly it will be too hot to touch. But put a pan of water on the same hot stove, and the time for a comparable rise in temperature is considerably longer, even if the pan contains a relatively small amount of water. Water has a very high capacity for storing internal energy. We say that water has a high *specific heat capacity*. The specific heat capacity c of a substance is the quantity of heat required to increase the temperature of one gram of the substance by one degree Celsius. This means that the amount of heat Q needed to increase the temperature of a mass m of material by a temperature difference ΔT is

$$Q = mc\Delta T$$

Turning this formula around, the specific heat capacity is related to the quantity of heat absorbed, the mass of the material, and the temperature change by

$$c = \frac{Q}{m\Delta T}$$

Each substance has its own specific heat capacity, which is characteristic of that substance. The specific heat capacity of pure water is 1.0 cal/g°C. So, if 1 calorie (cal) of heat is absorbed by 1 g of water, its temperature will rise by 1°C; or if 1 calorie of heat is extracted from 1 gram of water, its temperature will fall by 1°C.

Water has a higher specific heat capacity than most other materials. The high specific heat capacity of water makes it an excellent coolant. That's why it is used in an automobile to keep the engine from overheating. But water has a striking disadvantage in winter. It freezes at 0°C, and, what's even worse, it expands when it freezes. This expansion can crack the automobile engine block or fracture the radiator. To prevent such a mishap, antifreeze (ethylene glycol) is mixed with the water. The mixture has a much lower freezing point than water. The mixture has its lowest freezing point when the proportions are about 50% water and 50% antifreeze. But what effect does adding the antifreeze have on the mixture's specific heat capacity? In Part A of this experiment, you will determine the specific heat capacity of a 50% mixture of antifreeze and water.

To find the specific heat capacity, you will simply measure the quantity of heat that is absorbed and the corresponding temperature change. To supply heat, you will use an electric immersion heater.

An immersion heater is a small coil of nichrome wire commonly used to heat small amounts of liquids. It heats up much like the wire in a toaster. This is a very efficient device, for unlike a hot plate or flame, it transfers all of its energy to the material being heated, in this case a liquid. The energy dissipated by a heater is the same regardless of whether the liquid is pure water or a mixture of water and antifreeze.

You can use a computer with a temperature probe instead of a thermometer. Hook up a temperature probe to an interface box. Be sure to calibrate the temperature probe.

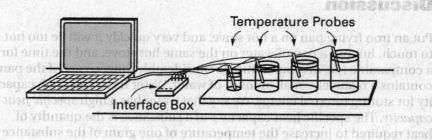

Procedure

Heat water.

Step 1: Heat 400 mL (400 g) of water with the heater for 200 seconds (a little over 3 minutes).

CAUTION: *Plug and unplug the immersion heater only when the heater element is submerged in liquid. Operating it in air destroys it immediately.*

Record the initial and final temperatures, and compute the change in temperature.

initial temperature = _____°C

final temperature = _____°C

change in temperature (ΔT) = _____°C

Step 2: Find the quantity of heat transferred to the water from the equation

Compare energy dissipated.

$$Q = mc\Delta T$$

where m = mass of water

c = specific heat capacity of water = 1 cal/g°C

ΔT = change in temperature

Q = _____ calories

Step 3: Pour 380 mL of a mixture of 50% antifreeze and 50% water into a beaker. Since antifreeze is slightly denser than water, 380 mL of 50% antifreeze mixture has a mass of 400 g. Heat the 400 g of antifreeze mixture for 200 seconds. Record the initial and final temperatures and the change in temperature.

Heat antifreeze mixture.

initial temperature = _____°C

final temperature = _____°C

change in temperature (ΔT) = _____°C

Step 4: With these data, compute the specific heat capacity of 50% antifreeze mixture from the equation

Compare specific heat capacities of antifreeze mixture.

$$c = \frac{Q}{m\Delta T}$$

specific heat c of antifreeze mixture = _____cal/g°C

Analysis

1. Which liquid has the lower specific heat capacity—pure water or a 50% mixture of antifreeze?

_____

_____

2. Which would warm from 25°C to 40°C faster with the same rate of energy input—pure water or a 50% mixture of antifreeze?

_____

_____

Part B
Discussion

By now you have found that the specific heat capacity of a mixture of antifreeze and water is lower than that of pure water. This suggests it is a poorer coolant than pure water. Yet it is advisable to continue using antifreeze in summer months. Is there an advantage, other than convenience, to leaving antifreeze in the radiator during summer, or should it be replaced with pure water?

To answer this question, you need to understand the role of the coolant in an automobile. Coolant draws heat from the engine block and then circulates it to the radiator, where it is dissipated to the atmosphere. The coolant is then recycled back to the engine.

The temperature of the coolant increases as it absorbs heat from the engine. But if it reaches its boiling point, the system boils over. So a coolant is effective only at temperatures below boiling. If the coolant is pure water at atmospheric pressure, this temperature is 100°C. (With a pressure cap on the radiator, both the pressure and the boiling point are higher.) Could an antifreeze mixture have a higher boiling point than pure water? If so, this would lessen the likelihood of boil-overs when the engine is overworked. You will experiment to find out.

Heat antifreeze mixture to its boiling point.

Step 5: Heat a sample of 50% antifreeze mixture with the immersion heater, and measure its boiling point. Record this temperature.

boiling point of antifreeze mixture = _____°C

Analysis

3. What effect does the boiling point of the antifreeze mixture have on the mixture's ability to act as a coolant?

_____

_____

_____

_____

4. Would it be appropriate to call ethylene glycol "antiboil" instead of "antifreeze" in climates where the temperature never goes below freezing?

_____

_____

_____

_____

58 The Bridge Connection

Purpose

To calculate the minimum length of the expansion joints for the Golden Gate Bridge

Required Equipment/Supplies

safety goggles
steel tube
thermal expansion apparatus
   (roller form)

micrometer
steam generator
bunsen burner
rubber tubing

Discussion

Gases of the same pressure and volume expand equally when heated, and contract equally when cooled—regardless of the kinds of molecules that compose the gas. That's because the molecules of a gas are so far apart that their size and nature have practically no effect on the amount of expansion or contraction. However, liquids and solids are individualists! Molecules and atoms in the solid state are close together in a variety of definite crystalline structures. Different liquids and solids expand or contract at different rates when their temperature is changed.

Expansions or contractions of metal can be critical in the construction of bridges. Temperatures at the Golden Gate Bridge in San Francisco can vary from –5°C to 40°C. The change in length of the bridge from winter to summer can be almost 2 meters! Clearly, engineers must keep thermal expansion in mind when designing bridges.

Suppose you owned an engineering firm *before* the Golden Gate Bridge was built and you were asked for advice on the minimum length to make expansion joints for the proposed bridge. (See a typical expansion joint in Figure 21.10 in your textbook.) Consider two expansion joints that connect the bridge to land at each end. The steel to be used is the same as that in the steel tubes you will use in this experiment. You are to measure how much the steel expands per meter for each degree increase in temperature. This ratio is called the *coefficient of linear expansion*. Then, compute the amount that the 2740-m structure will expand as its temperature increases. Now you can advise a minimum size of the expansion joints needed, to assure the success of the bridge.

You will determine the coefficient of linear expansion for steel by measuring the expansion of a steel tube when it is heated with steam at 100°C. The amount of expansion ΔL depends on the original length L, the change in temperature ΔT, and the coefficient of linear expansion α (which is characteristic of the type of material).

$$\Delta L = \alpha L \Delta T$$

The temperature change ΔT is simply 100°C minus room temperature. By measuring L, the original length the tube before heating, and ΔL, the change of the length after heating, you can compute α, the coefficient of linear expansion, by rearranging the equation.

$$\alpha = \frac{\Delta L}{L \Delta T}$$

It is difficult to measure how much the tube expands, because the expansion is small. One way to measure it is shown in Figure A. The end of the steel tube is arranged to be perpendicular to the axle of the pointer. When the steel tube resting on the axle expands, it rotates the axle and the pointer through an angle.

The pointer turns 360° (one full rotation) when the axle has rotated a distance equal to its circumference. The circumference C of the axle equals its diameter d times the number pi.

$$C = \pi d$$

If the expansion rotates the pointer through 180° (a half rotation), then the increase ΔL in length of the rod is equal to half the circumference of the axle. Ratio and proportion give you ΔL for other expansions. The ratio of the actual distance ΔL rotated to the distance πd rotated in one complete rotation equals the ratio of the angle θ through which the pointer rotates through to 360°.

$$\frac{\Delta L}{\pi d} = \frac{\theta}{360°}$$

Solve this equation for ΔL. Substituting this value into the second equation enables you to compute the coefficient of linear expansion. Once you have computed the value of α, you can compute the minimum length of the expansion joints by using the length of the bridge and the estimated temperature difference for summer and winter.

Procedure

Measure axle diameter.

Step 1: Using a micrometer, measure the diameter of the axle of the pointer.

$$d = \underline{\hspace{2cm}} \text{ mm}$$

Assemble apparatus.

Step 2: Assemble your apparatus as in Figure A, with the steam generator ready to go. Make sure the tube has a place to drain. Measure the distance in millimeters from the groove in the steel tube to the axle of the pointer (since you are measuring expansion between these two points). Do *not* measure the length of the entire tube.

$$L = \underline{\hspace{2cm}} \text{ mm}$$

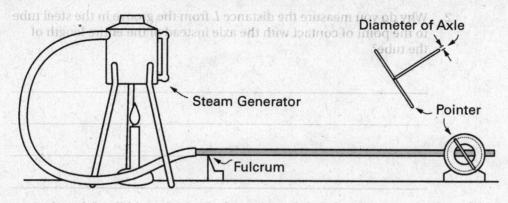

Fig. A

Step 3: Connect the steam generator and observe the change in length of the tube. Is the increase sudden or gradual? Record the change in temperature of your tube, assuming it started at room temperature.

Record temperature change and angle pointer turns.

$$\Delta T = \text{_____} °C$$

Record the angle θ through which the pointer turned due to the expansion of the tube.

$$\text{angle } \theta = \text{_____}°$$

Step 4: Compute the increase ΔL in length of the tube by substituting your measured values of θ and d into the following equation.

Compute increase in length of tube.

$$\Delta L = \frac{\pi \theta d}{360°} = \text{_____} \text{ mm}$$

Step 5: Compute the coefficient of linear expansion using your measured values of L, ΔT, and ΔL.

Compute coefficient of linear expansion.

$$\alpha = \frac{\Delta L}{L \Delta T} = \text{_____}$$

Step 6: Express the coefficient of linear expansion in scientific notation (that is, as a number times a power of ten).

$$\alpha = \text{_____}$$

Step 7: Compute the minimum length of the expansion joint(s). Show your work.

Compute length of expansion joint.

$$\Delta L = \text{_____}$$

Analysis

1. Why do you measure the diameter of the axle of the pointer in Step 1 instead of the diameter of the steel tube?

_____

_____

2. Why do you measure the distance L from the groove in the steel tube to the point of contact with the axle instead of the entire length of the tube?

_____

_____

_____

_____

3. Suppose you placed the pointer device in the middle of the tube. Would the coefficient of linear expansion for the steel tube be larger, less, or the same? Why?

_____

_____

4. What are the units of α?

_____

5. What are the sources of error in your experiment? List them along with an estimate of the percent contribution of each.

_____

_____

_____

_____

_____

6. In your consultation, suppose you experimentally determined that the expansion joints had to be a minimum of 2 m long. How large would you recommend them to be, taking your margin of error into account for safety?

_____

_____

_____

7. What do you think would be a good design for an expansion joint?

_____

_____

_____

_____

59 Cooling Off

Purpose

To compare the rates of cooling of objects of different colors and surface reflectances

Required Equipment/Supplies

4 empty soup cans of the same size (one covered with aluminum foil,
     one painted black, one white, and one any other color)
100-watt lightbulb and receptacle
4 thermometers (Celsius) or
     computer with temperature probes
printer
large test tube
one-hole rubber stopper, with thermometer or temperature probe
     mounted in it, to fit test tube
600-mL beaker
graduated cylinder
plastic foam cups with covers
hot water
crushed ice and water mixture
variety of different size, color, and shape containers made of various
     materials
meterstick
graph paper
computer and data-plotting software (optional)

Discussion

When you are confronted with a plate of food too hot to eat, you may have noticed that some things cool faster than others. Mashed potatoes can be comfortably eaten when boiled onions are still too hot. And blueberries in a blueberry muffin are still hot when the rest of the muffin has cooled enough to eat. Different materials cool at different rates. Explore and see.

Procedure

Step 1: Place the four cans 20 cm from an unshielded lightbulb. Place a thermometer in each can, and turn on the light. Record the temperature of each can after 1 minute, 2 minutes, and 3 minutes in Data Table A.

Can	Temperature (°C)		
	1 min	2 min	3 min
1			
2			
3			
4			

Data Table A

Activity

As an alternative, if a computer is available, use a temperature probe to read your data. Calibrate your probes, and monitor the temperature rise of each can. Save your data and make a printout.

1. For which can was the temperature rise the fastest?

_____

2. For which can was the temperature rise the slowest?

_____

3. After several minutes the temperatures of all the cans level off and remain constant. Does this mean that the cans stop absorbing radiant energy from the lightbulb?

_____

_____

4. For a can at constant temperature, what is the relationship between the amount of radiant energy being absorbed by the can and the amount of radiant energy being radiated and convected away from the can?

_____

_____

Monitor cooling of water in test tube.

Step 2: Place 25 mL of hot water from the tap in a test tube. Insert the thermometer mounted in the rubber stopper. Place the test tube in a beaker filled with crushed ice and water. Record the temperatures every 30 seconds over the next 5 minutes in Data Table B. (Once again, if you have a computer, use a temperature probe instead of a thermometer.) Draw a graph of temperature (vertical axis) vs. time (horizontal axis).

Time (min)	0	0.5	1.0	1.5	2.0	2.5	3.0	3.5	4.0	4.5	5.0
Temp. (°C)											

Data Table B

5. Describe your graph.

_____

_____

Monitor cooling of water in plastic foam cup.

Step 3: Fill a plastic foam cup with hot tap water. Monitor the temperature drop with either a thermometer or temperature probe. Make a graph of temperature (vertical axis) vs. time (horizontal axis).

	Temperatura (°C)		
3			
4			

Data Table A

Step 4: Repeat, but cover the cup with a plastic lid. Poke a hole (if it doesn't already have one), and insert the probe in the water to monitor the temperature.

6. How do the two cooling curves compare?

_____

_____

7. What cooling process is primarily responsible for the difference?

_____

_____

Going Further

Step 5: Place 200 mL of hot tap water in each of a variety of containers. You may want to wrap them with various materials. List the containers used.

Predict cooling rates of a variety of containers

_____

_____

_____

Predict which container will cool fastest and which container will cool most slowly.

Predicted fastest: _____

Predicted slowest: _____

Step 6: Monitor the cooling with either temperature probes or thermometers. Record which cooled the fastest and which the most slowly.

Observed fastest: _____

Observed slowest: _____

8. What factors determine the rate of cooling, based on your data from Step 6?

_____

_____

_____

_____

_____

Extra for Experts

Plot temperature vs. time.

Step 7: Using data-plotting software, plot data from Step 6 for each of your samples. Let time be the independent variable (horizontal axis), and, for convenience, set $t = 0$ at the origin. Let $T - T_2$ be the dependent variable (vertical axis), where T is the temperature of the sample and T_2 is room temperature. Can you think of a way to make your graph a straight line? (*Hint:* Try using some function of the vertical variable (temperature difference), such as its square or its square root or its logarithm.)

9. What does your graph look like? What mathematical relationship exists between the cooling rate and time? (The answer to this question requires some heavy-duty math—ask your teacher for help on this one!)

_____

_____

_____

_____

_____

_____

_____

_____

60 Solar Equality

Purpose

To measure the sun's power output and compare it with the power output of a 100-watt lightbulb

Required Equipment/Supplies

2-cm by 6-cm piece of aluminum foil with one side thinly coated with
   flat black paint
clear tape
meterstick
two wood blocks
glass jar with a hole in the metal lid
one-hole stopper to fit the hole in the jar lid
thermometer (Celsius, range –10°C to 110°C)
glycerin
100-watt lightbulb with receptacle

Discussion

If you told some friends that you had measured the power output of a
lightbulb, they would not be too excited. However, if you told them that
you had computed the power output of the whole sun using only house-
hold equipment, they would probably be quite impressed (or not believe
you). In this experiment, you will estimate the power output of the sun.
You will need a sunny day to do this experiment.

Procedure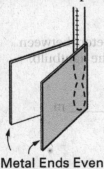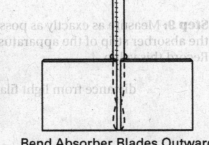

Step 1: With the blackened side facing out, fold the middle of the foil
strip around the thermometer bulb, as shown in Figure A. The ends of
the metal strip should line up evenly.

Assemble apparatus.

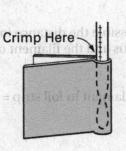

Crimp Here

Metal Ends Even

Bend Absorber Blades Outward

Fig. A   Fig. B   Fig. C

Step 2: Crimp the foil so that it completely surrounds the bulb, as in Figure B. Bend each end of the foil strip outward (Figure C). Use a meterstick to make a flat, even surface. Use a piece of clear tape on the unpainted side to hold the foil on the thermometer.

Step 3: Use glycerin to insert the free end of the thermometer into the one-hole stopper. Remove the lid from the jar, and place the stopper in the lid from the bottom side. Slide the thermometer until the foil strip is located in the middle of the jar. Place the lid on the jar.

Place apparatus outdoors in sun.

Step 4: Take your apparatus outdoors. Prop it at an angle so that the blackened side of the foil strip is exactly perpendicular to the rays of the sun.

Record maximum temperature reached.

Step 5: Leave the apparatus in this position in the sunlight until the maximum temperature is reached. Record this temperature.

maximum temperature = _____

Allow apparatus to cool to room temperature.

Step 6: Return the apparatus to the classroom, and allow the thermometer to cool to room temperature.

Set up apparatus using lightbulb.

Step 7: Set the meterstick on the table. Place the lightbulb with its filament located at the 0-cm mark of the meterstick (Figure D). Center the jar apparatus at the 95-cm mark with the blackened side of the foil strip exactly perpendicular to the light rays from the bulb. You may need to put some books under the jar apparatus.

Match outdoor temperature with lightbulb.

Step 8: Turn the lightbulb on. Slowly move the apparatus toward the lightbulb, 5 cm at a time, allowing the thermometer temperature to stabilize each time. As the temperature approaches that reached in Step 5, move the apparatus only 1 cm at a time. Adjust the distance of the apparatus 0.1 cm at a time until the temperature obtained in Step 5 is maintained for two minutes. Turn the lightbulb off.

Fig. D

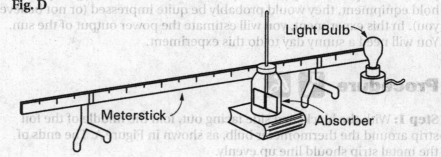

Light Bulb

Meterstick

Absorber

Measure distance to lightbulb.

Step 9: Measure as exactly as possible the distance in meters between the absorber strip of the apparatus and the filament of the lightbulb. Record this value.

distance from light filament to foil strip = _____ m

Step 10: For the distance obtained, use the following equation to compute the wattage of the sun. The sun's distance in meters is 1.5×10^{11} m. Show your work.

Compute wattage of the sun.

$$\text{sun's wattage} = (\text{bulb's wattage}) \times \frac{(\text{sun's distance})^2}{(\text{bulb's distance})^2}$$

sun's wattage = _____ W

Step 11: Use the value of the sun's wattage to compute the number of 100-watt lightbulbs needed to equal the sun's power. Show your work.

Compute number of lightbulbs.

number of 100-watt lightbulbs = _____

Analysis

1. Re-express the equation in Step 10 as a relationship between two ratios. Express the new equation as a sentence that begins, "The ratio of . . ."

_____

_____

_____

_____

_____

_____

2. Would it be possible to turn on the number of 100-watt lightbulbs you computed in Step 11 at once? Explain.

_____

_____

_____

_____

_____

3. The accepted value for the sun's wattage is 3.83×10^{26} W. List at least three factors that might account for the difference between your experimental value and the accepted value.

_____

_____

_____

_____

_____

_____

_____

_____

_____

_____

61 Boiling Is a Cooling Process

Purpose

To observe water changing its phase as it boils and then cools

Required Equipment/Supplies

safety goggles
paper towels
ring stand
wire gauze
2 plastic-coated test-tube clamps
1000-mL Florence flask (flat-bottomed) or Franklin's flask (crater-
    bottomed)
one-hole rubber stopper to fit flask, fitted with short (15-cm)
    thermometer or temperature probe
water
crushed ice or beaker of cool tap water
Bunsen burner
thermometer (Celsius), regular length (30 cm), or
    computer with temperature probe and
    printer
pan or tub
computer with data plotting software (optional)
graph paper (if computer is not used)

Discussion

When water evaporates, the more energetic molecules leave the liquid. This results in a lowering of the average energy of the molecules left behind. The liquid is cooled by the process of evaporation. Is this also true of boiling? Try it and see.

Procedure

Step 1: Attach an empty flask to the ring stand with a test-tube clamp. Insert the teacher-prepared stopper with the thermometer or temperature probe into the neck of the flask. Loosen the wing nut on the clamp so that when the flask is rotated upside down, the end of the thermometer clears the table top by about 3 cm.

Adjust height of flask.

Step 2: Before filling the flask with water, you need to practice the procedure you will be performing later. Remove the stopper from the flask. Attach a ring and gauze below the flask, and place an unlit Bunsen

Prepare setup for dry run.

burner below the ring. Attach a second thermometer or probe to the ring stand, and suspend it inside the flask.

Practice inverting flask.

Step 3: Imagine that you have been boiling water in the flask, and have just turned off the burner. Move the burner aside. Remove the second thermometer or probe and its clamp from the stand. Loosen the screw on the ring, and lower it and the gauze to the tabletop. Firmly grasp the clamp and neck of the "hot" flask with a damp paper towel. Insert the stopper into the neck. Loosen the wing nut on the clamp. Holding the flask firmly with a damp paper towel, rotate it in the clamp until it is upside down. Tighten the wing nut to keep it in this position.

Practice this procedure a few times so that you will be comfortable manipulating the apparatus in this way when the flask is filled with boiling-hot water.

Place the stopper aside for use in Step 5.

Monitor water temperature.

Step 4: Put on safety goggles. Fill the flask half full of water, and attach it to the ring stand. The ring and gauze should be below it for safety.

If you are using thermometers, attach a thermometer to the ring stand so that its bulb is in the water but not touching the flask. Make a data table so that you can record the temperature every 30 seconds until 3 minutes after the water begins boiling vigorously. Heat the water, and record your data.

Alternatively, if you are using a computer, attach a temperature probe to the ring stand in place of the thermometer. Calibrate your probe before heating the water. If available, use data plotting software to make a graph of temperature vs. time. Print out your graph.

Insert rubber stopper.

Step 5: When you stop heating the flask, remove the second thermometer. Drop the ring. Firmly grasp the clamp and neck with a damp paper towel. Insert the stopper with the thermometer or probe into the flask. Atmospheric pressure will make it fit snugly. Loosen the wing nut on the clamp. *Carefully* hold the flask, using a damp paper towel, and invert it by rotating it in the clamp. Tighten the wing nut on the clamp to keep the flask in the inverted position, as shown in Figure A.

Fig. A

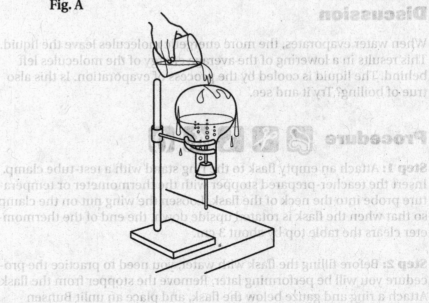

Step 6: Place a pan or tub under the flask. Pour cool tap water over the top half of the flask, or place crushed ice on it. Repeat the pouring several times. If you are using a computer, monitor the temperature of the water in the flask.

Cool flask.

1.   What do you observe happening inside the flask?

_____

_____

2.   What happens to the temperature of the water in the flask?

_____

_____

Step 7: Prepare a graph of temperature (vertical axis) vs. time (horizontal axis), either plotting data from your table or making a printout from the computer.

Make graph.

Analysis

3.   Does the temperature of boiling water increase when heat continues to be applied?

_____

_____

_____

4.   Explain your observations of the temperature of the water as it continues to boil.

_____

_____

_____

_____

5.   How does the amount of heat energy absorbed by a pot of water boiling on a stove compare with the amount of energy removed from the water by boiling?

_____

_____

6. Explain your observations of the inside of the inverted flask after cool water or ice was put on it.

_____

_____

_____

_____

_____

_____

_____

_____

_____

_____

_____

_____

_____

_____

_____

62 Melting Away

Purpose

To measure the heat of fusion for water

Required Equipment/Supplies

250-mL graduated cylinder
8-oz. plastic foam cup
water
ice cube (about 25 g)
paper towel
thermometer (Celsius) or
      computer with a temperature probe and
      printer
graph paper (if computer is not used)

Discussion

If you put heat into an object, will its temperature increase? Don't auto-
matically say yes, for there are exceptions. If you put heat into water at
100°C, its temperature will not increase until all the water has become
steam. The energy per gram that goes into changing the phase from liquid to gas is called the *heat of vaporization*. And when you put heat into
melting ice, its temperature will not increase until all the ice has melted.
The energy per gram that goes into changing the state from solid to liquid is called the *heat of fusion*. That's what this experiment is about.

Procedure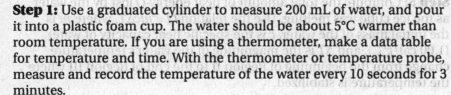

Step 1: Use a graduated cylinder to measure 200 mL of water, and pour
it into a plastic foam cup. The water should be about 5°C warmer than
room temperature. If you are using a thermometer, make a data table
for temperature and time. With the thermometer or temperature probe,
measure and record the temperature of the water every 10 seconds for 3
minutes.

Monitor temperature of water.

Step 2: Dry an ice cube by patting it with a paper towel. Add it to the
water. Continue monitoring the temperature of the water every 10
seconds while gently stirring it until 3 minutes *after* the ice cube has
melted. Record the data in a table or with the computer. Note the time at
which the ice cube has *just* melted.

Determine the final volume of water.

Step 3: Determine the final volume of the water.

final volume = _____

1. What was the mass of the water originally? What was the mass of the ice cube originally? Explain how you determined these masses.

_____

_____

_____

_____

Make graph.

Step 4: Plot your data to make a temperature (vertical axis) vs. time (horizontal axis) graph. If you are using a computer with data plotting software, print a copy for your analysis and report.

Study your graph. Draw vertical dashed lines to break your graph into three distinct regions. Region I covers the time before the ice cube was placed in the water. Region II covers the time while the cube was melting. Region III covers the time after the cube has melted.

2. What was the total temperature change of the water while the cube was melting (Region II)?

_____

_____

_____

3. How did placing the ice cube in the water affect the rate at which the water was cooling?

_____

_____

_____

Compute the energy lost by water.

Step 5: Compute the total amount of heat energy Q lost by the water as the ice cube was melting. Use the relation $Q = mc\Delta T$, where m is the initial mass of the water, c is the specific heat capacity of water (1.00 cal/g°C), and ΔT is the magnitude of the water's temperature change from the beginning of Region II to the end of Region III where the temperature is stabilized.

heat energy lost by original water = _____ cal

Compute heat energy absorbed during warming.

Step 6: Compute the amount of heat energy absorbed as the water from the melted ice warmed from 0°C to its final temperature.

heat energy absorbed by
melted ice during warming = _____ cal

Step 7: From the difference between the values found in Steps 5 and 6, compute the amount of heat energy that was absorbed by the ice as it melted.

Compute heat energy absorbed during melting.

> heat energy absorbed
> by ice during melting = _____ cal

Step 8: Compute the heat by fusion by dividing the value found in Step 7 by the mass of ice that melted in the cup.

Compute heat of fusion.

> heat of fusion = _____ cal/g

4. Compare this value to the standard value, 80 cal/g, and calculate the percentage difference.

_____

_____

_____

_____

_____

_____

_____

_____

Analysis

5. In order for the ice cube to melt, it has to extract heat energy from the warmer water, first a small amount of heat to warm up to 0°C (which we neglect in this experiment), then a larger amount to melt. The melting ice absorbs heat energy, and thus cools the water. The heat energy absorbed per gram when a substance changes from a solid to a liquid is called the heat of fusion. How is the amount of heat energy absorbed by the solid related to the heat of fusion and the mass of the solid?

_____

_____

6. The total amount of heat energy lost by the water is equal to the amounts of heat energy it took to do what things?

_____

_____

_____

7. What are some sources of error in this experiment?

_____

_____

_____

_____

_____

_____

_____

_____

63 Getting Steamed Up

Purpose

To determine the heat of vaporization for water

Required Equipment/Supplies

safety goggles
Bunsen burner
steam generator with rubber tubing and steam trap
3 large plastic foam cups
water
balance
thermometer (Celsius)

Discussion

The condensation of steam liberates energy that warms many buildings on cold winter days. In this lab, you will make steam by boiling water and investigate the amount of heat energy given off when steam condenses into liquid water. You will then determine the heat energy released per gram, or *heat of vaporization*, for the condensation of steam.

Procedure 🥽 🦺 🧤 👕 🧪 🔥

Step 1: Make a calorimeter by nesting 3 large plastic foam cups.
Measure the mass of the empty cups and record it in Data Table A.

Measure mass of cups.

Mass of Empty Cups	
Mass of Cups and Cool Water	
Mass of Cool Water	
Temperature of Cool Water	
Temperature of Warm Water	
Mass of Warm Water	
Specific Heat of Water	$1.00 \frac{cal}{g°C}$

Data Table A

Measure initial temperature and mass.	**Step 2:** Fill the inner cup half-full with cool water. Measure the mass of the triple cup and water to the nearest 0.1 g and record it in Data Table A. Also record the original temperature of the water to the nearest 0.5°C.
Assemble apparatus.	**Step 3:** Fill the steam generator half-full with water, and put its cap on. Place the end of the rubber tubing in the water in the calorimeter (Figure A).

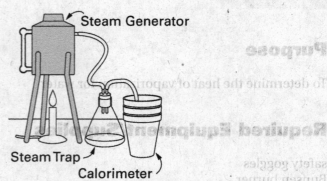

Fig. A

Ignite Bunsen burner.	**Step 4:** Put on safety goggles. Place the burner under the steam generator and ignite it to heat the water inside.
Adjust steam generator.	**Step 5:** Once the water in the steam generator starts boiling, adjust the rate at which steam comes out of the tubing so that it does not gurgle water out of the calorimeter. The steam should make the water bubble vigorously, but not violently. Gently stir the water with the thermometer. Bubble steam into the calorimeter until the water reaches a temperature no higher than 50°C.
Measure final temperature and mass.	**Step 6:** Shut off the burner, and remove the tubing from the water. Immediately determine the final mass and temperature of the warm water, and record them in Data Table A.
Compute mass of steam.	**Step 7:** Compute the mass of steam that condensed in your calorimeter from the change in mass of the water in the calorimeter.

mass of steam = _____ g

Compute heat energy gained.	**Step 8:** Compute the total amount of heat energy Q gained by the cool water using the relation $Q = mc\Delta T$, where m is the initial mass of the water, c is the specific heat of water (1.00 cal/g°C), and ΔT is the change in the temperature of the water. This heat comes in two steps: from the condensation of steam, and then from the condensed steam (now water) as it cools from 100°C to the final temperature. Show your work.

heat energy gained = _____ cal

Compute the energy lost during cooling.	**Step 9:** Compute the amount of heat energy lost by the water from the condensed steam as it cooled from 100°C down to its final temperature. Show your work.

heat energy lost during cooling
of water from the condensed steam = _____ cal

Step 10: From the difference between the values found in Steps 8 and 9, compute the amount of heat energy that was released by the steam as it condensed.

heat energy released during condensation = _____ cal

Step 11: Compute the heat of vaporization by dividing the value found in Step 10 by the mass of steam that condensed in the cup.

Compute heat of vaporization.

heat of vaporization = _____ cal/g

1. Compare this value to the standard value, 540 cal/g, and calculate the percentage difference.

_____

_____

_____

Analysis

2. There are two major energy changes involved in this experiment. One happens in the generator, and the other in the calorimeter. Where does the energy come from or go to during these changes?

_____

_____

_____

_____

3. Does the amount of steam that escapes into the air make any difference in this experiment?

_____

_____

_____

_____

4. Why does keeping the cap on when heating the water in the steam generator cause the water to boil more quickly?

_____

_____

_____

64 LN Is Cool Stuff

Purpose

To determine the specific heat of brass and the heat of vaporization of nitrogen

Required Equipment/Supplies

liquid nitrogen (Dewar flask required)
balance scale, digital preferred
50-g metal specimen, brass preferred
stopwatch
4 plastic foam cups
thermometer (to measure room temperature)

Discussion

The law of energy conservation is taught in every physics course nowadays, but in the 1700s it was unknown. It was at that time the American physicist Count Rumford in Bavaria performed experiments with heat. It makes sense that when heat is added to a substance, the temperature of the substance increases. Less noticed for many years is the *latent heat* that, *without* increasing the temperature, goes into breaking bonds between atoms when a substance changes phase. This experiment demonstrates Rumford's work on heat using some *really* cool stuff—liquid nitrogen!

CAUTION: *Liquid nitrogen is extremely cold—196°C below zero! Be careful not to spill it and make sure it does not come into contact with the skin. Only the teacher should transfer samples of liquid nitrogen.*

Part A: Determining the Evaporation Rate of LN

Procedure

Step 1: First, measure the mass of the empty cups—one placed inside the other as shown—so that you can determine the mass of the liquid nitrogen (LN) added to them.

mass of cups, $m =$ _____ g

Step 2: To determine the rate of evaporation of liquid nitrogen, ask the teacher to pour approximately 180 – 200 grams of LN into two plastic foam cups. After measuring its precise mass using a balance, immediately start a stopwatch and time how long it takes 10 grams to evaporate. This is very easy to observe with a digital balance. However, if using a Harvard Trip balance a convenient method of doing this is to set your balance for 10 grams *less* than the initial amount and watch for the balance arm to swing upwards. For example, if your initial amount of liquid nitrogen is 190 grams, set your balance to 180 grams and measure the time for the scale to balance again. Record the time it takes 10 grams of liquid nitrogen to evaporate.

time, $t =$ _____ s

Step 3: Calculate the rate of evaporation by dividing the mass by the time it took to evaporate.

rate of evaporation, $r =$ _____ g/s

Part B: Determining the Specific Heat of a Specimen

Procedure

Step 4: Immediately after 10 grams of liquid nitrogen have evaporated, place a 50-gram metal specimen in the LN (liquid nitrogen) and start the stopwatch. Assume the initial temperature of the metal mass is room temperature. After several minutes of rapid boiling, the rapid boiling of the LN will subside and become "quiet" as the LN and the specimen reach thermal equilibrium. Remove the specimen and measure the mass of the remaining LN. Record your data below.

$T_{initial} =$ _____°C

initial mass of LN + cups, $m_{initial} =$ _____ g

final mass of LN + cups, $m_{final} =$ _____ g

total mass of LN that evaporated: $m_{total} =$ _____ g

time that specimen was in the cup, $t =$ _____ s

Step 5: Use the rate of evaporation calculated in Step 3 and the time measured in Step 4 to determine the mass of nitrogen that would have evaporated during the same amount of time had you *not* put the specimen in the cup. Show your calculations.

mass due to evaporation = (rate of evaporation)(time)

$= rt$

mass due to evaporation, $m_{evap} =$ _____ g

Step 6: The total mass of LN that evaporates while the specimen is in the cup is the mass of LN that cools the specimen plus the mass of LN that would have evaporated in the same time without having placed the metal specimen in the cups.

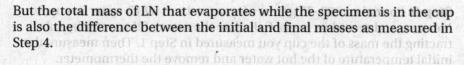

mass of LN that evaporates = (mass of LN to cool specimen) + (mass due to evaporation)

But the total mass of LN that evaporates while the specimen is in the cup is also the difference between the initial and final masses as measured in Step 4.

(initial mass – final mass) = (mass of LN to cool specimen) + (mass due to evaporation)

Therefore, the mass of LN that cools the specimen is the difference between the initial and final masses less the amount that would have evaporated.

mass of LN to cool specimen = (initial mass – final mass) – (mass due to evaporation)

Calculate the mass of liquid nitrogen that evaporated to cool the metal specimen. Show your calculations.

mass of LN that cools specimen, m_{LN} = _____ g

Step 7: The heat the specimen loses, which is the product of its mass, specific heat, and change in temperature ($m_s c_s \Delta t$) equals the heat that cooled the specimen and caused the LN to evaporate ($m_{LN} L_v$), where L_v is used for the latent heat of vaporization. Therefore,

$$m_s c_s \Delta T = m_{LN} L_v$$

If the heat of vaporization for LN is, L_v = 47.5 cal/g, determine the specific heat of the metal specimen. Assume the specimen was originally at room temperature and was cooled down to the temperature at which LN boils, –196°C. Show your calculations.

c_s = _____ $\frac{cal}{g\,°C}$

Part C: Determining the Heat of Vaporization of Nitrogen

Procedure

In Part A, you determined the specific heat of a sample by assuming the latent heat of vaporization for nitrogen, L_v = 47.5 cal/g. In this experiment, you will combine LN and warm water, and measure the temperature decrease of the water as the LN bubbles and boils away. This will enable you to calculate the latent heat of vaporization.

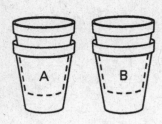

Step 8: Make two double-cup containers by nesting one plastic foam cup inside one inside the other as shown. Label one combination "A" and the other "B." Carefully measure the mass of containers.

mass of container A, m_A = _____ g

mass of container B, m_B = _____ g

Step 9: Pour about 60–75 grams of warm (about 60°C) water in cup A. Measure and record its mass. Calculate the mass of the water by subtracting the mass of the cup you measured in Step 1. Then measure the initial temperature of the hot water and remove the thermometer.

mass of container A+ mass of water, $m_{A + water}$ = _____ g

mass of water in A, m_{water} = _____ g

initial temperature of the water, T_i _____ °C

Step 10: Ask the teacher to pour about 40 grams of LN into cup B. To minimize the mass loss due to evaporation of LN, *quickly* measure the mass of cup B (containing LN) and pour the LN into cup A (containing warm water). This will generate a large white cloud. (What is it?) Measure the time it takes to evaporate and calculate the mass of LN as you did for the water in Step 2.

CAUTION: *Be careful not to add so much LN that it causes the water to freeze. If all of the water freezes, it will invalidate your data because this experiment does not take into account the latent heat of fusion for water. If it does, start over and repeat Step 3. The water should be cooled by the LN, but not frozen by it.*

mass of cups B + mass of LN, $m_{B + LN}$ = _____ g

mass of LN in B, m_{LN} = _____ g

time to evaporate, t = _____ s

Step 11: When evaporation of the nitrogen is complete, gently stir the water with the thermometer until all the ice, if any, has melted. Measure and record the final temperature of the water.

final temperature of the water, T_f = _____ °C

Assuming the heat that evaporated the LN cooled the water, determine the heat of vaporization for nitrogen, L_v. Be sure your calculations take into account the amount of LN that would have evaporated while the water was being cooled as you did in Step 2, Part A. Show all your calculations.

L_v = _____ cal/g

Analysis

1. How does your value for L_v compare with the accepted value of 47.5 cal/g?

   _____

   _____

2. In Step 3 of Part B, you were cautioned against adding so much LN that it would cause some of the water to freeze. Why would this invalidate your calculations?

   _____

   _____

   _____

   _____

   _____

Analysis

1. How does your value for L_f compare with the accepted value of 475 cal/g?

_____

_____

2. In Step 3 of Part B, you were cautioned against adding so much LN that it would cause some of the water to freeze. Why would this invalidate your calculations?

_____

_____

_____

_____

_____

65 Work for Your Ice Cream

Purpose

To measure the energy transfers occurring during the making and freezing of homemade ice cream

Required Equipment/Supplies

homemade ice cream machine
ice
rock salt
thermometer

insulated cups
ice cream mix
triple-beam balance
spring scale with maximum
    capacity of 50 N or 10 lb

Discussion

Energy must be supplied to a home to heat it on a cold winter day. Energy must also be supplied to an air conditioner that is cooling a home on a hot summer day. The air conditioner is transferring heat from the cooler indoors to the warmer outdoors. Energy input is always required to move heat from a region of lower temperature to a region of higher temperature.

Energy must be taken away from a liquid to make it a solid. If the liquid is cooler than the surrounding air, additional energy must be added to move heat from the liquid to the warmer air, just as extra energy is needed to move heat from a room to the warmer outdoors in summer. When the liquid is sweet cream, the solid that results is ice cream. (Making ice cream also involves swirling in air; ice cream is actually a mixture of a solid and a gas.)

The freezing of homemade ice cream involves several energy transfers.

1. Energy (work) is expended in turning the crank to overcome inertia and friction.
2. The slush of ice and rock salt takes up energy as it melts.
3. The ice cream mix cools from its original to its final temperature.
4. The metal container cools from its original to its final temperature.
5. The ice cream mix gives up energy as it freezes.

Procedure

Each group in the class should determine how it will make the measurements to determine the amount of energy transferred in one of the five processes above. If some constants for ice cream are needed, a group also should do a separate experiment to determine those constants. The constants might be the specific heat of the ice cream mix and the heat of fusion of ice cream. Each group should also carry out its method to determine the energy transferred.

You may have to sacrifice some of the ice cream you make to determine these constants and the energy transferred. Don't forget that many of the advances of science came only after great sacrifices! Organize your data to share with the class to make a profile of all the energy transfers.

Describe your procedure.

_____

_____

_____

Analysis

1. Which process of the five listed is the greatest absorber of energy?

_____

_____

2. How did the energy absorbed by the melting slush of ice and rock salt compare with the energy released by the other processes?

_____

_____

3. Salt is put on icy roads to promote melting. When you make home-made ice cream, salt is used to help promote freezing. Is this practice paradoxical, or does it make good physics sense?

_____

_____

66 The Drinking Bird

Purpose

To investigate the operation of a toy drinking bird

Required Equipment/Supplies

toy drinking bird
cup of water

Discussion

Toys often illustrate fundamental physical principles. The toy drinking bird is an example.

Procedure

Step 1: Set up the toy drinking bird with a cup of water as in Figure A. Position the cup to douse the bird's beak with each dip. The fulcrum may require some adjustment to let it cycle smoothly.

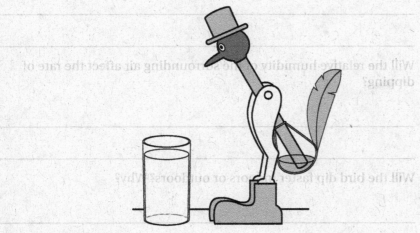

Fig. A

Step 2: After the bird starts "drinking," study its operation carefully. Your goal is to explain how it works. Answering the questions in the "Analysis" section will help you understand how it works.

1. What causes the fluid to rise up the toy bird's neck?

   _____

   _____

   _____

   _____

2. What causes the bird to dip?

   _____

   _____

3. What causes the bird to make itself erect?

   _____

   _____

   _____

4. What is the purpose of the fuzzy head?

   _____

5. Will the bird continue to drink if the cup is removed?

   _____

   _____

6. Will the relative humidity of the surrounding air affect the rate of dipping?

   _____

   _____

7. Will the bird dip faster indoors or outdoors? Why?

   _____

   _____

8. Under what conditions will the bird fail to operate?

   _____

   _____

9. Brainstorm with your lab partners about practical applications of the drinking bird.

_____

_____

_____

_____

_____

10. Explain how the bird works.

_____

_____

_____

_____

_____

_____

_____

_____

_____

_____

_____

_____

_____

67 The Uncommon Cold

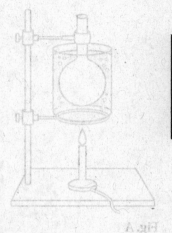

Fig. A

Purpose

To use linear extrapolation to estimate the Celsius value of the temperature of absolute zero

Required Equipment/Supplies

safety goggles
paper towel
Bunsen burner
wire gauze
ring stand with ring
250-mL Florence flask
flask clamp
short, solid glass rod
one-hole rubber stopper to fit flask
500-mL beaker
water
thermometer (Celsius)
ice bucket or container (large enough to submerge a 250-mL flask)
ice
large graduated cylinder
graph paper

Optional Equipment/Supplies

computer
data plotting software

Discussion

Under most conditions of constant pressure, the volume of a gas is proportional to the absolute temperature of the gas. As the temperature of a gas under constant pressure increases or decreases, the volume increases or decreases, in direct proportion to the change of absolute temperature. If this relationship remained valid all the way to absolute zero, the volume of the gas would shrink to zero there. This doesn't happen in practice because all gases liquefy when they get cold enough. Also, the finite size of molecules prevents liquids or solids from contracting to zero volume (which would imply infinite density).

In this experiment, you will discover that you can find out how cold absolute zero is even though you can't get close to that temperature. You will cool a volume of air and make a graph of its temperature-volume relation. Then you will extrapolate the graph to zero volume to predict the temperature, in degrees Celsius, of absolute zero.

Procedure

Set up ice bath.

Step 1: Make an ice bath of ice and water, using a bucket or container large enough to submerge a 250-mL flask. (Do not put the flask in it yet.)

Step 2: Put on safety goggles. Select a *dry* 250-mL Florence flask, and fit a *dry* single-hole stopper into the flask. Half-fill a 500-mL beaker with water, set it on the ring stand, and clamp the flask to the ring stand in the water with the water level approximately 4 cm below the top of the beaker (see Figure A). Boil the water for at least 3 minutes to make sure that the air in the flask is heated to the water temperature. Measure and record the water temperature.

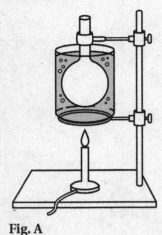

Fig. A

temperature of boiling water = _____

Step 3: Turn off the burner. Use a damp paper towel to grasp the clamp, and quickly place a solid glass rod into the hole of the rubber stopper to trap all the air molecules. Do this quickly while the air in the flask has the same temperature as the boiling water. Loosen the clamp from the ring stand, and lift the flask, stopper, and clamp assembly. Allow the flask to cool for a minute or so until it can be handled comfortably. Remove the clamp from the flask, and lower the flask upside down into the ice bath. Hold the flask and stopper below the water surface of the ice bath, and remove the glass rod.

Record bath temperature.

Step 4: Hold the flask upside down under the water surface for at least 3 minutes. Measure and record the temperature of the ice bath.

temperature of ice bath = _____

Remove flask from bath.

Step 5: Some water has entered the flask to take the place of the contracted air. The air in the flask now has the same temperature as the ice bath. With the flask totally submerged and the neck of the flask just under the water surface, place the glass rod or your finger over the hole of the stopper, and remove the flask from the ice bath.

Measure volumes of air.

Step 6: Devise a method to determine the volume of the trapped air at both temperatures. Record the volumes.

volume of air at temperature of boiling water = _____

volume of air at temperature of ice bath = _____

Graph and extrapolate.

Step 7: Plot the volume of air in the flask (vertical axis) vs. the temperature (horizontal axis) for the two conditions. Use a scale of –400 degrees Celsius to +100 degrees Celsius on the horizontal axis and a scale of 0 mL to 250 mL on the vertical axis. Draw a straight line through the two points and to the *x*-axis (where the extrapolated value for the volume of the gas is zero).

Analysis

1. Why did water flow into the flask in the ice bath?

_____

_____

_____

2. What is your predicted temperature for absolute zero in degrees Celsius? Explain how the graph is used for the prediction.

_____

_____

_____

_____

3. In what way does this graph suggest that temperature cannot drop below absolute zero?

_____

_____

_____

4. What can be done to improve the accuracy of this experiment?

_____

_____

_____

_____

_____

5. What are some assumptions that you made in conducting the experiment and analyzing the data?

_____

_____

_____

_____

6. What happens to air when it gets extremely cold?

_____

_____

_____

_____

Going Further

Use data plotting software to plot your data. Use the computer-drawn graph to check your prediction of the temperature of absolute zero.

7. How does the computer prediction compare with your earlier prediction?

_____

_____

_____

_____

_____

_____

_____

_____

68 Tick-Tock

Purpose

To construct a pendulum with a period of one second

Required Equipment/Supplies

ring stand   stopwatch or wristwatch
pendulum clamp   balance
pendulum bob   meterstick
string

Discussion

A simple pendulum consists of a small heavy ball (the bob) suspended by a lightweight string from a rigid support. The bob is free to oscillate (swing back and forth) in any direction. A pendulum completes one cycle or oscillation when it swings forth from a position of maximum deflection and then back to that position. The time it takes to complete one cycle is called its *period*.

If, during a 10-second interval, a pendulum completes 5 cycles, its period *T* is 10 seconds divided by 5 cycles, or 2 seconds. The period is then 2 seconds for this pendulum.

What determines the period of a pendulum? You will find out the factors by trying to make your pendulum have a period of exactly one second.

Procedure

Construct a pendulum with a period of *exactly* one second. To do this, change one variable at a time and keep track of which ones affect the period and which ones do not.

Questions

1. Briefly describe the method you used to construct your pendulum.

_____

_____

_____

2. What was the mass of your pendulum?

_____

_____

3. What effect, if any, does mass have on the period of a pendulum?

_____

_____

4. What effect, if any, does amplitude (size of swing) have on the period of a pendulum?

_____

_____

5. What was the length of your pendulum?

_____

_____

6. What effect, if any, does length have on the period of a pendulum?

_____

_____

_____

_____

7. If you set up your pendulum atop Mt. Everest, would the period be less than, the same as, or greater than it would be in your lab? Why?

_____

_____

_____

8. If you set up your pendulum aboard an orbiting space vehicle, would the period be less than, the same as, or greater than it would be in your lab?

_____

_____

_____

Chapter 25: Vibrations and Waves

69 Grandfather's Clock

Period of a Pendulum

55	
50	
45	
40	
35	
30	
25	
20	
15	
10	

Data Table A

Purpose

To investigate how the period of a pendulum varies with its length

Required Equipment/Supplies

ring stand
pendulum clamp
pendulum bob
string
graph paper or data plotting
software and printer

stopwatch or
computer with photogate
timing system
ring stands with clamps

Discussion

What characteristics of a pendulum determine its period, the time taken for one oscillation? Galileo timed the swinging of a chandelier in the cathedral at Pisa using his pulse as a clock. He discovered that the time it took to oscillate back and forth was the same regardless of its amplitude, or the size of its swing. In modern terminology, the period of a pendulum is independent of its amplitude (for small amplitudes, angles less than 10°).

Another quantity that does not affect the period of a pendulum is its mass. In Activity 68, Tick-Tock, you discovered that a pendulum's period depends only on its length. In this experiment, you will try to determine exactly *how* the length and period of a pendulum are related. Replacing Galileo's pulse, you will use a stopwatch or a computer.

Procedure

Step 1: Set up a pendulum using the listed equipment. Make its length 65 cm. Measure its period three times by timing the oscillations with the stopwatch or the computer system. (If you are using a computer to measure the period of your pendulum, set up the light probe. Use clamps and ring stands to position a light source (such as a flashlight) so that the pendulum bob eclipses the light probe somewhere in its path.) Record the average period in Data Table A.

Set up pendulum.

Measure pendulum length

Step 2: Shorten the pendulum length by 5 cm. Measure its period as in Step 1, and record the average period in Data Table A.

Shorten pendulum and repeat.

Length (cm)	Period (s)
65	
60	
55	
50	
45	
40	
35	
30	
25	
20	
15	
10	

Data Table A

Step 3: Complete Data Table A for the remaining pendulum lengths indicated there. Measure periods as you did in Step 1.

Step 4: Make a graph of the period (vertical axis) vs. the length of the pendulum (horizontal axis).

1. Describe your graph. Is it a straight line that shows that the period is directly proportional to the length? Or is it a curve that shows that the relationship between period and length is not a direct proportion?

_____

_____

Step 5: Often data points lie on a curve that is not a straight line. It is very difficult to determine the relationship between two variables from such a curve. It is virtually impossible to extrapolate accurately from a curve. Experimenters instead try to produce a straight-line graph by plotting appropriate functions (squares, cubes, logarithms, etc.) of the variables originally used on the horizontal and vertical axes. When they succeed in producing a straight line, they can more easily determine the relationship between variables.

The simplest way to try to "straighten out" a curve is to see if one of the variables is proportional to a power of the other variable. If your graph of period vs. length curves upward (has increasing slope), perhaps period is proportional to the square or the cube of the length. If your graph curves downward (has decreasing slope), perhaps it is the other way around; perhaps the square or the cube of the period is proportional to the length. Try plotting simple powers of one variable against the other to see if you can produce a straight line from your data. If you have a computer with data plotting software, use it to discover the mathematical relationship between the length and the period. A straight-line plot shows that the relationship between the variables chosen is a direct proportion.

2. What plot of powers of length and/or period results in a straight line?

_____

_____

Predict pendulum length.

Step 6: From your graph, predict what length of pendulum has a period of exactly two seconds.

predicted length = _____

Measure pendulum length.

Step 7: Measure the length of the pendulum that gives a period of 2.0 s.

measured length = _____

3. Compute the percentage difference between the measured length and the predicted length.

_____

_____

70 Catch a Wave

Purpose

To observe important wave properties

Required Equipment/Supplies

Slinky™ spring toy, long form
portable stereo with two detachable speakers
Doppler ball (piezoelectric speaker with 9-volt battery mounted inside
4"-diameter foam ball)

Discussion

When two waves overlap, the composite wave is the sum of the two
waves at each instant of time and at each point in space. The two waves
are still there and are separate and independent, not affecting each other
in any way. If the waves overlap only for some duration and in some
region, they continue on their way afterward exactly as they were, each
one uninfluenced by the other. This property is characteristic of waves
and is not observable for particles the size of billiard balls. Obviously,
you've never seen a cue ball collide with another billiard ball and
reappear on the other side! However, sound and water waves, if they are
weak enough, behave this way. That is, two sound waves can overlap
so that *no* sound results! Impressive!

Procedure

Part A: Longitudinal vs. Transverse Waves

Light is a *transverse* wave, meaning that the wave vibrates back and forth
perpendicular to the line of propagation. Sound is a *longitudinal* wave,
meaning that the wave vibrates along the line of propagation.

Step 1: Have your partner hold one end of a long Slinky and carefully—so as not to get it tangled or kinked—stretch it out on a smooth
(non-carpeted) floor or a long counter top. Give the Slinky a rapid jerk
by shaking it to one side then back so that you create a wave pulse that
travels to your partner. Be sure your partner holds the other end fixed.
Repeat several times, observing what happens to the wave pulse as it
travels to your partner and back.

Observe transverse waves.

1. How does the Slinky move with respect to the wave pulse?

_____

_____

2. Is the pulse transverse or longitudinal?

_____

_____

3. Why does the amplitude of the pulse decrease as it travels from its source?

_____

_____

_____

4. How does the reflected pulse differ from the original pulse?

_____

_____

_____

5. What happens to the wavelength of the pulse as it travels to and from your partner?

_____

Observe reflection of waves.

Step 2: Attach a piece of string about a meter long to one end of the Slinky. Have your partner hold the free end of the string. Send a pulse along the Slinky.

6. How does the reflected pulse differ from the original pulse?

_____

_____

Observe change in wave speed.

Step 3: Increase the tension in the Slinky by stretching it. Send a pulse along the Slinky. How does the tension affect the speed of the pulse? Does the tension in the Slinky affect other wave properties as well?

Observe longitudinal waves.

Step 4: Repeat steps 1 through 3 but this time jerk the Slinky back and forth along the direction of the outstretched Slinky. What kind of wave is produced? Record your observations.

_____

_____

_____

Step 5: Now for some real fun! This time you and your partner will create equal-sized pulses at the same time from opposite ends of the Slinky. It may require some practice to get your timing synchronized. Try it both ways—that is, with the pulses on the same side and then with the pulses on opposite sides of the line of propagation. Pay special attention to what happens as the pulses overlap. Record your observations.

Observe the sum of two waves.

_____

_____

_____

_____

_____

_____

_____

_____

Step 6: Detach two speakers from a portable stereo with both speakers in phase (that is, with the plus and minus connections to each speaker the same). Play in a mono mode so the signals of each speaker are identical. Note the fullness of the sound. Now reverse the polarity of one of the speakers by interchanging the plus and minus wires. Note that the sound is different—it lacks fullness. Some of the waves from one speaker are arriving at your ear out of phase with waves from the other speaker.

Observe interference of sound waves.

Now place the pair of speakers facing each other at arm's length apart. The long waves interfere destructively, detracting from the fullness of sound. Gradually bring the speakers closer to each other. What happens to the volume and fullness of the sound? Bring them face to face against each other. What happens to the volume now?

Part B: Standing Waves—Resonance

Have your partner hold one end of the Slinky. Shake the Slinky slowly back and forth until you get a wave that is the combination of a transmitted wave and its reflection—a standing wave—like the *fundamental* (or the first harmonic) shown in Figure A.

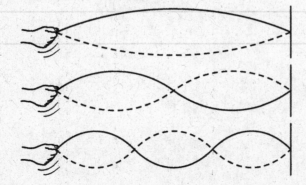

Fig. A

7. How long is the wave compared to the length of the Slinky?

_____

_____

Observe standing waves.

Step 7: Now shake the Slinky at a higher frequency so that a second-harmonic standing wave is created.

8. How long is the wave compared to the length of the Slinky?

_____

_____

Observe harmonics.

Step 8: See how many other harmonics you can create. Record your observations.

_____

_____

_____

Part C: The Doppler Effect

You are now going to investigate what happens when either the source or the receiver of waves is moving. For example, when a car whizzes by on the road, the pitch of its engine is higher when approaching and lower when receding. This change of frequency due to motion is called the Doppler effect.

Similarly, the whine of an airplane engine changes its pitch as it passes overhead. If the plane moves faster than the speed of sound, the Doppler shift is replaced by a shock wave, which produces a "sonic boom." It is interesting to note that any object traveling at supersonic speed creates its own shock wave—whether or not it is a sound emitter.

The Doppler effect occurs with *any* wave phenomenon (including light and other electromagnetic radiation) whenever there is relative motion between the source and receiver. For example, the decrease of frequency for the light of a receding star gives it a *red shift*. An approaching star is seen to be *blue shifted*. The Doppler effect is far reaching.

Observe Doppler effect.

Step 9: Play catch with your partner using a Doppler ball. How does the movement of the ball affect the pitch of the sound?

_____

_____

71   Ripple While You Work

Purpose

To observe wave phenomena in a ripple tank

Required Equipment/Supplies

ripple tank with light source and bottom screen
3/4-inch dowel
paraffin blocks
medicine dropper
length of large-diameter rubber hose
wave generator
large glass plate
cut rubber stoppers

Discussion

Water waves have simple properties when they have small amplitude, and they are familiar to everyone. Observing the behavior of water waves in a ripple tank will introduce you to the analysis of wave motion.

Procedure

Step 1: The ripple tank is set up for you. Turn on its light. Observe the screen at the base of the tank as you produce a pulse by touching your finger or pencil tip once to the water surface.

Observe pulse.

1. What is the shape of the pulse?

_____

_____

2. Does the speed of the pulse seem to be the same in all directions?

_____

_____

Step 2: Place the dowel in the water. Produce a straight wave front by rolling the dowel forward 1 cm, with the flat of your hand.

Generate straight wave front.

3. What is the shape of the pulse?

_____

_____

_____

Observe reflections.

Step 3: Place a paraffin block in the tank. With the dowel generate a pulse that strikes the barrier straight on.

4. What does the pulse do when it reaches the barrier?

_____

_____

_____

5. After the pulse strikes the barrier, what is the new direction of the pulse?

_____

_____

_____

Step 4: Move the paraffin block to change the angle at which the pulse strikes it.

6. What is the shape of the reflected pulse?

_____

_____

_____

Generate circular wave pulses.

Step 5: Produce circular wave pulses with water drops from the medicine dropper.

7. How do the pulses reflect from the paraffin block?

_____

_____

_____

8. From what point do the reflected pulses appear to be originating?

_____

_____

_____

Observe wave pulses reflected by a parabola.

Step 6: Bend a length of large-diameter rubber hose into the approximate shape of a parabola. Place it in the tank.

9. What do you observe when you use this tubing as a reflector for straight pulses?

_____

_____

_____

Step 7: Find the *point* at which the straight pulses reflected by the hose meet and mark it on the screen with your finger. This is the *focus* of the parabola. Generate a circular pulse with the dropper held straight above the focus of the parabola.

Observe wave pulses originating at the focus.

10. What is the shape of the reflected pulse?

_____

_____

11. Do any other points give the same pulse shape?

_____

Step 8: Start the wave generator to produce a straight wave. The distance between bright bars in the wave is the wavelength. Adjust the frequency of the wave generator.

Observe frequency change.

12. What effect does increasing the frequency have on the wavelength?

_____

_____

Step 9: Place a paraffin barrier halfway across the middle of the tank. Observe the part of the straight wave that strikes the barrier as well as the part that passes by it. Adjust the frequency of the wave generator so that the combination of the incoming and reflected wave appears to stand still. The combination then forms a standing wave.

Observe standing wave.

13. How does the wavelength of the standing wave compare with the wavelength of the wave traveling past the barrier?

_____

_____

Step 10: Support a piece of rectangular slab of glass with rubber stoppers so that it is 1.5 cm from the bottom of the tank and its top is *just* covered with water. Arrange the glass so that incoming wave fronts are parallel to one edge of the glass.

14. What happens as waves pass from deep to shallow water?

_____

_____

_____

_____

Compare wave speeds.

Step 11: Now turn the glass so that its edge is no longer parallel to the incoming wave fronts.

15. Are the wave fronts straight both outside and over the glass?

_____

_____

16. How do the speeds of the waves compare?

_____

_____

Observe wave spreading.

Step 12: Place paraffin blocks across the tank until they reach from side to side with a small opening in the middle. Generate straight waves with the wave generator.

17. How does the straight wave pattern change as it passes through the opening?

_____

_____

Step 13: Using a piece of paraffin about 4 cm long, modify your paraffin barrier so that it has two openings about 4 cm apart near the center. Generate a straight wave and allow it to pass through the pair of openings.

18. What wave pattern do you observe?

_____

_____

_____

Step 14: Put two point sources about 4 cm apart on the bar of the wave generator. Turn on the wave generator to produce overlapping circular waves.

19. What pattern do you now observe?

_____

_____

_____

_____

72 Mach One

Purpose

To determine the speed of sound using the concept of resonance

Required Equipment/Supplies

resonance tube approximately 50 cm long or golf club tube cut in half
1-L plastic graduated cylinder
meterstick
1 or 2 different tuning forks of 256 Hz or more
rubber band
Alka-Seltzer® antacid tablet (optional)

Discussion

You are familiar with many applications of *resonance*. You may have heard a vase across the room rattle when a particular note on a piano was played. The frequency of that note was the same as the natural vibration frequency of the vase. Your textbook has other examples of resonating objects.

Gases can resonate as well. A vibrating tuning fork held over an open tube can cause the air column to vibrate at a natural frequency that matches the frequency of the tuning fork. This is resonance. The length of the air column can be shortened by adding water to the tube. The sound is loudest when the natural vibration frequency of the air column is the same as (resonates with) the frequency of the tuning fork. For a tube open at one end and closed at the other, the lowest frequency of natural vibration is one for which the length of the air column is one fourth the wavelength of the sound wave.

In this experiment, you'll use the concept of resonance to determine the wavelength of a sound wave of known frequency. You can then compute the speed of sound by multiplying the frequency by the wavelength.

Procedure

Step 1: Fill the cylinder with water to about two thirds of its capacity. Place the resonance tube in the cylinder. You can vary the length of the air column in the tube by moving the tube up or down.

Step 2: Select a tuning fork, and record the frequency that is imprinted on it.

frequency = _____ Hz

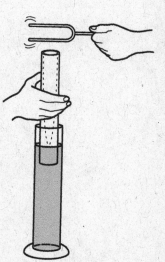

Strike the tuning fork on the heel of your shoe (NOT on the cylinder). Hold the tuning fork about 1 cm above the open end of the tube, horizontally, with its tines one above the other. Move both the fork and the tube up and down to find the air column length that gives the loudest sound. (There are several loud spots.) Mark the water level on the tube for this loudest sound with a rubber band stretched around the cylinder.

Measure air column length.

Step 3: Measure the distance from the top of the resonance tube to the water-level mark.

length of air column = _____ m

Measure the diameter.

Step 4: Measure the diameter of the resonance tube.

diameter of the resonance tube = _____ m

Compute corrected length.

Step 5: Make a corrected length by adding 0.4 times the diameter of the tube to the measured length of the air column. This corrected length accounts for the air just above the tube that also vibrates.

corrected length = _____ m

Compute the wavelength.

Step 6: The corrected length is one fourth of the wavelength of the sound vibrating in the air column. Compute the wavelength of that sound.

wavelength = _____ m

Compute the speed of sound.

Step 7: Using the frequency and the wavelength of the sound, compute the speed of sound in air. Show your work.

speed of sound in air = _____ m/s

Repeat using different tuning fork.

Step 8: If time permits, repeat Steps 2 to 7 using a different tuning fork.

frequency = _____ Hz   length of air column = _____ m

corrected length = _____ m   wavelength = _____ m

speed of sound in air = _____ m/s

Analysis

1. The accepted value for the speed of sound in dry air is 331 m/s at 0°C. This speed increases by 0.6 m/s for each additional degree Celsius above zero. Compute the accepted value for the speed of sound in dry air at the temperature of your room.

_____

_____

_____

2. How does your computed speed of sound compare with the accepted value? Compute the percentage difference.

_____

73 Shady Business

Purpose

To investigate the nature and formation of shadows

Required Equipment/Supplies

bright light source
book or other opaque object
screen or wall
meterstick

Discussion

If you look carefully at a shadow, you will notice that it has a dark central region and a fuzzy and less dark band around the edge of the central region. Why do shadows have two different regions?

Procedure

Step 1: Arrange a small light source so that a solid object such as a book casts a shadow on a screen or wall. Sketch the shadow formed, noting both its regions. Sketch the relative positions of the book, light source, and shadow.

Sketch shadow.

Step 2: Move the light source away from the object while keeping the position of the object fixed. Note and sketch any changes in the shadow. Sketch the new relative position of the light source.

Move light source.

1. What happens to the size of the fuzzy region around the edge of the central region when the light source is moved farther away?

_____

_____

Move object.

Step 3: Move the object closer to the light source while keeping the screen and the light source in the same position. Note and sketch any changes in the shadow. Sketch the new relative position of the object.

2. What happens to the size of the fuzzy region around the edge when the object is moved closer to the light source?

_____

_____

Analysis

3. Which relative positions of the object, light source, and screen result in a sharp distinct shadow with little or no fuzzy region around its edge?

_____

_____

_____

4. Which relative positions of the object, light source, and screen result in a large fuzzy region around a small or nonexistent central dark region?

_____

_____

_____

5. What causes the fuzzy region around the edge of a shadow?

_____

_____

74 Shades

Purpose

To investigate the effects of polarized light

Required Equipment/Supplies

3 small polarizing filters
light source
small plane mirror

Discussion

The vibrations of light waves reaching your eyes are mostly randomly oriented; they vibrate in many planes at once. In polarized light, the light waves vibrate in one plane only. Polarized light can be made by blocking all the waves except those in one plane with polarizing filters. The filters can also be used to detect polarized light.

Procedure

Step 1: Position one polarizing filter between your eyes and a light source. Slowly rotate the filter 360°. Observe the intensity of the light as seen through the filter. Note any intensity changes as you rotate the filter.

1. What happens to the intensity of the light as you rotate the filter?

_____

_____

_____

Step 2: Arrange one filter in a fixed position in front of the light source. Slowly rotate a second filter held between your eyes and the fixed filter. Note any intensity changes of the light as you rotate the filter 360°.

Rotate second filter.

2. What happens to the intensity of the light as you rotate the filter?

_____

_____

_____

Rotate other filter.

Step 3: Hold the filter at your eye in a fixed position while your partner slowly rotates the other filter next to the light source 360°. Note any intensity changes of the light as the filter as rotated.

3. What happens to the intensity of the light as the filter as rotated?

_____

_____

Rotate both filters.

Step 4: Rotate both of the filters through one complete rotation in the same direction at the same time. Note any intensity changes.

4. What happens to the intensity of the light as you rotate both filters together?

_____

_____

Rotate both filters in opposite directions.

Step 5: Rotate both of the filters through one complete rotation at the same time, but in opposite directions. Note any intensity changes.

5. What happens to the intensity of the light as you rotate both filters in opposite directions?

_____

_____

Rotate single filter for light reflected off a mirror.

Step 6: Repeat Step 1, except arrange the light source and a mirror so that you observe only the light coming from the mirror surface. Note any intensity changes of the light as you rotate the filter.

6. What happens to the intensity of the light as you rotate the filter?

_____

_____

_____

7. Is the light reflected off a mirror polarized?

_____

_____

View sky through filter.

Step 7: View different regions of the sky on a sunny day through a filter. Rotate the filter 360° while viewing each region.

CAUTION: *Do not look at the sun!*

_____

8. What happens to the intensity of the light as you rotate the filter?

_____

_____

_____

_____

9. Is the light of the sky polarized? If so, where is the region of maximum polarization in relation to the position of the sun?

_____

_____

_____

Step 8: View a liquid-crystal display (LCD) on a wristwatch or calculator using a filter. Rotate the filter 360°, and note any intensity changes.

View LCD with filter.

10. What happens to intensity of the light as you rotate the filter?

_____

_____

_____

11. Is the light coming from a liquid crystal display polarized?

_____

_____

Analysis

12. Why do polarized lenses make good sunglasses?

_____

_____

_____

_____

13. Explain why the effects seen in Steps 1 to 3 occur.

_____

_____

_____

_____

_____

_____

Going Further

Step 9: Position a pair of filters so that a minimum of light from a light source gets through. Place a third filter between the light source and the pair.

14. Does any light get through?

_____

_____

Step 10: Place the third filter beyond the pair.

15. Does any light get through?

_____

_____

Step 11: This time, sandwich the third filter between the other two filters at a 45° angle.

16. Does any light get through?

_____

_____

_____

_____

75 Flaming Out

Purpose

To observe the spectra of some metal atoms

Required Equipment/Supplies

safety goggles
spectroscope
incandescent lamp
Bunsen burner with matches
  or igniter
small beaker

7 20-cm pieces of platinum or
nichrome wire with a small
loop at one end
6 labeled bottles containing salts
  of lithium, sodium, potassium,
  calcium, strontium, and copper

Discussion

An element emits light of certain frequencies when heated to high
enough temperatures. Different frequencies are seen as different colors,
and each element emits (and absorbs) its own pattern of colors. This
allows us to identify these elements, whether they are nearby or far away.

Procedure

Step 1: Practice using the spectroscope by looking at an incandescent
lamp. The spectrum will appear as a rainbow of colors. Adjust the spectroscope until the spectrum is horizontal and clear.

Adjust spectroscope.

Step 2: Put on safety goggles. Ignite the Bunsen burner. Adjust it until
a blue, nearly invisible flame is obtained.

Step 3: Dip a loop of wire into the bottle of solid sodium chloride. Hold
the loop in the flame until the sodium chloride melts and vaporizes.
Observe the spectrum of the sodium atoms through the spectroscope.
You may also see a long, broad band image due to the glowing wire.
Ignore this image. In Data Table A, sketch any major lines you see, in the
appropriate position, for the color of the lines.

Step 4: Test each of the other salts as in Step 3. Each wire is to stay in its
proper bottle. Mixing the test wires contaminates them. If you should
make a mistake and place a wire in the wrong bottle, burn off all the salt
until the wire glows red hot, then return it to its proper bottle. In Data
Table A, sketch the major lines emitted by each salt.

Sketch spectral lines.

Data Table A

Salt of:	Major Spectral Lines				
	Red	Yellow	Green	Blue	Violet
Lithium					
Sodium					
Potassium					
Calcium					
Strontium					
Copper					

Observe spectrum of mixture.

Step 5: Mix small and equal amounts of the copper and lithium salts in the small beaker. Using the extra test wire, hold a loopful of the mixture in the flame, and observe the resulting spectrum through the spectroscope.

1. Does the spectrum of the mixture of copper and lithium salts contain a combination of the copper and lithium lines?

_____

Step 6: Mix a trace of lithium salt with a larger amount of copper salt. Observe the resulting spectrum through the spectroscope, using the same wire.

2. Did you see the characteristic colors of both copper and lithium?

_____

Analysis

3. How do you know that the bright yellow lines you observed when looking at sodium chloride are due to the sodium and not to the chlorine in the compound?

_____

_____

4. From your observations in Steps 5 and 6, draw conclusions about the relative amounts of metal elements present in each mixture.

_____

5. In steel mills, large amounts of scrap steel of unknown composition are melted to make new steel. Explain how the laboratory technicians in the steel mills can tell exactly what is in any given batch of steel in order to adjust its composition.

_____

76 Why the Sky Is Blue

Purpose

To investigate the mechanism that causes light to scatter

Required Equipment/Supplies

long, skinny tank (fish tank will do)
Mop & Glo (liquid floor cleaning fluid)
flashlight (mini Maglite or equivalent preferred)
laser pointers
sympathetic tuning forks
tuning fork (same frequency as sympathetic tuning forks)
colored pencils (optional)

Discussion

Everybody enjoys a nice day when white puffy clouds dot a bright blue sky. Why *is* the sky blue? And why are sunsets and sunrises red? Did you know the sky is actually violet? Many people think the sky is blue because it reflects off the blue oceans. That might be true for people who lived on the coast near the ocean. But why are the skies blue over Nebraska or other places where the ocean is a long way away? Have you ever noticed that a glass of water looks clear, yet a glass of nonfat milk has a faint bluish tint to it? That's because the milk has tiny little particles that cause the light to interact, or *scatter* in all directions. Let's do some experimenting and see how light behaves in these circumstances and see if we can understand why the sky is blue!

Procedure

Step 1: Your teacher will perform a series of demonstrations to help you understand the basic ideas of resonance and how it applies to scattering.

Listen to the sound of the tuning fork as your teacher strikes it. Notice both the pitch and the intensity (loudness). Now observe when the tuning fork is struck and the handle is placed against the table. Notice how the sound gets louder, but the pitch remains the same. That's because the vibration of the tuning fork is transmitted to the table that in turn vibrates. The vibration of the handle causes the tabletop in turn to vibrate *sympathetically*, hence the term sympathetic vibration. It's a form of *resonance*.

Your teacher will demonstrate a (single) tuning fork mounted on a wooden box open on one end. Notice the increase in volume. That's because the wooden box vibrates (sympathetically) as well as the tuning fork, which causes much more air to be moved—hence the louder sound.

Your teacher will demonstrate what happens when two tuning fork resonators are placed a meter apart and one fork is struck. Record your observations. Explain.

_____

_____

_____

_____

Step 2: Fill the long-skinny tank with clean water. Shine the beam of the flashlight down the long axis of the tank by holding the flashlight up next to one end the tank. The water in the tank should look reasonably clear except for a few small bubbles.

Step 3: Slowly add a few drops of Mop & Glo to the tank. Stir completely. View the side of the tank from all angles. View the bulb of the flashlight by peering down the long axis of the tank. Record all your observations.

_____

_____

_____

Step 4: Now slowly add Mop & Glo drops to the tank while your lab partner stirs the tank until the end of the tank opposite to the flashlight begins to take on a slight reddish-hue. View the bulb of the flashlight by peering through the tank of water. Record all your observations.

_____

_____

_____

Step 5: Add enough Mop & Glo until the end opposite of the flashlight is red-orange.

Analysis

1. How did the light change as you added more and more Mop & Glo from the side of the tank?

   _____

   _____

   _____

   _____

2. How did the color of the bulb change as you added more and more Mop & Glo?

   _____

   _____

   _____

   _____

3. Think about the tuning fork demonstrations performed by your teacher at the beginning of the lab. In effect, the sound from the first tuning fork that was struck was "scattered" by the second tuning fork. How does this apply to why the sky is blue?

   _____

   _____

   _____

   _____

   _____

4. Draw and label the light from the sun that passes through the atmosphere as it reaches the three observers on the ground. Be sure to indicate what color the observer sees as a result of the light as it passes through the atmosphere.

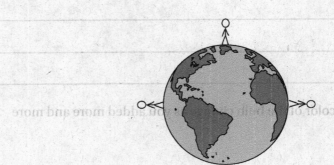

_____

_____

_____

5. As you added more and more Mop & Glo, the water in the tank appeared white. Why? Can you explain why clouds are white? Name other examples of this effect.

_____

_____

_____

_____

_____

77 Images

Purpose

To formulate ideas about how reflected light travels to your eyes

Required Equipment/Supplies

2 small plane mirrors
supports for the mirrors
2 single-hole rubber stoppers
2 pencils
2 sheets of paper
transparent tape

Discussion

Reflections are interesting. Reflections of reflections are fascinating. Reflections of reflections of reflections are . . . you will see for yourself in this activity.

Procedure

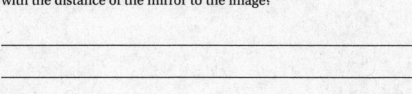

Fig. A

Step 1: Place the pencils in the rubber stoppers. Set one plane mirror upright in the middle of a sheet of paper, as shown in Figure A. Stand one pencil vertically in front of the mirror. Hold your eye steady at the height of the mirror. Locate the image of the pencil formed by the mirror. Place the second pencil where the image of the first appears to be. If you have located the image correctly, the image of the first pencil and the second pencil itself will remain "together" as you move your head from side to side.

1. How does the distance from the first pencil to the mirror compare with the distance of the mirror to the image?

   _____

   _____

Step 2: On the sheet of paper, draw the path you think the light takes from the first pencil to your eye as you observe the image. Draw a dotted line to where the image appears to be located as seen by the observing eye.

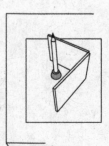

Fig. B

Formation of Virtual Images

Step 3: Hinge two mirrors together with transparent tape. Set the mirrors upright and at right angles to each other in the middle of a second sheet of paper. Place a pencil in its stopper between the mirrors, as in Figure B.

2. How many images do you see?

_____

_____

Draw ray diagram.

Step 4: On the paper, show where the images are located. Draw the paths you think the light takes as it goes from the pencil to your eye.

Decrease angle between mirrors.

Step 5: Decrease the angle between the two mirrors.

3. What happens to the number of images you get when you decrease the angle between the two mirrors?

_____

_____

Fig. A

Fig. B

78 Pepper's Ghost

Purpose

To explore the formation of mirror images by a plate of glass

Required Equipment/Supplies

safety goggles
two candles of equal size, in holders
1 thick plate of glass, approximately 30 cm × 30 cm × 1 cm
2 supports for the glass plate
matches

Discussion

John Henry Pepper (1821–1900), a professor in London, used his knowledge of image formation to perform as an illusionist. One of his illusions was based on the fact that glass both reflects and transmits light.

Procedure

Step 1: Put on safety goggles. Light one candle, and place it about 6 cm in front of a vertical thick glass plate. Place a similar, but unlighted, candle at the position on the other side of the glass plate at the point where the flame of the lighted candle appears to be on the unlighted candle.

1. How does the distance from the lighted candle to the glass plate compare with the distance from the glass plate to the unlighted candle?

_____

_____

Step 2: Look carefully, and you should see a double image of the candle flame.

Find double image.

2. How would you explain the double image?

_____

_____

_____

Find multiple images.

Step 3: Look at the glass plate such that your line of vision makes a small angle with the surface of the glass. You will see three or more "ghost" images of the candle flame.

3. Explain these "ghost" images.

_____

_____

_____

_____

79 The Kaleidoscope

Purpose

To apply the concept of reflection to a mirror system with multiple reflections

Required Equipment/Supplies

2 plane mirrors, 4 in. × 5 in.   viewing object
transparent tape   protractor
clay   toy kaleidoscope (optional)

Discussion

Have you ever held a mirror in front of you and another mirror in back of you in order to see the back of your head? Did what you saw surprise you?

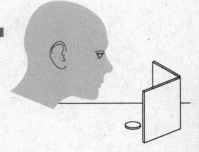

Procedure

Step 1: Hinge the two mirrors together with transparent tape to allow them to open at various angles. Use clay and a protractor to hold the two mirrors at an angle of 72°. Place the object to be observed inside the angled mirrors. Count the number of images resulting from this system and record in Data Table A.

Step 2: Reduce the angle of the mirrors by 5 degrees at a time, and count the number of images at each angle. Record your findings in Data Table A.

Step 3: Study and observe the operation of a toy kaleidoscope, if one is available.

Analysis

1. Explain the reason for the multiple images you have observed.

_____

_____

_____

Angle	Number of Images
72°	
67°	
62°	
57°	
52°	
47°	
42°	
37°	
32°	
27°	

Data Table A

2. What effect does the angle between the mirrors have on the number of images?

_____

_____

_____

_____

3. Using the information you have gained, explain the construction and operation of a toy kaleidoscope.

_____

_____

_____

_____

_____

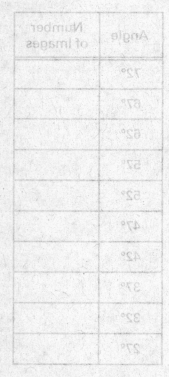

Angle	Number of Images
72°	
67°	
62°	
57°	
52°	
47°	
42°	
37°	
32°	
27°	

Data Table A

80   Funland

Purpose

To investigate the nature, position, and size of images formed by a concave mirror

Required Equipment/Supplies

concave spherical mirror
cardboard
night-light with clear 7-watt bulb
small amount of modeling clay
meterstick

Optional Equipment/Supplies

computer
data plotting software

Discussion

The law of reflection states that the angle of reflection equals the angle of incidence. Parallel light rays that strike a plane mirror head on bounce directly backward and are still parallel. If the parallel rays strike that mirror at another angle, each bounces off at the same angle and the rays are again parallel. A plane mirror cannot bring light rays to a focus because the reflected light rays are still parallel and do not converge. Images observed in a plane mirror are always *virtual* images because *real* images are made only by converging light.

    A parabolic mirror is able to focus parallel rays of light to a single point (the *focal point*) because of its variable curvature. A small spherical mirror has a curvature that deviates only a little from that of a parabolic curve and is cheaper and easier to make. Spherical mirrors can, therefore, be used to make real images, as you will do in this experiment.

Procedure

Step 1: The distance from the center of a spherical mirror surface to the focal point is called the *focal length*. Measure the focal length of your mirror by having it convert a parallel beam of light into a converging beam that comes to a point on a screen. Use the filament of a lit, clear 7-watt bulb as a source of approximately parallel light and a piece of

Measure focal length of mirror.

d_O(cm)	d_i (cm)

cardboard as a screen. Record your measurement below to the nearest 0.1 cm. Also, record the number of your mirror.

focal length = _____ cm

mirror number = _____

Step 2: The rays of light striking your mirror from the bulb may not be exactly parallel. What effect, if any, would this have on your measured value for the focal length? What effect would moving the light source farther away from the mirror have? Increase the distance between the mirror and the light source to see if the focal length changes. (If a better source of parallel light is available, use it to find the focal point of your mirror). Record your measurement to the nearest 0.1 cm.

focal length f = _____ cm

Fig. A   Fig. B

Find a real image with mirror.

Step 3: Use a small amount of modeling clay at the bottom of the mirror to act as a mirror holder. Arrange a screen and a light source as shown in Figure A. Position your screen so that the image is slightly off to one side of the object, as shown in Figure B. Move the mirror so that it is farther than one focal length f from the nightlight. Move the screen to form a sharp image of the filament on the screen. Can a real image be formed on the screen? Is it magnified or reduced, compared with the object? Is the image erect (right-side up) or inverted (upside down)? Record your findings in Data Table A.

Data Table A

Position of Object	Nature of Image		
	Real or Virtual?	Magnified?	Inverted or Erect?
Beyond f			
At f			
Within f			

d_o (cm)	d_i (cm)

Data Table B

Step 4: Where, in relation to one focal length from the mirror, is the object when the image appears right-side up (erect)? What is the relative size of the image (magnified or reduced) compared with the object? Is the image real or virtual? Record your findings in Data Table A.

Step 5: Is there a spacing between object and mirror for which no image appears at all? Where is the object in relation to the focal length? Record this position in Data Table A.

Step 6: Position the mirror two focal lengths away from the light source. The mirror will then form an image of the filament on a screen placed slightly to one side of the light source. The distance between the *focal point* and the object is the object distance d_o and the distance between the focal point and the image is the image distance d_i. Record the distances d_o and d_i in Data Table B. Move the mirror 5 cm farther away from the light source, and reposition the screen until the image comes back into focus. Progressively extend d_o by repeating these 5-cm movements five more times. Record d_o and d_i each time.

Step 7: Plot d_i (vertical axis) vs. d_o (horizontal axis), then different powers of each to discover the mathematical relation between d_i and d_o. Is there any combination that makes a linear graph through the origin and thus a direct proportion? If available, use data plotting software to plot your data.

1. What mathematical relationship exists between d_i and d_o?

_____

_____

_____

_____

Step 8: You can locate the position of the image of the object in Figure C using the ray-diagram method. Draw the path of the light rays that leaves the tip of the arrow parallel to the principal axis.

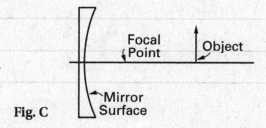

Fig. C

2. Where does this ray go after it is reflected?

_____

_____

_____

Draw the light ray that leaves the tip of the arrow and passes through the focal point.

3. Where does this light ray go after it is reflected?

_____

_____

_____

Now draw the paths of these two light rays after they are reflected. At the point where they cross, an image of the tip of the arrow is formed.

Step 9: Use the ray-diagram method to locate the image of the object in Figure D. Draw the path of the ray that leaves the tip of the arrow parallel to the principal axis and is reflected by the mirror. Trace another ray that heads toward the mirror in the same direction as if it *originated* from the focal point and is reflected by the mirror.

Fig. D

4. Where do the two reflected rays *appear* to cross? _____

_____

_____

_____

5. Could the image be projected onto a screen? Explain.

_____

_____

_____

_____

Name _____ Period _____ Date _____

Chapter 30: Lenses

Pinhole Camera

81 Camera Obscura

Purpose

To observe images formed by a pinhole camera and to compare images formed with and without a lens

Required Equipment/Supplies

covered shoe box with a pinhole and a converging lens set in one end,
 an open end opposite, and glassine paper inside the box (as in Figure A)
piece of masking tape

Discussion

The first camera, known as a *camera obscura*, used a pinhole opening to let light in. The light that passes through the pinhole forms an image on the inner back wall of the camera. Because the opening is small, a long time is required to expose the film sufficiently. A lens allows more light to pass through and still focuses the light onto the film. Cameras with lenses require much less time for exposure, and the pictures have come to be called "snapshots."

Procedure

Step 1: Use a pinhole camera constructed as in Figure A. Tape the foil flap down over the lens so that only the pinhole is exposed. Hold the camera with the pinhole toward a brightly illuminated scene, such as the scene through a window during the daytime. Light enters the pinhole and falls on the glassine paper. Observe the image of the scene on the glassine paper.

1. Is the image on the screen upside down (inverted)?

_____

2. Is the image on the screen reversed left to right?

_____

Step 2: Now seal off the pinhole with a piece of masking tape, and open the foil door to allow light through the lens. Move the camera around. You can watch people or cars moving by.

Observe images on screen of camera with pinhole.

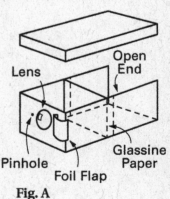

Fig. A

Observe images with lens.

3. Is the image on the screen upside down (inverted)?

_____

4. Is the image on the screen reversed left to right?

_____

Step 3: A pinhole camera focuses equally well on objects at all distances. Point the camera lens at a nearby object to determine whether the lens focuses on nearby objects.

5. Does the lens focus on nearby objects?

_____

_____

Draw ray diagram.

Step 4: Draw a ray diagram as follows. Draw a ray for light that passes from the top of a distant object through a pinhole and onto a screen. Draw another ray for light that passes from the bottom of the object through the pinhole and onto the screen. Show the image created on the screen by the pinhole.

Analysis

6. Why is the image created by the pinhole dimmer than the one created by the lens?

_____

7. How is a pinhole camera similar to your eye? Do you think that the images formed on the retina of your eye are upside down?

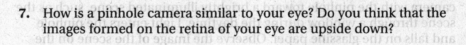

_____

_____

_____

_____

Chapter 30: Lenses   **Convex and Concave Lenses**

82   Thin Lens

Purpose

To explore concave and convex lenses

Required Equipment/Supplies

convex lens
concave lens

Discussion

Lenses are not to read about, but to experiment with. Before study-ing Chapter 30 in the text, some hands-on experience is important for understanding lenses. This activity should help guide you to discover some of their interesting properties.

Procedure

Move an object to different distances from a convex lens and you will see an image form at different locations. At some locations, the image will appear upside-down; other times, it will appear right-side up, and in others it will disappear entirely.

Initially, locate the object at a distance 2*f* from the lens. Is the image larger or smaller than the object? Is the image *erect* (right-side up) or *inverted* (upside down)? Can the image be projected (a *real* image) or not (a *virtual* image)? Is there any position of the object for which no image is formed? Record your observations as to the nature of the image you observe in Data Table A and Data Table B for both kinds of lenses.

Analysis

1. When the image appears right-side up (erect) using a converging lens, how many focal lengths is the object from the lens?

_____

2. Under what circumstances is the image formed by a converging lens magnified? Under what circumstances is it reduced? When is it real? When is it virtual?

_____

_____

_____

3. Can an object be located in a position where a converging lens forms no real image?

_____

4. For a diverging lens, is the virtual image enlarged or reduced?

_____

5. Can you form a real image with a diverging lens?

_____

6. When the object is moved, does the image formed by a converging lens always move in the same direction? What about the image formed by a diverging lens?

_____

_____

Data Table A

	Nature of Image Converging Lens		
Position of Object	Real or Virtual	Magnified or Reduced	Inverted or Erect
Beyond 2f			
At 2f			
At f			
Within f			

Data Table B

	Nature of Image Diverging Lens		
Position of Object	Real or Virtual	Magnified or Reduced	Inverted or Erect
Beyond 2f			
At 2f			
At f			
Within f			

83 Lensless Lens

Purpose

To investigate the operation of a pinhole "lens"

Required Equipment/Supplies

3 in. × 5 in. card
straight pin
meterstick

Discussion

The image formed through a pinhole is in focus no matter where the object is located. In this activity, you will use a pinhole to enable you to see nearby objects more clearly than you can without it.

Procedure

Step 1: Bring this printed page closer and closer to your eye until you cannot focus on it any longer. Even though your pupil is relatively small, your eye does not function as a pinhole camera because it does not focus well on nearby objects.

Look at print close up.

Step 2: With a straight pin, poke a pinhole about 1 cm from the edge of a 3" × 5" card. Hold the card in front of your eye and read these instructions through the pinhole. Bright light is needed. Bring the page closer and closer to your eye until it is a few centimeters away. You should be able to read clearly. Quickly take the pinhole away and see if you can still read the words.

1. Did the print appear magnified when observed through the pinhole?

   _____

   _____

Analysis

2. Did the pinhole actually magnify the print?

   _____

   _____

   _____

   _____

   _____

   _____

   _____

3. Why was the page of instructions dimmer when seen through the pinhole than when seen using your eye alone?

   _____

   _____

4. A nearsighted person cannot see distant objects clearly without corrective lenses. Yet, such a person can see distant objects clearly through a pinhole. Explain how this is possible. (And if you are nearsighted yourself, try it!)

   _____

   _____

   _____

84   Air Lens

Purpose

To apply knowledge of lenses to a different type of lens system

Required Equipment/Supplies

2 depression microscope slides
light source
screen

Discussion

Ordinary lenses are made of glass. A glass lens that is thicker at the center than at the edge is convex in shape, converges light, and is called a converging lens. A glass lens that is thinner at the middle than at the edge is concave in shape, diverges light, and is called a diverging lens.

Suppose you had an air space that was thicker at the center than at the edges and was surrounded by glass. This would comprise a sort of "convex air lens." What would it do to light? This activity will let you find out.

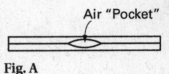

Fig. A

Procedure 🖐

Step 1: A convex air lens encased in glass can be produced by placing two depression microscope slides together, as shown in Figure A.

Construct convex air lens.

1. Predict whether this arrangement makes a diverging or converging lens. Explain your prediction.

_____

_____

_____

_____

_____

_____

Step 2: Use your lens with a light source and screen to check your prediction.

2. What do you discover?

_____

_____

_____

_____

Analysis

3. Why is the statement "The shape of a lens determines whether it is a converging or diverging lens" not always true?

_____

_____

_____

4. Draw ray diagrams for both a *convex* and a *concave* air lens encased in glass to show what these lenses do to light rays passing through them.

_____

_____

_____

_____

_____

_____

85 Bifocals

Purpose

To investigate the nature, position, and size of images formed by a converging lens.

Required Equipment/Supplies

converging lens
small amount of modeling clay
cardboard
meterstick
night-light with clear, 7-watt bulb

Optional Equipment/Supplies

data plotting software
computer

Discussion

The use of lenses to aid vision may have occurred as early as the tenth century in China. Eyeglasses came into more common use in Europe in the fifteenth century. Have you ever wondered how they work? In Experiment 80, Funland, you learned that the size and location of an image formed by a concave mirror is determined by the size and location of the object. In this experiment, you will investigate these relationships for a converging glass lens.

Procedure 🔧

Step 1: A converging lens focuses parallel light rays to a *focal point*. The distance from the center of a lens to the focal point is called the *focal length, f*. Measure the focal length of the lens by having it convert a parallel beam of light into a converging beam that comes to a small spot on a screen. Use the filament of a lit, clear, 7-watt bulb as a source of approximately parallel light and a piece of cardboard as a small screen. Record your measurement below to the nearest 0.1 cm. Also, record the number of your lens.

focal length = _____ cm

lens number = _____

Measure focal length.

Length
f

Parallel
Light

Focal
Point

Step 2: The rays of light striking the lens may not be parallel. What effect, if any, would this have on your measured value for the focal length? What effect would moving the light source farther away have? Move it farther away and record the focal length to the nearest 0.1 cm. (If a better source of parallel light is available, use it to find the focal length of your lens.)

focal length $f =$ _____ cm

Find inverted image with lens.

7-W Bulb   Lens   Screen

Fig. A

Step 3: Use a small amount of modeling clay at the bottom of the lens as a lens holder. Arrange a screen and a light source as shown in Figure A. Observe the image of the filament on the screen, and move the screen until the image of the filament is as sharp as possible. Where, in relation to one focal length from the lens, is the object when the image appears upside down (inverted)? What is the relative size of the image (magnified or reduced) and the object (the filament)? Is the image real or virtual? Record your findings in Data Table A.

Data Table A

Position of Object	Nature of Image		
	Real or Virtual?	Magnified?	Inverted or Erect?
Beyond f			
At f			
Within f			

Find erect image with lens.

Step 4: Where, in relation to one focal length from the lens, is the object when the image appears right-side up (erect)? What is the relative size of the image compared with the object? Is the image real or virtual? Record your findings in Data Table A.

Step 5: Is there a distance of the object from the lens for which no image appears at all? If so, what is this distance relative to the focal length? Record this position in Data Table A.

Measure d_i and d_o.

d_o (cm)	d_i (cm)

Data Table B

Step 6: Position the lens two focal lengths away from the light source to form an image on the screen on the other side of the lens as in Figure A. The distance between the object and the *focal point* closest to it is the distance d_o, and the distance between the other focal point and the image is the image distance d_i. Record the distances d_o and d_i in Data Table B. Move the lens 5 cm farther away from the light source, and reposition the screen until the image comes back into focus. Repeat these 5-cm movements five more times, recording d_o and d_i each time.

Step 7: Plot d_i (vertical axis) vs. d_o (horizontal axis), then different powers of each, to discover the mathematical relation between d_i and d_o. Does any combination give a linear graph through the origin and, thus, a direct proportion? If available, use data plotting software to plot your data.

1.   What mathematical relationship exists between d_i and d_o?

_____

Step 8: You can locate the position of the image in Figure B using the ray-diagram method. Draw the path of the light ray that leaves the tip of the arrow parallel to the principal axis.

Fig. B

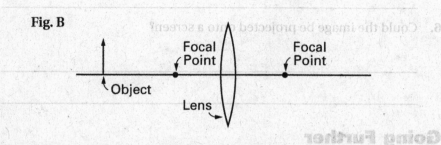

2. Where does this ray go after it is refracted?

_____

Draw the light ray that leaves the tip of the arrow and passes through the focal point.

3. Where does this light ray go after it is refracted?

_____

_____

Now, draw the paths of these two light rays after they are refracted. At the point where they cross, an image of the tip of the arrow is formed.

Step 9: Use the ray-diagram method to locate the image of the object in Figure C. Draw the path of the ray that leaves the tip of the arrow parallel to the principal axis and is refracted by the lens. Trace another ray that heads toward the lens in the same direction as if it *originated* from the focal point and is refracted by the lens.

Fig. C

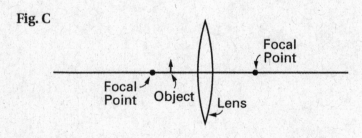

4. Do the refracted rays *actually* cross?

_____

_____

5. Where do they *appear* to cross?

_____

_____

6. Could the image be projected onto a screen?

_____

_____

Going Further

Step 10: Use two converging lenses to see if you can create a magnified image of a distant object. Sketch your arrangement of lenses with their relative positions and focal lengths. (Had you been the *first* person to have discovered, 400 years ago, that two converging lenses can make a telescope, your name would be the answer to questions in science classes today!)

_____

_____

_____

_____

_____

_____

_____

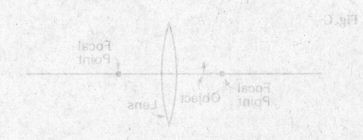

_____

_____

         Focal Length of a Diverging Lens

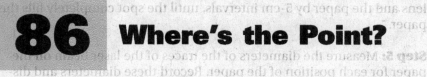

86 Where's the Point?

	15
	20

Data Table A

Purpose

To measure the focal length of a diverging lens

Required Equipment/Supplies

low-powered helium-neon laser
diverging lens
sheet of white paper
meterstick
graph paper (if computer is not used)

Optional Equipment/Supplies

computer
data plotting software
printer

Discussion

Parallel light rays are brought to a focus at the focal point of a converging lens. Ray diagrams are useful for understanding this. Parallel light rays are *not* brought to a focus by a diverging lens. Ray diagrams or other techniques are essential for understanding this. In this experiment, you will use a laser to simulate a ray diagram for a diverging lens. Lasers are fun!

Procedure

Step 1: Carefully (lasers are delicate!) place the laser on a table. Do not point it at any mirrors, windows, or persons.

Set up laser.

Step 2: Place a diverging lens in front of the laser. Turn on the laser. Use the sheet of white paper to observe that the beam is very narrow as it comes out of the laser, but after going through the lens, it spreads out into an ever-widening cone.

Observe diverging laser beam.

Step 3: Place the sheet of paper against a book. Hold the paper 5 cm beyond the lens that is in the laser beam. The red spot made by the beam should be in the center of the paper. With a pen or pencil, trace the outline of the red spot. Label the outline "distance 5 cm."

Distance From Lens (cm)	Diameter of Laser Spot (cm)
5	
10	
15	
20	

Data Table A

Step 4: Move the paper 5 cm farther away from the lens, and again trace the outline of the spot that is produced. Label the outline with the new distance. Repeat this procedure, increasing the distance between the lens and the paper by 5-cm intervals, until the spot completely fills the paper.

Step 5: Measure the diameters of the traces of the laser beam on the paper for each position of the paper. Record these diameters and distances from the lens in Data Table A.

Step 6: Plot a graph of the beam diameter (vertical axis) vs. the distance (horizontal axis) between the lens and the paper. Allow room on your graph for negative distances (to the left of the vertical axis.) If available, use data plotting software to plot your data.

Step 7: To find the distance from the lens at which the beam diameter would be zero, extend your line until it intersects the horizontal axis. The negative distance along the horizontal axis is the focal length of the diverging lens. If you are using data plotting software, include a printout of the graph with your lab report.

focal length of lens = _____ cm

Analysis

The focal length of a convex lens is the distance from the lens where parallel light rays are brought to a focus. Why is it impossible to find the focal length of a diverging lens in this manner?

_____

_____

_____

_____

87 Rainbows Without Rain

Purpose

To observe and develop a hypothesis about the phenomenon of light interference

Required Equipment/Supplies

soap-bubble solution
wire frame for soap films
large, flat, rimmed pan (such as a cookie sheet)
oil
2 microscope slides or glass plates
2 rubber bands

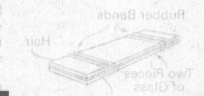

Discussion

A rainbow is produced by the refraction and reflection of light from drops of water in the sky. Rainbow colors, however, can be produced in a variety of ways. Some of these ways will be explored in this lab activity.

Procedure

Step 1: Pour some of the bubble solution into the flat pan. Place the loop of the wire frame into the solution. Hold the frame in a vertical position. Look at the soap film with the room lights behind you, reflecting off the film.

1. List as many observations as you can of what you saw in the soap film.

_____

_____

2. How would you explain these observations?

_____

_____

Step 2: During or after a rainfall, you may have noticed brilliant colors on a wet driveway or parking lot where oil has dripped from a car engine. To reproduce this situation, cover the bottom of the pan with a thin layer of water. Place a drop of oil on the water, and look at the oil slick with various angles of incident light.

3. List as many observations as you can of the oil on the water.

_____

_____

_____

4. How would you explain these observations?

_____

_____

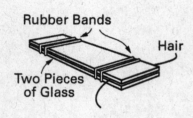

Rubber Bands

Hair

Two Pieces
of Glass

Step 3: Make a very thin wedge of air between two glass plates or microscope slides. You can do this by placing a hair across one end between the two. Fasten both ends together with rubber bands. Try to observe small repeating colored bands in the air wedge.

5. List your observations.

_____

_____

_____

6. How would you explain these observations?

_____

_____

Analysis

7. Summarize any patterns in your observations.

_____

_____

_____

88   What's My Lambda?

Purpose

To use the basic principles of diffraction and interference to measure the wavelength of laser light

Required Equipment/Supplies

laser
metersticks or measuring tape
diffraction grating(s)
CD, DVD, and large binder clip

Discussion

Diffraction is a beautiful example of interference. When waves overlap and reinforce each other, they *constructively interfere*. Likewise, when two waves overlap and cancel one another, they *destructively interfere*.

Study Figure A. Waves from S spread out in all directions. Waves that impinge on the slits of a grating at S1 and S2 likewise spread out in all directions. Look at the waves from S1 and S2 which converge at "a." Since they travel exactly the same distance they arrive at the same time; they are in phase with each other. They constructively interfere and form a bright fringe called the *central maximum* (also called the *zeroth* fringe).

Now look at the waves from S1 and S2 that converge at "b." Since the waves from S2 travel exactly one-half wavelength farther than those from S1, the waves from S2 lag behind those from S1 by one-half wavelength; they are out of phase with each other. Therefore, they destructively interfere and form a dark fringe.

Now look at the waves from S1 and S2 that converge at "c." The waves from S2 travel exactly one wavelength farther than those from S1. Since the waves from S2 lag behind those of S1 by one complete wavelength, they are back in step with each other; they are in phase and constructively interfere. They form a bright fringe called the first-order bright fringe.

In summary, when the path-lengths differ by whole-number multiples of wavelengths (1λ, 2λ, 3λ, etc.), the result is constructive interference and bright fringes occur. Likewise, when the path-lengths differ by *odd* numbers of half-wavelengths ($\frac{1}{2}\lambda$, $\frac{3}{2}\lambda$, $\frac{5}{2}\lambda$, etc.), the result is destructive interference and dark fringes occur.

Let's take a closer look at waves that form the bright fringes. To see how these path differences cause fringes for

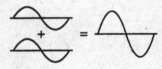

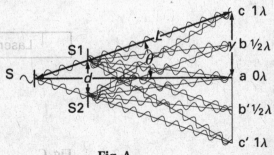

Fig. A

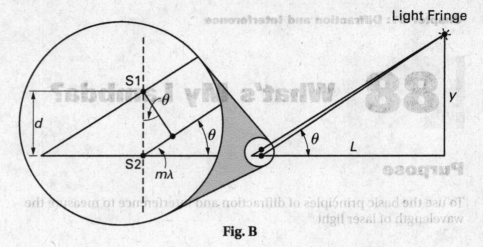

Fig. B

gratings, study Figure B. Since the distance between the slits of the grating is very small compared to the distance to the screen, the waves from each slit are very nearly parallel. Notice that the small triangle next to the slits is similar to the large triangle with the screen where the fringes are formed. Upon careful inspection, the extra distance that waves travel from S2 compared to S1 equals $d \sin \theta$. Since $\sin \theta$ is y/L, this relationship can be summarized by the following formula:

$$m\lambda = d \sin \theta$$

where m is the order of the spectrum (or the number of fringes from the central fringe), λ is the wavelength of the light being diffracted, d is the distance between slits in the grating, and θ is the angle between the central fringe and the mth fringe.

Since we know the spacing of the slits or grooves of the diffraction grating, we can measure the angle the laser light is diffracted to compute the wavelength of laser light.

Procedure ⚠

CAUTION: *Avoid shining laser light into people's eyes.*

Step 1: The distance between slits or grooves (usually referred to as *lines*) on the grating will be supplied by your teacher. Typically, this is in lines/mm or lines/inch. If it's lines/inch, you'll need to convert it using conversion 1 inch = 25.4 mm. Obtain the value for n from your teacher.

$n = \underline{\qquad}$ lines/mm

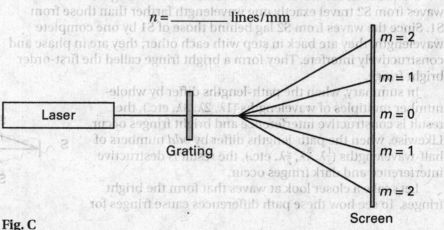

Fig. C

Step 2: Arrange the laser so that it shines directly into the diffraction grating producing a fringe pattern on a screen located about a meter away as shown in Figure C. If space permits, you can use a white board as a screen. Measure the distance from the grating to the screen, L, and the distance to the first ($m = 1$) bright fringe, y. Record your values for y and L, and then compute the wavelength of the laser.

$$y = \underline{\hspace{3cm}}$$

$$L = \underline{\hspace{3cm}}$$

Since $\sin \theta = y/L$, calculate $\sin \theta$ by measuring y and L, where y is the distance between the zeroth fringe and the first-order fringe and L is the distance the laser light travels to the first fringe. You'll note the fringe spacings are *nonlinear* (not equally spaced), becoming closer with higher m's. Depending on distance from the laser and ruler, y is likely to be several centimeters. Since $m = 1$ for the first fringe, the wavelength formula becomes:

$$\lambda = \frac{1}{m} (d \sin \theta) = d\frac{y}{(L)}$$

Step 3: Calculate the wavelength of the laser light.

$$\lambda_{\text{measured}} = \underline{\hspace{3cm}} \text{ m}$$

Step 4: How well does your computed value of the wavelength compare with the actual value (as supplied by your teacher)? If they are available, repeat using lasers of different wavelengths. Record your results.

$$\lambda_{\text{given}} = \underline{\hspace{3cm}} \text{ m}$$

_____

_____

Step 5: Use a laser of known wavelength to figure out how many lines or slits per millimeter that grating has. This time, shine a laser directly through the diffraction grating so that you get a horizontal pattern on a screen. Position the screen a meter away from the laser and grating. Measure the distance from the central maximum to the second-order maximum. Use the formula $m\lambda = d \sin \theta$ to find d, the width of the slits or lines on the diffraction grating. Show your calculations.

$$d = \underline{\hspace{3cm}} \text{ mm/line}$$

Step 6: The number of lines per millimeter, n, is the reciprocal of d. Compare your calculated value for n to the value stamped on the grating or supplied by your teacher.

$n = 1/d = \underline{\hspace{2cm}}$ lines/mm   % difference = $\underline{\hspace{2cm}}$

_____

_____

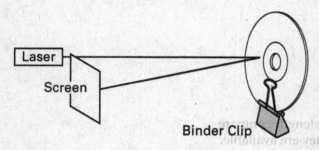

d

Disc Rotation

← Pit

Focused Laser Beam

Fig. D

Going Further

The bottom side of a compact disc is a highly reflective surface containing a spiral of "pits." If stretched out, this spiral would be about 5 km long! The pits are arranged in a fashion similar to that shown in Figure D. Each pit is 0.5 μm (0.5×10⁻⁶m) wide and is separated from each adjoining row by a distance of 1.6 μm—an industrial standard. The spiral of pits behaves much the same as a diffraction grating. You probably suspected this because of the rainbow of colors reflected from them.

When a laser beam is reflected off the bottom side of the disc, a familiar diffraction pattern is formed. If the angle of the laser beam is small, the distance between the rows of pits, d, can be estimated by:

$$d = \frac{m\lambda}{\sin \theta}$$

where m is the diffraction order, and θ is the angular position of the mth maximum (bright fringe).

Laser

Screen

Binder Clip

Fig. E

Step 7: Arrange a disc, laser, and screen as shown in Figure E. Direct the laser beam so that it strikes the disc approximately halfway up the CD, as shown in Figure F. Mount the CD using a large binder clip as shown. The binder clip makes it easy to adjust the height of the CD so that the laser beam strikes the horizontal diameter of the CD. This arrangement will give you a horizontal diffraction pattern on the screen so that the first-, second-, third-order (etc.) maximums will appear on either side of the bright central maximum.

Step 8: Determine the angular position, θ, of the first-order maximum, from the geometry of your experiment. Since the angle is large, you *cannot* use the small angle approximation that sin θ = tan θ.

$\theta =$ _____

Step 9: Calculate the distance d between the pits. How does your value compare with 1.6 μm? Compute the percentage difference.

$d_{CD} =$ _____

% difference = _____

Step 10: Repeat using a DVD. How does your measured value for the distance between the pits for a CD and a DVD compare?

$d_{DVD} =$ _____

_____

_____

_____

_____

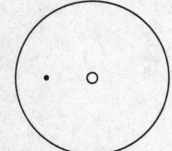

Fig. F

89 Static Cling

Purpose

To observe some of the effects of static electricity

Required Equipment/Supplies

electroscope
hard rubber rod and fur *or* glass rod and silk
plastic golf-club tube
foam rubber
plastic foam "peanuts" or packing material
coin with insulated connected string
empty soup or soda can, with insulated connecting string

Discussion

Have you ever been shocked after walking on a carpet and reaching for
a doorknob? Have you ever found your sock hiding inside one of your
shirts just after it came out of the clothes dryer? Have you ever seen a
lightning bolt from closer range than you might like? All of these situations arise due to *static electricity*. After this activity, you should understand its behavior a bit better.

Procedure

Step 1: Make sure the electroscope is discharged (neutral) by touching
the probe with your finger. The leaves will drop down as far as possible.

   CAUTION: *Do not open the electroscope in an effort to adjust the
position of the leaves. NEVER touch the leaves.*

Step 2: Rub a hard rubber rod with fur, or a glass rod with silk. The rubber rod will become negatively charged, while the glass rod will become
positively charged. Touch the probe of the electroscope with the charged
rod.

1. What happens to the leaves of the electroscope?

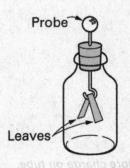

Probe

Leaves

Activity

2. What kind of charge is on the leaves?

_____

_____

Charge plastic tube.

Step 3: Discharge the electroscope by touching the probe with your finger. Charge a plastic tube by rubbing it with a piece of foam rubber. Observe what happens when you bring the charged tube close to (but not touching) the electroscope, and then move the tube away.

3. Record what happens.

_____

_____

Charge electroscope by induction.

Step 4: Devise a way to leave a charge on the electroscope, using the charged plastic tube but without touching the tube to the probe.

4. Record the method you used to charge the electroscope by induction.

_____

_____

_____

Test charge on electroscope.

Step 5: Test whether the charge on the electroscope is positive or negative by bringing a charged glass or rubber rod close to (but not touching) the probe.

5. Is the charge on the electroscope positive or negative? Explain how you can tell.

_____

_____

Explore packing "peanuts."

Step 6: Charge the plastic tube. Now put some packing "peanuts" out on the table. Try to pick them up with the charged tube, or pour some over the charged tube. See how many different ways you can make the "peanuts" interact with the charged tube.

6. Describe and explain the behavior of the "peanuts."

_____

_____

Explore charge on tube.

Step 7: Charge the plastic tube by rubbing it with different materials. Each time, charge the electroscope by induction, as in Step 4, and test whether the charge on the electroscope is positive or negative.

90 Sticky Electrostatics

Purpose

To investigate the nature of static electricity

Required Equipment/Supplies

3/4" tape, Scotch Magic Tape (no substitutes)
fresh balloons
digital voltmeter (DVM), with 10 mega-ohm input impedance or greater

Discussion

When discussing static electricity, many people focus on the need to rub materials together in order to generate separations of charge. Some state that friction creates the separation of charge. Is this statement always true—or only some of the time? What *is* the nature of electrostatic charge?

Forget rubbing for now and consider two objects simply touched together. Their surfaces adhere slightly. Chemical bonds form at the regions of contact between the molecules of both surfaces. If the surfaces are not of the same material, the bonds will probably be *polarized*, with the shared bonding electrons staying with one surface more than with the other. When the two objects are pulled apart again, the bonds rupture and one surface may end up with electrons from the other surface. Now the surfaces are no longer neutral. One surface has extra electrons (electron *surplus*) while the other surface has fewer electrons (electron *deficient*) compared to the number of protons in each substance. These charges are then separated as the surfaces are pulled apart. As the objects are separated, the charges move with them.

If the surfaces involved are rough or fibrous, friction *does* play a part in surface charging. If you touch a balloon to someone's hair, the hair really only touches the balloon in tiny spots, and the total area of contact is extremely small. However, if the balloon is *dragged* across the hair, then the successive areas of contact add up. Rubbing a balloon on your head increases the total area of contact, so it increases the amount of charge that is separated. However, the friction does not *cause* the charging. You can rub two balloons together as much as you like, and you will never create any "static electricity." Contact between *dissimilar* materials is required.

Activity

Procedure

Step 1: Pull a couple of strips of plastic adhesive tape from a roll. Each one should be about 12–20 cm long. Hold them up by their ends, then slowly bring them side by side. What happens? Notice that they repel each other. If you try to get the dangling lengths of tape to touch each other, the tape will swerve and gyrate to frustrate your efforts. Obviously the tape has become electrically charged. But how? No friction was involved.

_____

_____

Step 2: One at a time, pass each of the strips of tape lightly between your fingers so as to discharge or neutralize them, then hold the two strips near each other again. Now how do the strips behave? If discharged, they will not repel each other. You've managed to discharge the strips by touching them.

Step 3: Fold over a couple of centimeters of the end of each strip. This gives you a non-sticky handle to work with. Carefully stick the two strips to each other so the sticky side of one strip adheres to the "dry" side of the other. You should end up with a double-thick layer of tape which is sticky on one side, and which has two tabs at the end. Now grasp the tabs and rapidly peel the strips apart. Keep them distantly separated, then slowly bring them together again. How do the strips behave this time?

_____

Step 4: Blow-up two fresh balloons. Do not rub them against your hair or clothing. See if you can "create" static electricity by rubbing two electrically neutral balloons together. What is your result?

_____

Step 5: Discharge your two strips of tape by running each one between your fingers. Hold them near each other to verify that they neither attract nor repel one another. Now stick the two strips together, but this time do it with the adhesive sides facing one another. Peel the strips apart again, then bring them near each other. Are the strips now neutral, or do they attract one another?

Step 6: Finally, peel four separate strips from a roll and neutralize them with your fingers. Then stick them together in pairs with the sticky side of one stuck to the dry side of the other. Now peel each pair apart so you have four charged strips.

Hold pairs of these strips together in different combinations. What do you discover? You can determine the polarity of the four strips by rubbing a balloon on your hair (rubber always acquires a negative charge when it touches hair), then holding it near the strip being investigated. If the balloon and the tape strip repel, the strip is negatively charged.

Analysis

1. How did the strips of tape become charged in Step 3?

2. How do you explain why the strips of tape are *not* charged when peeled apart in Step 5 while they *are* in Step 4?

3. Paper is a reasonably good conductor compared to plastic tape. Explain why masking tape does not work well for this activity.

Going Further

A digital voltmeter (DVM) can be used to detect the sign of the charge that accumulates on an object. Turn the "DC Volts" scale of the meter to maximum sensitivity (some newer models are auto-ranging and only require being set to "DC Volts"). When brought near a charged object, the digital display not only indicates a small voltage, but the sign of the charge on the object as well. Place the common, or ground probe, off to one side out of the way. The meter may give a small positive or negative readout—depending on its environment. Allow the meter to stabilize.

Use the positive probe to investigate the sign of the charge on objects. When a positively charged object is brought near the probe, the positive charge on the object "pushes" on positive charges on the probe through the meter, causing the reading on the meter to incre ase. When a negatively charged object is brought near the probe, the negative charge on the object "pushes" on negative charges on the probe, causing the reading on the meter to decrease. Therefore, the sign of the charge on the object is related to the change of the reading on the meter—regardless of the sign of the original readout. As you investigate the sign of the charge of objects, you will note that the change in the readout "decays." The readout of the meter decays due to the transient nature of how the meter works—not because the charge on the object is dissipating. The decay rate depends on the input impedance of your particular meter. The greater the input impedance is, the slower the decay. The lower the input impedance is, the faster the decay.

Step 7: Pull a 12–20 cm strip of tape from a roll. Being careful not to neutralize the tape, use a DVM to determine the sign of the charge on the strip of tape. Repeat for several strips. Record your results below.

sign of the charge on the strip _____

Use the DVM to probe the roll of tape after pulling a strip of tape from the roll. What do you find?

_____

_____

_____

_____

_____

_____

91   Sparky, the Electrician

Purpose

To study various arrangements of a battery and bulbs and the effects of those arrangements on bulb brightness

Required Equipment/Supplies

size-D dry cell (battery)
6 pieces of bare copper wire
3 flashlight bulbs
3 bulb holders
second size-D dry cell (optional)

Discussion

A dry cell (commonly called a battery) is a source of electric energy. Many arrangements are possible to get this energy from dry cells to flashlight bulbs. In this activity, you will test these arrangements to see which makes the bulbs brightest.

Procedure

Step 1: Arrange one bulb (without a holder), one battery, and wire in as many ways as you can to make the bulb emit light. Sketch each of your arrangements, including failures as well as successes. Label the sketches of the successes.

1. Describe the similarities among your successful trials.

_____

_____

_____

_____

_____

_____

Step 2: Use a bulb in a bulb holder (instead of a bare bulb), one battery, and wire. Arrange these in as many ways as you can to make the bulb light.

2. What two parts of the bulb does the holder make contact with?

_____

_____

_____

Step 3: Using one battery, light as many bulbs in holders as you can. Sketch each of your arrangements, and note the ones that work.

3. Compare your results with those of other students. What arrangement(s), using only one battery, made the most bulbs glow?

_____

_____

_____

Step 4: Diagrams for electric circuits use symbols like the ones in Figure A.

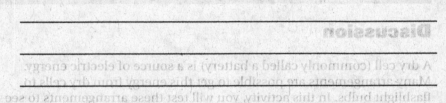

——————— Wire

——|·|—— Battery

Fig. A   —WWW— Light bulb or any device that uses electrical energy in a circuit

Connect the bulbs in holders, one battery, and wire as shown in each circuit diagram of Figure B. Circuits like these are examples of *series circuits*.

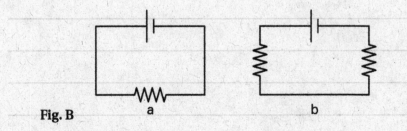

Fig. B   a   b

4. Do the bulbs light in each of these series circuits?

_____

_____

_____

Step 5: In the circuit with two bulbs, unscrew one of the bulbs.

5. What happens to the other bulb?

_____

_____

Step 6: Set up the circuit shown in the circuit diagram of Figure C. A circuit like this is called a *parallel circuit*.

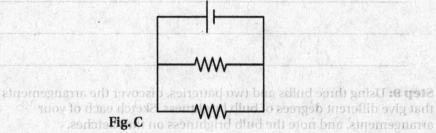

Fig. C

6. Do both bulbs light in this parallel circuit?

_____

_____

Step 7: Unscrew one of the bulbs in the parallel circuit.

7. What happens to the other bulb?

_____

_____

8. In your own words, describe the differences between series and parallel circuits.

_____

_____

_____

_____

Going Further

Step 8: Using two batteries, light as many bulbs as you can. Sketch each of your arrangements, and note the ones that work.

_____

_____

9. What arrangement(s), using two batteries, lit the most bulbs?

_____

_____

_____

Step 9: Using three bulbs and two batteries, discover the arrangements that give different degrees of bulb brightness. Sketch each of your arrangements, and note the bulb brightness on the sketches.

_____

_____

10. How many different degrees of brightness could you obtain using three bulbs and two batteries? Did other students use different arrangements?

_____

_____

_____

_____

_____

92 Brown Out

Purpose

To investigate charging and discharging a capacitor

Required Equipment/Supplies

CASTLE Kit (available from PASCO)
  or
1 25,000 μF capacitor (20 volts nonpolar)
2 #14 lightbulbs (round) (no substitutions allowed!)
2 #48 lightbulbs (long) (no substitutions allowed!)
4 lightbulb sockets
1 packet of 12 alligator leads
1 D-cell battery holder and 3 D-cells

Discussion

When you switch on a flashlight, the maximum brightness of the bulb occurs immediately. If a capacitor is in the circuit, however, there is a noticeable delay before maximum brightness occurs. When the circuit contains a capacitor, the flow of charge through the circuit may take a noticeable time. How much time depends upon the resistance of the resistor and the charge capacity of the capacitor. In this activity, we will place a resistor (lightbulb) between the battery and the capacitor to be charged. By using bulbs of different resistances, the charging and discharging times are easily observed.

Procedure

Step 1: Connect a battery, two long bulbs, and a blue capacitor (25,000 μF) as shown in Figure A. Leave one wire (lead) to the battery disconnected. *Close* the circuit by connecting the lead to the battery and observe how long the bulb remains lit. You are *charging the capacitor*.

Step 2: Disconnect the leads from the battery and remove the battery from the circuit. Connect the two leads that were connected to the battery to each other as shown in Figure B. Observe the length of time the bulbs remain lit. This process is called *discharging the capacitor*.

Step 3: Replace the long (#48) bulbs in the circuit with round (#12) bulbs and charge the capacitor. Observe the length of time the bulbs remain lit. Remove the battery from the circuit as in Step 2 and discharge the capacitor through the round bulbs. Observe the time the bulbs remain lit. Which bulbs remain lit longer as the capacitor charges and discharges—long or round bulbs?

Assemble the circuit and charge the capacitor.

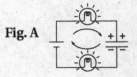

Fig. A

Fig. B

To account for the different times the bulbs are lit, we can make the following hypotheses:

- If bulbs affect the amount of charge that passes through them, bulbs that remain lit longer allow more charge to pass through them. The charge would be stored in the capacitor.
- If, however, bulbs affect the rate of charge flow rather than the amount of charge that flows, then bulbs that remain lit longer will increase the time during which charge flows through them.

Charge the capacitor.

Step 4: Charge the capacitor through two long bulbs. Now remove the long bulbs from their sockets and replace them with round bulbs, being careful not to accidentally discharge the capacitor.

1. Suppose the capacitor stores the same amount of charge no matter what type of bulbs are used during charging. Will discharging through round bulbs take more, less, or the same time as in Step 3—when the capacitor was *charged* through round bulbs?

2. If, instead, a longer charging time indicates more charge is stored in the capacitor than occurs with a shorter charging time, will discharging now through round bulbs take more, less, or the same time as it did in Step 4?

Discharge the capacitor.

Step 5: Remove the battery from the circuit and discharge the capacitor. Is the time the bulbs remain lit longer, shorter, or the same as in Step 3?

Analysis

3. (a) What is one use of a capacitor?

(b) Does the amount of charge stored in a capacitor depend on the type of bulbs through which it was charged? Explain.

4. Is it true that the type of bulb affects the rate at which charge flows through it? Why or why not?

93 Ohm Sweet Ohm

Purpose

To investigate how current varies with voltage and resistance

Required Equipment/Supplies

nichrome wire apparatus with bulb
4 1.5-volt batteries
  or
2 Genecon hand-crank generators

Discussion

Normally, it is desirable for wires in an electric circuit to stay cool. Red-hot wires can melt and cause short circuits. There are notable exceptions, however. Nichrome wire is a high-resistance wire capable of glowing red-hot without melting. It is commonly used as the heating element in toasters, ovens, stoves, hair dryers, and so forth. In this experiment, nichrome wire is used as a variable resistor. Doubling the length of a piece of wire doubles the resistance; tripling the length triples the resistance, and so on.

Tungsten wire is capable of glowing white-hot and is used as filaments in lightbulbs. Light and heat are generated as the current heats the high-resistance tungsten filament. The hotter the filament, the brighter the bulb. For the same voltage, a bright bulb (such as a 100-watt bulb) has a *lower* resistance than a dimmer bulb (such as a 25-watt bulb). Just as water flows with more difficulty through a thinner pipe, electrical resistance is greater for a thinner wire. Manufacturers make bulbs of different wattages by varying the thickness of the filaments, so we find that a 100-W bulb has a lower resistance and a thicker filament than a 25-W bulb.

In this lab, the brightness of the bulb will be used as a current indicator. A bright glow indicates a large current is flowing through the bulb; a dim glow means a small current is flowing.

Procedure

Step 1: Connect four D-cell batteries in series, so that the positive terminal is connected to the negative terminal in a battery holder as shown in Figure A. This arrangement, with Terminal #1 as ground, will provide you with a variable voltage supply as indicated in Table A.

Assemble the battery with four D-cells.

Data Table A

Terminal Numbers	Voltage (V)
1–2	1.5
1–3	3.0
1–4	4.5
1–5	6.0

Assemble the circuit and draw a circuit diagram.

Step 2: Assemble the circuit as shown in Figure B. Label one binding post of the nichrome wire "A" and the other "B." Attach the ground lead (#1) of the voltage supply to one side of a knife switch. Connect the other side of the switch to binding Post A on the thickest nichrome wire. Connect the 3-volt lead (#3) from the voltage supply to a clip lead of a test bulb. Attach the other clip lead of the test bulb to the other binding Post B on the nichrome wire.

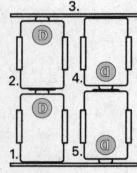

Fig. A

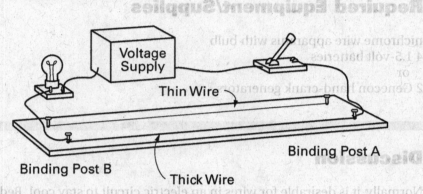

Fig. B

The voltage supply is now connected so that the current passes through two resistances: the bulb and the nichrome wire. You will vary the resistance in the circuit by moving the clip lead of the test bulb from binding Post B to binding Post A. Using the standard symbols for the circuit elements, draw a diagram that represents this series circuit.

Note: *Always apply power from battery packs by closing a switch and make your measurements quickly.* Leave the power on just long enough to make your measurements and then open the switch. *Leaving the power on in the circuit for long periods of time will drain your batteries and heat the wire, thereby changing its resistance.*

Observe the brightness of the bulb.

Step 3: After carefully checking all your connections, apply power to the circuit by closing the switch. Observe the intensity of the bulb as you move the test bulb lead from binding Post B toward A.

1. What happens to the brightness of the bulb as you move it from Binding Post B to A?

_____

_____

Repeat with thinner wire.

Step 4: Repeat using the thinner nichrome wire. Observe the relative brightness of the bulb as you move the bulb's lead closer to Binding Post A.

2. How does the brightness of the bulb with the thinner wire compare with the brightness of the bulb when connected to a thicker wire?

_____

_____

_____

3. What effects do the thickness and length of the wire have on its resistance?

_____

_____

_____

4. Does the current of the circuit increase or decrease as you move the lead closer to Binding Post B? As you move the lead from B to A, does the resistance of the circuit increase or decrease?

_____

_____

Step 5: Repeat Steps 1–2 using the 4.5 and 6-volt leads instead of the 3-volt leads.

5. How does the brightness of the test bulb compare for the two nichrome wires using 4.5 volts instead of 3 volts?

_____

_____

_____

6. Combining your results from Questions 4 and 5, how does the current in the circuit depend upon voltage and resistance?

_____

_____

Going Further

Step 6: Now insert an ammeter into the circuit as illustrated in Figure C. With the thicker piece of nichrome wire in the circuit, place the ammeter in series with the voltage supply between Terminal #1 of the voltage supply and the switch. The ammeter will read total current in the circuit. Measure the current in the circuit as you move the test bulb lead from B to A. Be sure to apply power *only* while making the measurements to prevent draining the batteries. Repeat using the thinner wire.

Note: *If you are not using a digital meter, you may have to reverse the polarity of the leads if the needle of the meter goes the wrong way (–) when power is applied.*

Install ammeter in the circuit and measure current.

Voltage
Supply

Fig. C

7. Do your results show a decrease in current as the resistance (or length of the wire) is increased?

_____

_____

8. Do your results show an increase in current as the voltage is increased?

_____

_____

9. How do the currents in the thicker and thinner wires compare when the same voltage is applied to the same lengths of wire?

_____

_____

_____

_____

94 Getting Wired

Purpose

To build a model that illustrates electric current

Required Equipment/Supplies

4 D-cells (1.5 volt batteries)
D-cell battery holder
3 alligator clip leads
2 bulbs and bulb holders

Discussion

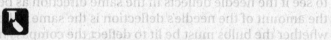

While we can float on a raft gliding down the Mississippi or ride in cars moving in traffic, nobody can *see* electric current flow. Even in the case of lightning, we are seeing the flash of hot glowing gases produced by electric current—not the current itself. However, we can infer the presence of electric current using lightbulbs and magnetic compasses in much the same way as a flag indicates the presence of wind. In this activity, you will build a *model* to study electric current.

Part A: What Is Happening in the Wires?

Procedure 🖐

Step 1: With the circuit arranged as shown in Figure A, turn the bulbs on and off by connecting and disconnecting one of the wires.

Observe the wires when the circuit is closed.

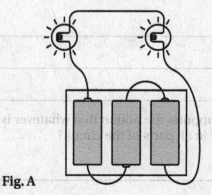

Fig. A

1. Is there any visual evidence that something is moving around the circuit when the bulbs are lit? For example, does one bulb light before the other? Does one bulb go out before the other? Is one bulb brighter than the other?

_____

_____

_____

_____

Position a compass underneath the wire.

Step 2: Place a magnetic compass on the table near the circuit with the needle pointing to the "N." With the bulbs unlit, place one of the wires on top of the compass parallel to the needle as in Figure B. Connect and disconnect a lead in the circuit several times while you observe the compass needle. Observe what happens to the needle when the bulb lights. Observe what happens to the needle when the bulbs go out.

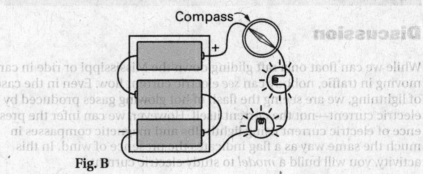

Fig. B

Step 3: Place the compass beneath the wire in different parts of the circuit. Be sure the needle is parallel to the wire when the bulbs are not lit. Observe the needle as you open and close the circuit several times. Look to see if the needle deflects in the same direction as before. Look to see if the amount of the needle's deflection is the same as before. Also, observe whether the bulbs must be lit to deflect the compass needle.

2. What evidence supports the notion that something is happening in the wires while the bulbs are energized?

_____

_____

_____

3. What evidence supports the notion that whatever is happening occurs uniformly in all parts of the circuit?

_____

_____

Part B: Is There Directionality to What Is Happening in the Circuit?

Procedure

Step 4: Arrange the circuit as in Figure A. Place one of the wires on top of the compass parallel to the needle. Open and close the circuit while you carefully observe the needle. Note whether the needle deflects clockwise or counterclockwise.

Observe the deflection of the compass.

Step 5: Reverse the leads from the battery without altering the circuit and compass. Do this by simply exchanging the lead connected to the positive terminal of the battery with the lead connected to the negative terminal. Open and close the circuit while you watch the compass needle. Watch the needle deflect and note whether it is clockwise or counterclockwise.

Reverse the leads from the battery and observe the deflection of the compass.

4. Is the direction of the deflection the same as in Step 4, before the leads to the battery were reversed? Is the amount of the needle's deflection the same as before?

_____

_____

_____

_____

5. Suppose something is flowing in the wires. Do you think the *direction* the needle is deflected is caused by the amount of the flow or the direction of the flow?

_____

_____

_____

Step 6: Remove one of the D-cells from the battery holder so that the battery holder only has two cells instead of three. Carefully observe deflection of the needle while you repeat Steps 4 and 5.

Remove one of the cells from the battery.

6. How do the size and direction of the compass needle's deflections compare when you use two cells instead of three?

_____

_____

_____

_____

Add two cells to the battery.

Step 7: Install two more D-cells in the battery holder so that it has four D-cells. Carefully observe deflection of the needle as you repeat Steps 4 and 5.

7. How do the deflections of the compass needle compare with those with two and three D-cells? Do you think the *size* of the needle's deflection is caused by *amount of the flow* or the *direction of the flow*?

_____

_____

Analysis

8. Hypothesize what is happening in the circuit when bulbs are lit.

_____

_____

9. Hypothesize what is happening in the circuit when the direction of the compass deflection reverses.

_____

_____

10. Hypothesize what is happening in the wires when the amount of the needle's deflection increases or decreases.

_____

_____

_____

11. What do you think the battery does?

_____

_____

_____

95 Cranking Up

Purpose

To observe and compare the work done in a series circuit and the work done in a parallel circuit

Required Equipment/Supplies

4 lightbulbs, sockets and clip leads   voltmeter
Genecon hand-crank generator   ammeter
parallel bulb apparatus

Procedure

Part A: Qualitative Investigation

Step 1: Assemble four bulbs in series as shown in Figure A. Screw all the bulbs into their sockets. Connect the sockets with clip leads.

     Connect one lead of a Genecon to one end of the string of bulbs and the other lead to the other end of the string. Crank the Genecon so that all the bulbs light up. Now, disconnect one of the bulbs from the string and reconnect the Genecon. Crank the Genecon so that the three remaining bulbs are energized to the same brightness as the four-bulb arrangement. How does the crank feel now? Repeat, removing one bulb at a time and comparing the cranking torque each time.

Assemble the circuit and crank the Genecon as you unscrew bulbs in series.

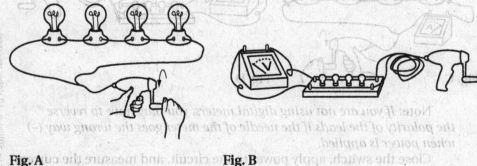

Fig. A   **Fig. B**

Step 2: Assemble the circuit with the parallel bulb apparatus, as shown in Figure B. Each end of the bulb apparatus has two terminals. Connect the leads of a voltmeter to one pair of terminals on one end of the apparatus. Connect the leads of the Genecon to the terminals on the other end of the apparatus. Crank the Genecon with all the bulbs unscrewed in the sockets so that they don't light. Then, have your partner screw them in one at a time as you crank on the Genecon. Try to keep the bulbs energized at the same brightness as each bulb is screwed into its socket.

Assemble the parallel circuit and crank the Genecon as you screw in the bulbs.

1. What do you notice about the *torque* required to crank the Genecon at a constant speed as more bulbs are added to the circuit?

_____

2. How would you describe the amount of torque required to crank the Genecon to energize four bulbs in series compared with that required for four bulbs in parallel?

_____

3. If all the bulbs in the series and parallel circuits are glowing equally brightly, is the energy expended (the work you are doing to crank the Genecon) the same?

_____

Part B: Quantitative Investigation— Resistors in Series

Now repeat Part A in a quantitative fashion using a voltmeter and an ammeter.

Assemble the circuit in series.

Step 3: Assemble four bulbs in a series circuit and connect the meters, as shown in Figure C. Connect the voltmeter in parallel with all four bulbs so you can measure the total voltage applied to the circuit. Then you will connect it in parallel with single bulbs to measure the voltage across each bulb. Connect the 3-volt lead from the voltage supply to one terminal of the bulbs and the ground connection to one lead of an ammeter. Connect the other lead of the ammeter to the second terminal of the bulbs. The ammeter will measure the *total* current in the circuit.

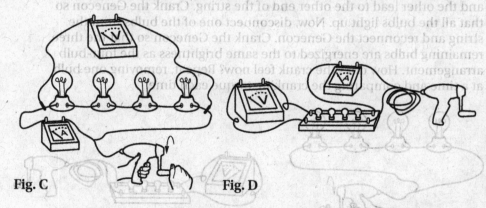

Fig. C   **Fig. D**

Note: *If you are not using digital meters, you may have to reverse the polarity of the leads if the needle of the meter goes the wrong way (–) when power is applied.*

Close the switch, apply power to the circuit, and measure the current in the circuit, the voltage applied to the circuit, and the voltage across each bulb. Record your results in Data Table A.

Step 4: Now remove one of the bulbs from the string, close the gap in the circuit, and repeat your measurements for three bulbs. Then remove the other bulbs one at a time, closing the gap in the circuit each time, and repeat the measurements. Record your data in Data Table A.

Number of Bulbs	Total Current (A)	Total Voltage (V)	Voltage Across Each Bulb (V)
1			
2			
3			
4			

Data Table A

Number of Bulbs	Total Current (A)	Total Voltage (V)	Voltage Across Each Bulb (V)
1			
2			
3			
4			

Data Table B

Step 5: Repeat using the 4.5-volt terminal of the voltage supply instead of the 3-volt terminal. Record your data in Data Table B.

Repeat using a different voltage.

4. Is there any change in brightness as the number of bulbs changes?

5. Does the voltage applied in the circuit change as you add more bulbs?

_____

6. How are the voltages across each bulb related to the applied voltage?

_____

_____

7. How does the current supplied by the battery change when more bulbs are added?

_____

8. Did any of the rules you discovered relating voltages and currents change when you applied 4.5 volts instead of 3 volts?

_____

Part C: Quantitative Investigation—Resistors in Parallel

Step 6: Assemble the circuit and connect the meters, as shown in Figure D. Connect the voltmeter in parallel with the bulbs by connecting the voltmeter to two terminals on one end of the parallel bulb apparatus. Connect the 3-volt lead from the voltage supply to one terminal of the parallel bulb apparatus. Connect the ground lead from the voltage supply to one lead of an ammeter; connect the other lead of the ammeter to the second terminal of the parallel bulb apparatus. The ammeter will measure the total current in the circuit.

Make sure the bulbs are not loose in their sockets. Close the switch and apply power to the circuit. Observe the brightness of the bulbs, then unscrew the bulbs one at a time.

Assemble the circuit in parallel.

Record your measurements of current and voltage.

Step 7: Screw the bulbs back in, one at a time, each time measuring the current in the circuit, the voltage applied to the circuit, and the voltage drop across each bulb. Record your data in Data Table C.

Number of Bulbs	Total Current (A)	Total Voltage (V)	Voltage Across Each Bulb (V)
1			
2			
3			
4			

Data Table C

Number of Bulbs	Total Current (A)	Total Voltage (V)	Voltage Across Each Bulb (V)
1			
2			
3			

Data Table D

Repeat using a different voltage.

Step 8: Repeat Steps 3 and 4 using the 4.5-volt terminal of the voltage supply instead of the 3-volt terminal. Record your data in Data Table D.

9. Is there any change in brightness as the number of bulbs changes?

    _____

10. Does the voltage across each bulb change as more bulbs are added to or subtracted from the circuit?

    _____

11. Does the applied voltage to the circuit change as you add more bulbs?

    _____

12. How does the current supplied by the battery change as the number of bulbs in the circuit changes?

    _____

    _____

    _____

    _____

13. Did the ratio of voltage and current change when you applied 4.5 volts instead of 3 volts?

    _____

96   3-Way Switch

Purpose

To explore ways to turn a lightbulb on or off from either one of two switches.

Required Equipment/Supplies

2.5-V DC lightbulb with socket
connecting wire
2 single-pole double-throw switches
2 1.5-V size-D dry cells connected in series in a holder

Discussion

Frequently, multistory homes have hallways with ceiling lights. It is convenient if you can turn a hallway light on or off from a switch located at either the top or bottom of the staircase. Each switch should be able to turn the light on or off, regardless of the previous setting of either switch. The same arrangement is often adopted in a room with two doors. In this activity, you will see how simple, but tricky, such a common circuit really is!

Procedure

Step 1: Examine a 3-volt battery (formed from two 1.5-volt dry cells with the positive terminal of one connected to the negative terminal of the other). Connect a wire from the positive terminal of the battery to the center terminal of a single-pole double-throw switch. Connect a wire from the negative terminal of the same battery to one terminal of the lightbulb socket. Connect the other terminal of the lightbulb socket to the center terminal of the other switch.

Step 2: Now interconnect the free terminals of the switches so that the bulb turns on or off from either switch. That is, when both switches are closed in either direction, moving either switch from one side to the other will always turn an unlit bulb on or a lit bulb off.

Step 3: Draw a simple circuit diagram of your successful circuit.

Single Pole
Double-Throw Switch

Devise working circuit.

Diagram 3-way switch.

Activity

Reverse polarity of battery.

Step 4: The polarity of a battery can be reversed in a circuit by switching the connections to the positive and negative terminals. Predict whether your successful circuit will work if you reverse the polarity of the battery.

prediction: _____

Now reverse the polarity and record the result.

result: _____

Interchange battery and bulb.

Step 5: Predict whether your successful circuit will work if you reconnect the circuit so that the battery is where the lightbulb is now, and vice versa.

prediction: _____

Now try it and record your results.

results: _____

Analysis

An ordinary switch has an "on" setting, which closes the circuit at that point, and an "off" setting, which opens the circuit at that point. On the switches you used in this activity, what function do the two "closed" settings on each switch have? Can either setting keep the circuit open independently of how the other switch is set?

_____

_____

_____

_____

_____

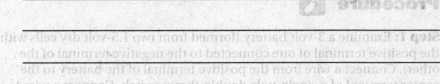

Single Pole
Double-Throw Switch

Chapter 36: Magnetism

97   3-D Magnetic Field

Purpose

To explore the shape of magnetic fields

Required Equipment/Supplies

2 bar magnets
iron filings
strong horseshoe magnet
sheet of clear plastic

5 to 10 small compasses
jar of iron filings in oil
paper

Discussion

A magnetic field cannot be seen directly, but its overall shape can be seen by the effect it has on iron filings.

Procedure

Step 1: Vigorously shake the jar of iron filings. Select the strongest horseshoe magnet available. Place the jar over one of the poles of the magnet and observe carefully. Place the jar at other locations around the magnet to observe how the filings line up.

1. What happened to the iron filings when they were acted upon by the magnetic field of the magnet?

_____

_____

_____

_____

Step 2: From all your observations, draw a sketch showing the direction of the magnetic field all around your magnet, as observed from the side. Also, draw a sketch as viewed from the end of the magnet.

Sketch magnetic field.

_____

_____

Observe orientation of compasses.

Step 3: Obtain two bar magnets and 5–10 small compasses. Note which end of each compass points toward the north. As you proceed with the activity, represent each compass as an arrow whose point is the north-pointing end.

Trace magnetic field lines.

Step 4: Trace one of the bar magnets on a piece of paper. Move the compasses around the magnet, and use arrows to draw the directions they point at each location. Link the arrows together by continuous lines to show the magnetic field.

Sketch magnetic field lines.

Step 5: Obtain a small quantity of iron filings and a sheet of clear plastic. Place the plastic on top of one of the bar magnets, and sprinkle a small quantity of iron filings over the plastic. It may be necessary to gently tap or jiggle the plastic sheet. The filings will line themselves up with the magnetic field. In the following space, sketch the pattern that the filings make. Repeat this step using the other bar magnet.

Repeat using two magnets.

Step 6: Repeat Step 5 for two bar magnets with like poles facing each other, such as N and N or S and S, and with unlike poles facing each other. Sketch the pattern of the filings in both situations.

2. Compare the methods of Steps 4 and 5 in terms of their usefulness in obtaining a quick and accurate picture of the magnetic field.

_____

_____

_____

3. Are there any limitations to either method?

_____

_____

_____

4. What generalizations can you make about magnetic field lines?

_____

_____

_____

98 You're Repulsive

Purpose

To observe the force on an electric charge moving in a magnetic field, and the current induced in a conductor moving in a magnetic field

Required Equipment/Supplies

cathode ray oscilloscope or computer with monitor
horseshoe magnet
bar magnet
compass
50-cm insulated wire
galvanometer or sensitive milliammeter
masking tape

Discussion

In this lab activity, you will explore the relationship between the magnetic field of a horseshoe magnet and the force that acts on a beam of electrons that move through the field. You will see that you can deflect the beam with different orientations of the magnet. If you had more control over the strength and orientation of the magnetic field, you could use it to "paint" a picture on the inside of a cathode ray tube with the electron beam. This is what happens in a television set.

A moving magnetic field can do something besides make a television picture. It can induce the electricity at the generating station to power the television set. You will explore this idea, too.

CAUTION: Do not bring a strong, demonstration magnet near a color TV or monitor.

Procedure

Step 1: If you are using an oscilloscope, adjust it so that only a spot occurs in the middle of the screen. This will occur when there is no horizontal sweep.

If you are using a computer monitor for the cathode ray tube, use a graphics program to create a spot at the center of the screen. Make a white spot on a black background.

Adjust monitor or oscilloscope so dot is centered.

Activity

You're Repulsive

1. The dot on the screen is caused by an electron beam that hits the screen. In what direction are the electrons moving?

_____

_____

Make sketches of different orientations of the magnet.

Step 2: If the north and south poles of your magnets are not marked, use a compass to determine whether a pole is a north or south pole, and label it with tape.

CAUTION: *Do not use large, demonstration magnets in this activity. Such magnets should not be brought close to any cathode ray tube, as they can cause permanent damage.*

Place the poles of the horseshoe magnet 1 cm from the screen. Try the orientations of the magnet shown in Figure A. Sketch arrows on Figure A to indicate the direction in which the spot moves in each case. Try other orientations of the magnet, and make sketches to show how the spot moves.

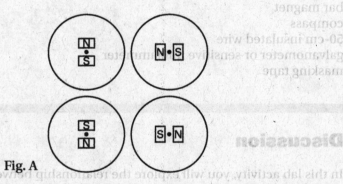

Fig. A

2. Recall that the magnetic field lines outside a magnet run from the north pole to the south pole. The spot moves in the direction of the magnetic force on the beam. How is the direction of the magnetic force on the beam related to the direction of the magnetic field?

_____

_____

_____

Note effects of bar magnet on spot.

Step 3: Aim one pole of a bar magnet directly toward the spot. Record your observations.

_____

_____

Step 4: Change your aim so that the pole of the bar magnet points to one side of the spot. Record your observations.

_____

_____

3. In general, what are the relative directions of the electron beam, the magnetic field, and the magnetic force on the beam for maximum deflection of the electron beam?

_____

_____

_____

Step 5: With a long insulated wire, make a three-loop coil with a diameter of approximately 8 cm. Tape the loops together. Connect the ends of the wire to the two terminals of a galvanometer or sensitive milliammeter. Explore the effects of moving a bar magnet into and out of the coil to induce electric current and cause the galvanometer to deflect. Vary the directions, poles, and speeds of the magnet. Also, vary the number of loops in the coil, and try different strengths of magnets.

Explore how moving magnet affects coil of wire.

4. Under what conditions can you induce the largest current and get the largest deflection of the galvanometer?

_____

_____

_____

_____

5. What do you need to do to cause the galvanometer to deflect in the opposite direction?

_____

_____

_____

_____

_____

99 Motors and Generators

Purpose

To observe the effects of electromagnetic induction

Required Equipment/Supplies

2 Genecon hand-crank generators
DC power supply; 3–6 volt
voltmeter (digital or analog)
stopwatch
2 large demonstration horseshoe magnets
2 coils of magnet wire
1 Farad capacitor (optional)

Discussion

Generators and motors are similar devices with input and output reversed. Both involve wire loops in a magnetic field. The input in a motor is electric current, which is deflected as it enters the magnetic field inside the device. This deflection turns the wire loop and mechanical energy is the output. In a generator, the wire loop is forced to rotate by mechanical means. Initially, static charges in the wire are deflected to produce an electric-current output.

In a generator, the wire loop is rotated through a magnetic field. The wire loop provides a conducting path for the charges as they are deflected at right angles by the magnetic field.

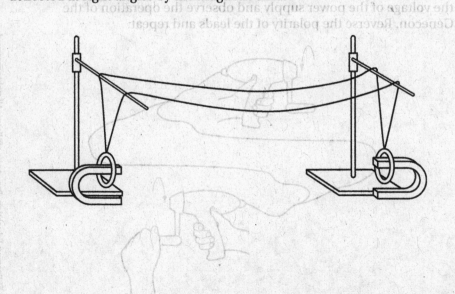

Procedure

Step 1: Set up the magnets and the wires as shown. Move one coil to one side and then back again.

1. What happens to the other coil? Explain.

_____

_____

_____

_____

_____

2. Does the same thing happen if the coils are not connected to each other?

_____

_____

_____

3. What happens if the poles of the other magnet are reversed?

_____

Step 2: Study the construction of a Genecon. Note that it consists of a DC motor whose armature shaft is connected to the hand crank via gears. Adjust the range of a DC power supply so that voltage output is a maximum of 5 volts. Attach the leads of the Genecon to the power supply. Hold the Genecon so that its handle is free to rotate. Slowly increase the voltage of the power supply and observe the operation of the Genecon. Reverse the polarity of the leads and repeat.

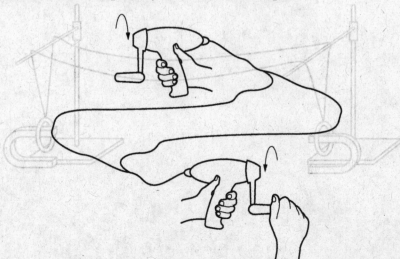

4. What did you observe?

Step 3: Connect the leads of one Genecon to the leads of another. Have your partner hold one Genecon while you turn the crank on the other.

5. What happens to the other Genecon when you turn the crank on yours:

a. in the clockwise direction?

_____

b. in the counterclockwise direction?

_____

c. fast?

_____

d. slowly?

_____

e. with the leads reversed?

_____

Analysis

6. Does the Genecon behave any differently when connected to another Genecon rather than a power supply? What is the principal difference in this case?

_____

_____

_____

Going Further—Efficiency

Step 4: Attach the leads of the Genecon to a voltmeter whose range is set to a maximum of 10 volts. Crank the handle at various speeds. Observe the readings on the voltmeter.

Attach the leads of a Genecon to the terminals of a single bulb in a socket. Attach the leads of a voltmeter to the same terminals of the bulb. The voltmeter should be adjusted so that the full-scale reading is 5 or 10 volts. Turn the handle of the Genecon at a steady fixed speed so that the voltmeter reads 0.5 volt. Have your partner time you for ten seconds as you count the number of turns of the crank. Record your data in Data Table A.

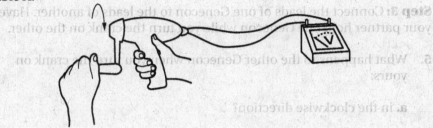

Data Table A

Number of Turns	Voltage

Repeat this procedure up to 4 volts in 1/2-volt increments. Observe the intensity of the light bulb.

Step 5: The speed at which the armature moves through the magnetic field inside the generator is proportional to the number of turns per second. Use your data to make a graph of Voltage (volts) vs. Speed (turns/s).

Analysis

7. How does the intensity of the lamp vary as you increase the crank speed?

_____

_____

8. How does the voltage of the generator vary with the speed of the armature as it moves through the magnetic field?

_____

_____

9. What is the optimum speed required (that is, the speed after which there is very little increase in voltage with an increase in crank speed) to generate voltage using this generator?

_____

_____

10. Where does the energy to light the bulb originate?

_____

_____

Going Even Further—
Increasing Your Capacity

A capacitor is an electronic device that stores electric charge and electric energy. The flash attachment for cameras uses a capacitor to store the energy needed to provide a sudden flash of light. Capacitors are used to smooth out alternating current ripples in a direct current voltage supply such as those used to power your calculator or radio.

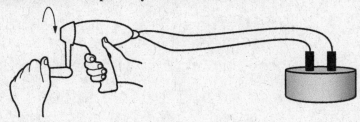

Step 6: Attach the leads of a Genecon to a large capacitor—a 1.0 farad capacitor. Crank the Genecon briskly for a minute or so. Feel and observe the force required to turn the crank as you go. Then, after a minute or so, disconnect one of the leads to the capacitor (either one is OK). Predict what will happen when you re-connect the crank.

Prediction:

_____

_____

11. Does the crank rotate? If so, does it rotate in the same direction you had been cranking or in the opposite direction? Are you surprised? Why? Can you explain why it rotated the way it did?

_____

_____

_____

_____

_____

_____

_____

_____

_____

100 Particular Waves

Purpose

To observe the photoelectric effect

Required Equipment/Supplies

electroscope
electrostatic kit, containing strips of white plastic and clear acetate and
  swatches of wool and silk
zinc plate (approximately 5 cm × 5 cm × 0.1 cm) or magnesium ribbon,
  10 cm long
steel wool
lamp with 200-watt bulb
60-watt ultraviolet light source (mercury vapor lamp)

Discussion

Albert Einstein was best known for his discovery of special and general relativity. Interestingly enough, he was awarded the Nobel Prize for something entirely different—the rules governing the photoelectric effect. In this activity, you will observe the photoelectric effect, which is the ejection of electrons from certain metals (in this case, zinc or magnesium) when exposed to light.

Procedure

Step 1: Scrub the zinc plate (or magnesium ribbon) with the steel wool to make it shiny; then place the plate on the probe of the electroscope.

Scrub metal until shiny.

Step 2: Rub the white plastic strip with the wool cloth to charge the strip negatively. Touch the strip to the zinc plate on the electroscope. Notice that the leaves separate—evidence that the electroscope is charged.

Observe electroscope.

Step 3: Observe the leaves of the electroscope for one minute.

1.   Did the electroscope discharge by itself during that time?

_____

_____

Step 4: Touch the zinc plate on the electroscope with your finger. Note that the electroscope discharges.

2. Why did the electroscope discharge when you touched it?

_____

_____

_____

_____

Step 5: Rub the clear acetate strip with the silk cloth to charge the strip positively. Touch the strip to the zinc plate on the electroscope. Observe the leaves for one minute. Now touch the zinc plate to see whether the electroscope discharges.

3. Describe what happened to the electroscope from the time you touched the charged acetate strip to the zinc plate.

_____

_____

_____

_____

Shine white light from 200-watt bulb on zinc plate.

Step 6: Perhaps electrons can be "blown away" from a negatively charged electroscope by bombarding it with high-intensity light. Charge the electroscope negatively, as in Step 2. Shine white light from a 200-watt lightbulb onto the zinc plate from a distance of 10 cm.

4. How does the electroscope react to the high-intensity white light?

_____

_____

_____

Shine weak ultraviolet light on zinc plate.

Step 7: Recharge the electroscope negatively if its leaves have dropped. Now shine light from a 60-watt ultraviolet light source on the zinc plate.

5. How does the electroscope react to the weak, ultraviolet light?

_____

_____

_____

Step 8: Possibly the ultraviolet light is somehow making the air conductive. Charge the strip with a positive charge as in Step 5, and shine the ultraviolet light on the zinc plate again.

6. Does the electroscope discharge?

_____

_____

_____

Step 9: In Data Table A, indicate in each box whether or not the electroscope discharged during your tests.

	Bright Visible Light Caused the Electroscope to:	*Weak* Ultraviolet Light Caused the Electroscope to:
Negatively Charged Electroscope		
Positively Charged Electroscope		

Data Table A

Analysis

7. If the *intensity* of the light is responsible for discharging the electroscope, which light source should discharge the electroscope better?

_____

_____

8. If the electroscope could not be discharged by high-intensity white light, but was discharged by weak, ultraviolet light, the *intensity* of the light did not cause it to discharge. How is ultraviolet light different from visible light?

_____

_____

_____

9. Although light is a wave phenomenon, it also behaves like a stream of particles called *photons*. Each photon carries a discrete amount of energy. When a photon is absorbed, its energy is given to whatever absorbs it. According to your data, which type of photons seem to have more energy—those of visible light or those of ultraviolet light?

_____

_____

_____

10. The energy of a photon is proportional to the frequency of the light. Photons of ultraviolet light possess enough energy to "kick free" electrons trapped in the zinc metal. When the electroscope was positively charged, why did it not discharge when it was exposed to ultraviolet light?

_____

_____

_____

11. Which would be better at discharging a negatively charged electroscope, an infrared heat lamp or a dentist's X-ray machine? Why?

_____

_____

_____

_____

_____

_____

101 Energy of a Photon

Purpose

To determine the energy of a photon emitted by an LED and to estimate the value of Planck's constant

Required Equipment/Supplies

one each of red, green, and blue LEDs
three 200-ohm resistors
voltmeter
adjustable DC voltage supply (1–3 volts or more), or
    9-volt battery and holder and 1k-ohm potentiometer
electronic circuit assembly or circuit board
spectroscope with nm scale (available from Sargent Welch)
low-wattage clear filament bulb with gooseneck or other suitable
    lamp variac

Potentiometer

Diode

Resistor

Fig. B

Discussion

Light is a tiny fraction of the entire electromagnetic spectrum created by accelerating electric charges, usually electrons. When electrons move from a higher energy state to a lower one, they emit a photon. The energy of the photon equals the energy difference between the two energy states. A famous physicist named Max Planck discovered that the energy of a photon was directly related to its frequency, and this relationship is now known as Planck's law:

$$E = hf$$

where f is the frequency of the photon and h is Planck's constant, which has a value of

$$h = 6.6 \times 10^{-34} \text{ J-s}$$

Light emitting diodes, or LEDs, convert the energy change of one electron into one photon of light. In this experiment, you will slowly increase the energy of the electrons by increasing the voltage across the LEDs and observe what happens and also compare and contrast this with the operation of an ordinary filament bulb.

Procedure 🔧 🔬

Step 1: Observe a clear filament bulb with a spectroscope when your classroom is darkened. Your teacher will assist you with the operation of the spectroscope. The trick is to point the slit towards the bulb but look through the grating off to one side to see the colors. Your teacher will then turn up the voltage to the bulb with a variac (which stands for "variable AC"—essentially a variable transformer capable of supplying variable voltages).

What do you observe? What colors do you see through the spectroscope? What happens as the voltage supplied to the bulb is increased? How is the intensity of the light connected to the voltage applied to the bulb? Summarize your observations below.

_____

_____

_____

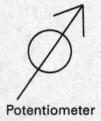

Potentiometer

Step 2: Assemble the circuit, as shown in Figure A. First, connect each LED in series with a 200-ohm resistor. Then connect the three LED/resistor combinations in parallel with each other and connect the two ends of this parallel combination to the variable-voltage supply.

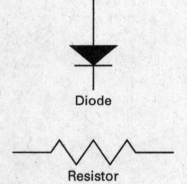

Variable Voltage

1–3 V

RGB LEDs

200 Ohms

Fig. A

Diode

Step 3: Predict what you think is going to happen when you apply voltage to the LEDs.

_____

_____

_____

Resistor

Fig. B

Now *slowly* increase the voltage across the LEDs. Record your findings. Compare and contrast your findings with your prediction. Turn the LEDs off when done.

_____

_____

Step 4: Repeat, this time measuring the voltage across each LED as it comes on. Record the voltage across each LED in Data Table A. Turn the LEDs off when done.

Data Table A

The Voltage Across Each LED

LED Color	Voltage (volts)
red	
green	
blue	

Step 5: *Slowly* increase the voltage across the LEDs and use a spectroscope to measure the wavelength of each color. Record your data in Data Table B. You can then calculate the frequency f of each color in Hz by using the equation $f = c/\lambda$, where c is 3×10^8 m/s and λ is wavelength in meters.

Data Table B

The Voltage Across Each LED Using a Spectroscope

LED Color	Wavelength (m)	Frequency (Hz)
red		
green		
blue		

Analysis

1. Express 1 volt in terms of joules (energy) and coulombs (charge).

_____

_____

2. If V is the voltage needed to light an LED and the charge of one electron is $e = 1.6 \times 10^{-19}$ C, write an equation to find the energy that a single electron gives up to make a single photon. Calculate the energy for each color LED and put the values in the last column of Data Table C.

_____

Data Table C

The Energy Emitted from Photons

LED Color	Frequency (Hz)	Energy (J)
red		
green		
blue		

3. Planck's law, $E = hf$, is of the same form as the equation $y = mx + b$ where m is the slope and b is the y-intercept. For Planck's law, h is the slope of the line of E vs. f. Make a graph of the energy of the photons vs. their frequency. Make a slope triangle and calculate the slope of the graph.

    a. How does the slope of your graph compare to the accepted value $h = 6.6 \times 10^{-34}$ J-s?

        slope of the line m = _____

    b. Compute the percent error.

        percent error = _____ %

4. Compare and contrast the operation of a filament light bulb with that of LEDs.

_____

_____

_____

_____

_____

_____

_____

102 Nuclear Marbles

Purpose

To determine the diameter of a marble by indirect measurement

Required Equipment/Supplies

7–10 marbles
3 metersticks

Discussion

People sometimes have to resort to something besides their sense of sight to determine the shape and size of things, especially for things smaller than the wavelength of light. One way to do this is to fire particles at the object to be investigated, and to study the paths of the particles that are deflected by the object. Physicists do this with particle accelerators. Ernest Rutherford discovered the tiny atomic nucleus in his gold-foil experiment. In this activity, you will try a simpler but similar method with marbles.

You are not allowed to use a ruler or meterstick to measure the marbles directly. Instead, you will roll other marbles at the target "nuclear" marbles and, from the percentage of rolls that lead to collisions, determine their size. This is a little bit like throwing snowballs at a tree trunk while blindfolded. If only a few of your throws result in hits, you can infer that the trunk is small.

First, use a bit of reasoning to arrive at a formula for the diameter of the nuclear marbles (NM). Then, at the end of the experiment, you can measure the marbles directly and compare your results.

When you roll a marble toward a nuclear marble, you have a certain probability of a hit between the rolling marble (RM) and the nuclear marble (NM). One expression of the probability P of a hit is the ratio of the path width required for a hit to the width L of the target area (see Figure A). The path width is equal to two RM radii plus the diameter of the NM, as shown in Figure B. The probability P that a rolling marble will hit a lone nuclear marble in the target area is

$$P = \frac{\text{path width}}{\text{target width}}$$

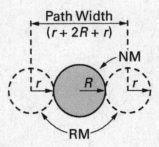

Fig. A

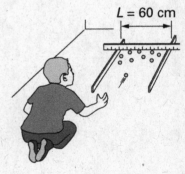

Fig. B

$$= \frac{2R + 2r}{L} = \frac{2(R + r)}{L}$$

where $\qquad R$ = the radius of the NM

r = the radius of the RM

$R + r$ = the distance between the centers of an RM and an NM that are touching

and $\qquad L$ = the width of the target area.

If the number of nuclear marbles is increased to N, the probability of a hit is increased by a factor of N (provided N is small enough that the probability of multiple collisions is small). Thus, the probability that the rolling marble will hit one of the N widely spaced nuclear marbles is

$$P = \frac{2N(R + r)}{L}$$

The probability of a hit can also be determined experimentally by the ratio of the number of hits to the number of trials.

$$P = \frac{H}{T}$$

where $\qquad H$ = the number of hits

and $\qquad T$ = the number of trials.

You now have two expressions for the probability of a hit. These two expressions may be equated. If the radii of the rolling marble and nuclear marble are equal, then $R + r = d$, where d is the diameter of any of the marbles. Combine the last two equations for P, and write an expression for d in terms of H, T, N, and L.

marble diameter $d =$ _____

This is the formula you are now going to test.

Procedure

Step 1: Place 6–9 marbles in an area 60 cm wide ($L = 60$ cm), as in Figure A. Roll additional marbles randomly, one at a time, toward the whole target area from the release point. If a rolling marble hits two nuclear marbles, count just one hit. If a rolling marble goes outside the 60-cm-wide area, do not count that trial. A significant number of trials—more than 200—need to be made before the results become statistically significant. Record your total number of hits H and total number of trials T.

$H =$ _____

$T =$ _____

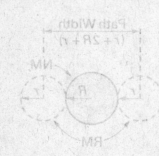

Set up nuclear targets.

Step 2: Use your formula from the Discussion to find the diameter of the marble. Show your work.

computed diameter = _____

Step 3: Measure the diameter of one marble.

measured diameter = _____

Analysis

1. Compare your results for the diameter determined indirectly in the collision experiment and directly by measurement. What is the percentage difference in these two ways of measuring the diameter?

_____

_____

_____

_____

_____

_____

2. State a conclusion you can draw from this experiment.

_____

_____

_____

_____

_____

_____

Step 2: Use your formula from the Discussion to find the diameter of the marble. Show your work.

computed diameter = _____

Step 3: Measure the diameter of one marble.

measured diameter = _____

Analysis

1. Compare your results for the diameter determined indirectly in the collision experiment and directly by measurement. What is the percentage difference in these two ways of measuring the diameter?

_____

_____

_____

_____

_____

2. State a conclusion you can draw from this experiment.

_____

_____

_____

_____

_____

103 Half-Life

Purpose

To develop an understanding of half-life and radioactive decay

Required Equipment/Supplies

shoe box and lid
200 or more pennies
graph paper

Optional Equipment/Supplies

jar of 200 brass fasteners
computer
data plotting software

Discussion

Many things grow at what is called an exponential rate: population, money bearing interest in the bank, and the thickness of paper that is repeatedly folded over onto itself. Many other things decrease exponentially: the value of money stuffed under a mattress, the amount of vacant area in a place where population is growing, and the remaining amount of a material that is undergoing radioactive decay. A useful way to describe the rate of decrease is in terms of *half-life*—the time it takes for the quantity to be reduced to half its initial value. For *exponential* decrease, the half-life stays the same. This means that the time to go from 100% of the quantity to 50% is the same as the time to go from 50% to 25% or from 25% to 12.5%, or from 4% to 2%.

    Radioactive materials are characterized by their rates of decay and are rated in terms of their half-lives. You will explore this idea in this activity.

Procedure

Step 1: Place the pennies in a shoe box, and place the lid on the box. Shake the box for several seconds. Open the box and remove all the pennies with the head-side up. Count these and record the number in Data Table A. Do *not* put the removed pennies back in the box.

Remove all pennies with head-side up.

Step 2: Repeat Step 1 over and over until one or no pennies remain. Record the number of pennies removed each time in Data Table A.

Repeat Step 1.

Total Pennies:					
Shake Number	Number of Pennies Removed	Number of Pennies Remaining	Shake Number	Number of Pennies Removed	Number of Pennies Remaining
1			6		
2			7		
3			8		
4			9		
5			10		

Data Table A

Compute number of pennies remaining each time.

Step 3: Add the numbers of pennies removed to find the total number of pennies. Now, find the number of pennies remaining after each shake by subtracting the number of pennies removed each time from the previous number remaining, and record in Data Table A.

Plot your data.

Step 4: Graph the number of pennies remaining (vertical axis) vs. the number of shakes (horizontal axis). Draw a smooth line that best fits the points.

Analysis

1. What is the meaning of the graph you obtained?

_____

_____

_____

2. Approximately what percent of the remaining pennies were removed on each shake? Why?

3. Each shake represents a half-life for the pennies. What is meant by a half-life?

_____

Going Further

Step 5: Shake a jar of brass paper fasteners and pour them onto the table. Remove the fasteners that are standing on their heads, as you did the pennies with the head side up. Repeat until all the fasteners are gone.

Step 6: Plot your data on the computer, using data plotting software. Try to discover what changes in the value of your vertical or horizontal axis will make your graph come out a straight line. Ask your teacher for assistance if you need help.

104 Chain Reaction

Purpose

To simulate a simple chain reaction

Required Equipment/Supplies

100 dominoes
large table or floor space
stopwatch

Discussion

You could give your cold to two people; they in turn could give it to two others, each of whom in turn could give it to two others. Before you knew it, everyone in school would be sneezing. You would have set off a chain reaction. Similarly, electrons in a photomultiplier tube in an electronic instrument multiply in a chain reaction so that a tiny input produces a huge output. Another example of a chain reaction occurs when one neutron triggers the release of two or more neutrons in a piece of uranium, and each of these neutrons triggers the release of more neutrons (along with the release of nuclear energy). The results of this kind of chain reaction can be devastating.

In this activity, you will explore chain reactions using dominoes.

Procedure

Step 1: Set up a string of dominoes about half a domino length apart in a straight line, as you did back in Activity 9, The Domino Effect. Push the first domino and measure how long it takes for the entire string to fall over. Also notice whether the number of dominoes being knocked over per second increases, decreases, or remains about the same as the pulse runs down the row of dominoes.

Step 2: Set up the dominoes in an arrangement similar to the one in Figure A. When one domino falls, another one or two will be knocked over. When you finish setting up all your dominoes, push the first domino over, and time how long it takes for all or most of the dominoes to fall over. Also, notice whether the number of dominoes being knocked over per unit time increases, decreases, or remains about the same.

Analysis

1. Which approach results in the shorter time to knock over all the dominoes, the one with a line of dominoes or the one with randomly arranged dominoes?

_____

_____

_____

2. How did the number of dominoes being knocked over per unit time change in each procedure?

_____

_____

3. What made each sequence of falling dominoes?

_____

_____

4. Imagine that the dominoes represent the neutrons released by uranium atoms when they fission (split apart). Neutrons from the nucleus of each fissioning uranium atom hit other uranium nuclei and cause them to fission. In a big enough piece of uranium, this chain reaction continues to grow if there are no controls. An atomic explosion would then result in a split second. How is the domino reaction in Step 2 similar to the atomic fission process?

_____

_____

_____

5. How is the domino reaction in Step 2 dissimilar to the atomic fission process?

_____

_____

_____

105 Roll Out the π

Purpose

To learn the proper use of a meterstick, a vernier caliper, and a micrometer

Required Equipment/Supplies

meterstick
vernier caliper
micrometer
several 4–6" length dowels or metal cylinders of various diameters

Discussion

When making measurements, it's important to keep both the *precision* (the smallest unit that is measurable) and the *significant figures* in mind. The number of significant figures in an actual measurement depends on the instrument and its precision. For example, a micrometer is capable of greater precision than a vernier caliper. However, when a micrometer is used to measure the thickness of a single piece of paper, it has fewer significant figures (i.e., one) than a vernier caliper measuring the thickness of 1000 pages (i.e., three).

Procedure

Step 1: Use a meterstick to measure the length, width, and thickness of your lab table. Record the data along with the precision of each measurement. Make each measurement five times each time at a different location on the lab table.

Data Table A: The Dimensions of a Lab Table

Measurement	Length (cm)	Width (cm)	Thickness (cm)	Precision
1				
2				
3				
4				
5				
Average				

Step 2: Find the average of the length, width, and thickness of the lab table. Use these average values for each dimension of the lab table to compute the volume of the top. Be sure to indicate the proper number of significant figures in your calculation and to attach the appropriate units to your answer. Show your calculations.

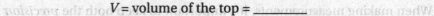

V = volume of the top = _____

Step 3: Determine the thickness of a single page in your textbook two ways. Do this by measuring the thickness of the book (excluding the cover) and dividing by the number of pieces of paper. First make your measurements of the book with a meterstick and then repeat using a vernier caliper. Make each measurement three times and obtain an average value. Record all measurements with the proper number of significant figures.

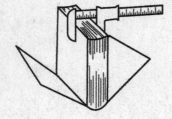

number of pieces of paper = _____

Data Table B: Determining the Thickness of a Textbook Page using Two Different Instruments

Trial	Thickness (mm) (Using Meterstick)	Thickness (mm) (Using Vernier Caliper)
1		
2		
3		
Average		

thickness of single page using meterstick = _____

thickness of single page using vernier caliper = _____

Step 4: Now measure the thickness of a single page using a micrometer. Make note of its precision.

thickness = _____ precision _____

1. Which instrument results in the greater number of significant figures?

_____

_____

2. How do the two values for the thickness per page compare?

_____

_____

Step 5: Calculate π by rolling a cylinder on a piece of paper beginning and ending at the same point on the circumference. Roll the cylinder as many times as possible without exceeding the maximum distance the vernier caliper can measure. Make your measurement three times and compute the average value of the circumference.

Data Table C: Circumference of a Cylinder Using a Vernier Caliper

Trial	Distance Rolled (cm)
1	
2	
3	
Average	

Measure the diameter of the cylinder using a micrometer. Make your measurement three times and compute the average value for the diameter.

Data Table D: Diameter of a Cylinder Using a Micrometer

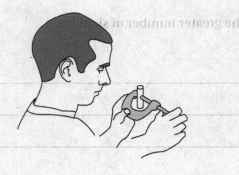

Trial	Diameter (cm)
1	
2	
3	
Average	

Use the average value of the circumference and the average value of the diameter to calculate π. Show your calculations. Be sure to include the proper number of significant figures and appropriate units. Show your calculations.

$$\pi = \underline{\hspace{3cm}}$$

Repeat using cylinders of different diameters.

Analysis

Mathematical methods estimate π to be 3.14159. How does your experimental value compare? Compute the percentage error by using 3.14159 as the accepted value.

$$\text{percentage error} = \frac{|\text{measured value} - \text{accepted value}|}{\text{accepted value}} \times 100\%$$

106 You're on Your Own

Many of the labs in this manual are intended to help you better understand a physics principle or concept or to give you experience in performing some specific task. As such, they often contain very specific directions. Sometimes you may know the "answer" to a lab before you do it. That's okay—because the answer is secondary to the important practice you gain in gathering, organizing and interpreting data.

The following labs are open-ended and do not entail specified steps for you to follow. The purpose of these open-ended investigations is to give you experience at attempting to find the solutions to problems for which the answer is not known. In these cases, you must devise your own method. A list of such labs is shown below.

Choose one of the investigations from the list or come up with one of your own. It is important that you define exactly what your investigation will and will not accomplish. Formulate a hypothesis. As a safety precaution, be sure to have your teacher approve your experimental procedure and/or apparatus before you begin experimenting. Acquire and organize your data—graphically, if appropriate. Specify as many factors as you can that influenced your experimental outcome. Does your experiment affirm or refute your hypothesis? Remember, some of the most famous experiments in physics had null results—e.g., the Michelson–Morley experiment—so do not despair if your experimental results refute your hypothesis. Do and *enjoy*!

- Find a relationship between the area covered by jigsaw pieces that are unconnected and the same pieces when connected. Predict the area needed to lay out pieces for a puzzle that when put together is known to have a certain area.

- Determine the factors that influence the toppling speed of dominoes. What is the maximum speed for a chain of dominoes at least one meter long?

- Devise and build an accelerometer. Calibrate the accelerometer so that it measures acceleration in m/s^2. Explain its operation.

- Devise an experiment that shows how the applied force (or *net* force) and mass of a system are related to its acceleration.

- Devise a method to measure free-fall acceleration.

- Devise a method to measure the speed of an object, such as a whiffle ball, tennis ball, baseball, etc., as it strikes the ground when dropped.

- Find quantitative relationships among the height, speed, mass, kinetic energy, and potential energy of a projectile ejected by a physical pendulum apparatus (such as in Releasing Your Potential available from Arbor Scientific) or a child jumping from a swing while swinging.

- Devise a simulation using *Interactive Physics* software.

- Devise an experiment that demonstrates: (a) constant speed, (b) constant velocity, (c) constant acceleration, and (d) variable acceleration (jerks).

- Devise an experimental procedure that measures the important variables for a damped harmonic oscillator, such as a loaded spring.

- Devise an experimental procedure to measure the vertical temperature gradient over a 24-hour period in your physics classroom during: (a) a school day and (b) on the weekend. Compare the temperature gradients between days during both warm and cold seasons. How thermally efficient is the classroom? A computer with multiple temperature probes may be very helpful.

- Estimate the average force you exert on a baseball with your hand when pitched. Express your estimate in terms of the distance the ball is thrown and the time of flight—both quantities you can measure.

- Devise a method by measure the coefficient of rolling friction for a toy car.

- Use the CASTLE Kit (available from PASCO) to devise an experiment that investigates the effect different numbers of bulbs have on the charging/discharging times of a capacitor.

- Calculate the uphill incline of a hill, θ, which you can cycle on at constant speed as a function of the gear radii. Test your predictions by cycling on a nearby incline.

- Segments of a short span bridge are observed to deflect downwards as vehicles cross it. Likewise, rails on a railroad track are deflected as a train rolls by. Devise a technique that will enable you to safely measure the deflection of the roadbed or the train track.

- Use LabQuest from Vernier Software to devise an experiment.

- Use one or more of the physics principles you have learned to explain and test the operation of an instrument used in a biology, chemistry, or biotechnology classroom, such as a spectrophotometer, gel electrophoresis box, power supply, centrifuge, −20°C freezer, orbital shaker, or a pH meter.

Appendix: Significant Figures and Uncertainty in Measurement

Units of Measurement

All measurements consist of a unit that tells what was measured and a number that tells how many units were measured. Both are necessary. If you say that a friend is going to give you 10, you are telling only *how many*. You also need to tell *what*: 10 fingers, 10 cents, 10 dollars, or 10 corny jokes. If your teacher asks you to measure the length of a piece of wood, saying that the answer is 36 is not correct. She or he needs to know whether the length is 36 centimeters, feet, or meters. All measurements must be expressed using a number and an appropriate unit. Units of measurement are more fully covered in Appendix A of the *Conceptual Physics* text.

Numbers

Two kinds of numbers are used in science—those that are counted or defined and those that are measured. There is a great difference between a counted or defined number and a measured number. The exact value of a counted or defined number can be stated, but the exact value of a measured number cannot be known.

For example, you can count the number of chairs in your classroom, the number of fingers on your hand, or the number of nickels in your pocket with absolute certainty. Counted numbers are not subject to error (unless the number counted is so large that you can't be sure of the count!).

Defined numbers are about exact relations, defined to be true. The exact number of seconds in an hour and the exact number of sides on a square are examples. Defined numbers also are not subject to error.

Every measured number, no matter how carefully measured, has some degree of uncertainty. What is the width of your desk? Is it 98.5 centimeters, 98.52 centimeters, 98.520 centimeters, or 98.5201 centimeters? You cannot state its exact measurement with absolute certainty.

Uncertainty in Measurement

The uncertainty in a measurement depends on the precision of the measuring device and the skill of the person who uses it. There are nearly always some human limitations in a measurement. In addition, uncertainties contributed by limited precision of your measuring instruments cannot be avoided.

Uncertainty in a measurement can be illustrated by the two different metersticks in Figure A. The measurements are of the length of a tabletop. Assuming that the zero end of the meterstick has been carefully and accurately positioned at the left end of the table, how long is the table?

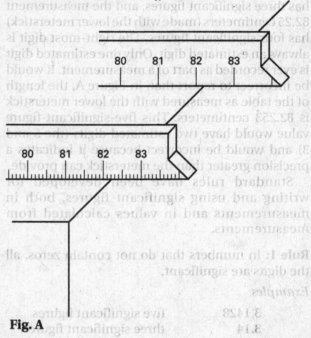

Fig. A

The upper scale in the figure is marked off in centimeter intervals. Using this scale, you can say with certainty that the length is between 82 and 83 centimeters. You can say further that it is closer to 82 centimeters than to 83 centimeters; you can estimate it to be 82.2 centimeters.

The lower scale has more subdivisions and has a greater precision because it is marked off in millimeters. With this meterstick, you can say that the length is definitely between 82.2 and 82.3 centimeters, and you can estimate it to be 82.25 centimeters.

Note how both readings contain some digits that are exactly known, and one digit (the last one) that is estimated. Note also that the uncertainty in the reading of the lower meterstick is less than that of the top meterstick. The lower meterstick can give a reading to the hundredths place, and the top meterstick to the tenths place. The lower meterstick is more precise than the top one.

No measurements are exact. A reported measurement conveys two kinds of information: (1) the magnitude of the measurement and (2) the precision of the measurement. The location of the decimal point and the number value gives the magnitude. The precision is indicated by the number of significant figures recorded.

Significant Figures

Significant figures are the digits in any measurement that are known with certainty plus one digit that is uncertain. The measurement 82.2 centimeters (made with the top meterstick in Figure A) has three significant figures, and the measurement 82.25 centimeters (made with the lower meterstick) has four significant figures. The right-most digit is always an estimated digit. Only one estimated digit is ever recorded as part of a measurement. It would be incorrect to report that, in Figure A, the length of the table as measured with the lower meterstick is 82.253 centimeters. This five-significant-figure value would have two estimated digits (the 5 and 3) and would be incorrect because it indicates a precision greater than the meterstick can provide.

Standard rules have been developed for writing and using significant figures, both in measurements and in values calculated from measurements.

Rule 1: In numbers that do not contain zeros, all the digits are significant.

Examples:

3.1428	five significant figures
3.14	three significant figures
469	three significant figures

Rule 2: All zeros between significant digits are significant.

Examples:

7.053	four significant figures
7053	four significant figures
302	three significant figures

Rule 3: Zeros to the left of the first nonzero digit serve only to fix the position of the decimal point and are not significant.

Examples:

0.0056	two significant figures
0.0789	three significant figures
0.000001	one significant figure

Rule 4: In a number with digits to the right of a decimal point, zeros to the right of the last nonzero digit are significant.

Examples:

43	two significant figures
43.0	three significant figures
43.00	four significant figures
0.00200	three significant figures
0.40050	five significant figures

Rule 5: In a number that has no decimal point, and that ends in one or more zeros (such as 3600), the zeros that end the number may or may not be significant. The number is ambiguous in terms of significant figures. Before the number of significant figures can be specified, further information is needed about how the number was obtained. If it is a measured number, the zeros are probably not significant. If the number is a defined or counted number, all the digits are significant (assuming perfect counting!).

Confusion is avoided when numbers are expressed in scientific notation. All digits are taken to be significant when expressed this way.

Examples:

3.6×10^5	two significant figures
3.60×10^5	three significant figures
3.600×10^5	four significant figures
2×10^{-5}	one significant figure
2.0×10^{-5}	two significant figures
2.00×10^{-5}	three significant figures

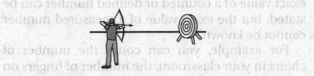

Good Precision
Poor Accuracy

Poor Precision
Poor Accuracy

Good Precision
Good Accuracy

Rounding Off

A calculator displays eight or more digits. How do you round off such a display of digits to, say, three significant figures? Three simple rules govern the process of deleting unwanted (nonsignificant) digits from a calculator number.

Rule 1: If the first digit to be dropped is less than 5, that digit and all the digits that follow it are simply dropped.

Example:

54.234 rounded off to three significant figures becomes 54.2.

Rule 2: If the first digit to be dropped is a digit greater than 5, or if it is a 5 followed by digits other than zero, the excess digits are all dropped and the last retained digit is increased in value by one unit.

Example:

54.36, 54.359, and 54.3598 rounded off to three significant figures all become 54.4.

Rule 3: If the first digit to be dropped is a 5 not followed by any other digit, or if it is a 5 followed only by zeros, an odd-even rule is applied. That is, if the last retained digit is even, its value is not changed, and the 5 and any zeros that follow are dropped. But if the last digit is odd, its value is increased by one. The intention of this odd-even rule is to average the effects of rounding off.

Examples:

54.2500 to three significant figures becomes 54.2.

54.3500 to three significant figures becomes 54.4.

Significant Figures and Calculated Quantities

Suppose that you measure the mass of a small wooden block to be 2 grams on a balance, and you find that its volume is 3 cubic centimeters by poking it beneath the surface of water in a graduated cylinder. The density of the piece of wood is its mass divided by its volume. If you divide 2 by 3 on your calculator, the reading on the display is 0.6666666. It would be incorrect to report that the density of the block of wood is 0.6666666 gram per cubic centimeter. To do so would be claiming a degree of precision that is not warranted. Your answer should be rounded off to a sensible number of significant figures.

The number of significant figures allowable in a calculated result depends on the number of significant figures in the data used to obtain the result, and on the type of mathematical operation(s) used to obtain the result. There are separate rules for multiplication and division, and for addition and subtraction.

Multiplication and Division For multiplication and division, an answer should have the number of significant figures found in the number with the fewest significant figures. For the density example above, the answer would be rounded off to one significant figure, 0.7 gram per cubic centimeter. If the mass were measured to be 2.0 grams, and if the volume were still taken to be 3 cubic centimeters, the answer would still be rounded to one significant figure, 0.7 gram per cubic centimeter. If the mass were measured to be 2.0 grams and the volume to be 3.0 or 3.00 cubic centimeters, the answer would be rounded off to two significant figures: 0.67 gram per cubic centimeter.

Study the following examples. Assume that the numbers being multiplied or divided are measured numbers.

Example A:

8.536 × 0.47 = 4.01192 (calculator answer)
The input with the fewest significant figures is 0.47, which has two significant figures. Therefore, the calculator answer 4.01192 must be rounded off to 4.0.

Example B:

3840 ÷ 285.3 = 13.459516 (calculator answer)
The input with the fewest significant figures is 3840, which has three significant figures. Therefore, the calculator answer 13.459516 must be rounded off to 13.5.

Example C:

360.0 ÷ 3.000 = 12 (calculator answer)
Both inputs contain four significant figures. Therefore, the correct answer must also contain four significant figures, and the calculator answer 12 must be written as 12.00. In this case, the calculator gave too few significant figures.

Addition and Subtraction For addition or subtraction, the answer should not have digits beyond the last digit position common to all the numbers being added and subtracted. Study the following examples:

Example A:

      34.6
      17.8
+   15
      67.4 (calculator answer)

The last digit position common to all numbers is the units place. Therefore, the calculator answer of 67.4 must be rounded off to the units place to become 67.

Example B:

```
  20.02
  20.002
+ 20.0002
  60.0222 (calculator answer)
```

The last digit position common to all numbers is the hundredths place. Therefore, the calculator answer of 60.0222 must be rounded off to the hundredths place, 60.02.

Example C:

345.56 − 245.5 = 100.06 (calculator answer)

The last digit position common to both numbers in this subtraction operation is the tenths place. Therefore, the answer should be rounded off to 100.1.

Percentage Uncertainty

If your aunt told you that she had made $100 in the stock market, you would be more impressed if this gain were on a $100 investment than if it were on a $10,000 investment. In the first case, she would have doubled her investment and made a 100% gain. In the second case, she would have made a 1% gain.

In laboratory measurements, the *percentage* uncertainty is usually more important than the *size* of the uncertainty. Measuring something to within 1 centimeter may be good or poor, depending on the length of the object you are measuring. Measuring the length of a 10-centimeter pencil to ±1 centimeter is quite a bit different from measuring the length of a 100-meter track to the same ±1 centimeter. The measurement of the pencil shows a relative uncertainty of 10%. The track measurement is uncertain by only 1 part in 10,000, or 0.01%.

Percentage Error

Uncertainty and error can easily be confused. *Uncertainty* gives the range within which the actual value is *likely* to lie relative to the measured value. It is used when the actual value is not known for sure, but is only inferred from the measurements. Uncertainty is reflected in the number of significant figures used in reporting a measurement.

The *error* of a measurement is the amount by which the measurement differs from a known, accepted value as determined by skilled observers using high-precision equipment. It is a measure of the accuracy of the method of measurement as well as the skill of the person making the measurement. The *percentage* error, which is usually more important than the actual error, is found by dividing the difference between the measured value and the accepted value of a quantity by the accepted value, and then multiplying this quotient by 100%.

$$\% \text{ error} = \frac{|\text{accepted value} - \text{measured value}|}{\text{accepted value}} \times 100\%$$

For example, suppose that the measured value of the acceleration of gravity is found to be 9.44 m/s^2. The accepted value is 9.80 m/s^2. The difference between these two values is $(9.80 \text{ m/s}^2) - (9.44 \text{ m/s}^2)$, or 0.36 m/s^2.

$$\% \text{ error} = \frac{0.36 \text{ m/s}^2}{9.80 \text{ m/s}^2} \times 100\%$$

$$= 3.7\%$$